Architecting Microsoft Azure Solutions Study & Lab Gu
Harinder Kohli

All progress happens outside the comfort zone
Michael John Bobak

Architecting Microsoft Azure Solutions Study & Lab Guide Part 1
Exam 70-535

Harinder Kohli

Published by:

kindle | direct publishing

This edition has been published by arrangement with **Kindle Direct Publishing**.

ISBN
ISBN: 9781983007149

Edition: 2018

Contents at a Glance

Contents

Case Studies

1. Designing Virtual Networks and Network Security Groups
2. User Defined Route
3. Workload Isolation with Hub and Spoke VNETs using VNET Peering
4. Availability Set
5. Choosing VM size and Designing IOPs
6. Load Balancing e-commerce server
7. Highly Available Multisite Website
8. Federating On-premises Active Directory and Azure AD
9. Website authentication using on-premises ADFS as SAML Identity Provider
10. Identity Management
11. Licensing Case Study 1
12. Licensing Case Study 2
13. Secure Remote Access to on-premises Application

Lab Exercises

Chapter 1 Virtual Network
1. Creating Virtual Network
2. Add Additional Subnets
3. Creating Network Security Groups and add inbound rules
4. Associating NSG with Subnet
5. VNET Peering
6. Setting up Virtual Network Service Endpoints

Chapter2 Azure Compute
7. Creating Virtual Machine wvm535
8. Logging on to VM using RDP
9. Installing IIS Web Server on Virtual Machine
10. Virtual Machine Host Level Monitoring
11. Virtual Machine Guest Level Monitoring
12. Demonstrating additional functionalities of the Virtual Machine

Chapter 3 Storage Account
13. Creating Storage Account Gpv2
14. Demonstrating Functionalities of Storage Account

Chapter 4 Azure Storage
15. Creating Blob Storage
16. Generating shared access signature (SAS)
17. Creating and Mounting File Share
18. Creating Queue Storage

Chapter 5 Virtual Machine Scale Set
19. Deploying Virtual Machine Scale Set

Chapter 6 Azure Backup
20. Create Recovery Services Vault
21. Backup Files & Folder on Windows Server VM using Backup Agent option
22. Azure VM-level backup

Chapter 7 Azure Site Recover
23. Enabling Disaster Recovery for Azure VM using Azure Site Recovery

Chapter 8 Containers
24. Deploying Containers on Azure Ubuntu Linux VM
25. Deploying Container Instances
26. Deploying Web App for Containers
27. Deploying Azure Kubernetes Services

Introduction

Architecting Microsoft Azure Solutions Study & Lab Guide Part 1: Exam 70-535 is being published after a delay of 7 Months. Originally to be published in Oct 2017 was delayed because of multiple reasons including MS changing the exam from 70-534 to 70-535.

70-535 Exam is targeted toward Azure Architects who can design Cloud Solutions using Azure Services. 70-535 Exam focuses both on **Infrastructure Topics** such as Virtual Servers, Networks, Storage, Azure Active Directory, Azure CDN and **Database & PaaS Topics** such as SQL Database, Web Apps, IoT Solutions & Service Bus. One of the key success points to pass the exam is to work with Azure portal and practice configuring various Azure services.

Architecting Microsoft Azure Solution Lab & Study Guide helps you prepare for 70-535 Exam. It contains Topic lessons, Design Case Studies & Lab Exercises. It is being published in 2 separate Books.
Part 1 (Which is this book) focuses on Infrastructure Topics.
Part 2 Focuses on Database & PaaS Topics and is being published separately.

The twin focus of this book is to get your fundamental on Azure Services on strong footing and prepare you to design cloud solutions using Azure Services. Topic lessons, Design case studies and lab exercises are all geared towards making you understand Azure fundamentals. 70-535 Exam heavily focuses on fundamentals of Azure Services.

Best of Luck for 70-535 Exam.

I would be pleased to hear your feedback and thoughts on the book. Please comment on Amazon or mail to: harinder-kohli@outlook.com.

Harinder Kohli

How to contact the Author

Email: harinder-kohli@outlook.com
Linkedin: www.linkedin.com/in/harinderkohli
Azure Blog @ https://mykloud.wordpress.com

Updates

Information about Book Updates will be published on my blog site.

Register and get bonus full scale case study

Send your amazon e-mail as proof of purchase of the book and receive full scale case study.

Download TOC and Sample Chapter from Box.com

https://app.box.com/s/4jrkw1m2f232wsnwpfows2wweh2tuzyg

Chapter 1 Virtual Networks

This Chapter covers following

- Virtual Networks
- Network Security Groups
- Public & Private IP Addresses in Azure
- Default System Route
- User Defined Route (UDR)
- Virtual Network Peering
- Global VNET Peering
- Virtual Network Service Endpoints

This Chapter Covers following Case Studies

- Designing Virtual Networks and Network Security Groups
- User Defined Route
- Workload Isolation with Hub and Spoke VNETs using VNET Peering

This Chapter Covers following Lab Exercises

- Creating Virtual Network
- Add Additional Subnets
- Creating Network Security Groups and add inbound rules
- Associating NSG with Subnet
- VNET Peering
- Setting up Virtual Network Service Endpoints

Chapter Topology

In this chapter we will create below topology. Default Azure AD is created when you sign for Azure subscription.

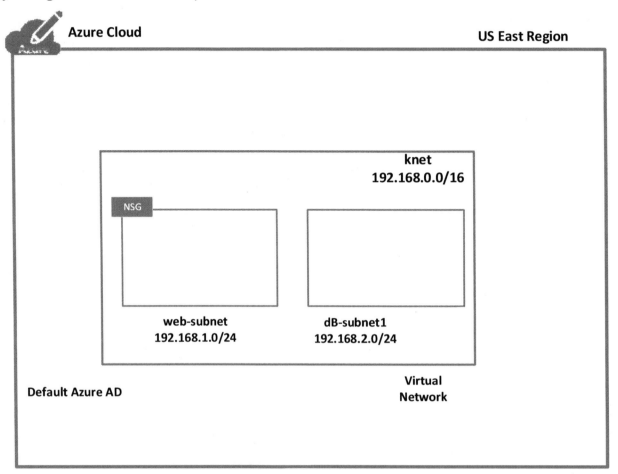

Following Topology will be used for VNET Peering Lab.

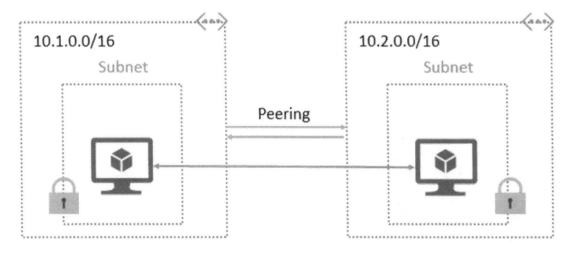

Virtual Networks (VNET)

An Azure virtual network (VNET) is Virtual Data Center in the cloud. Virtual Network is further segmented into subnets. Access to the subnets can be controlled using Network Security groups. Virtual Machines are created in Subnets.

End customer create Virtual Networks. End customers define the IP address blocks, security policies, and route tables within this network.

Figure below shows virtual network KNET1 with 2 subnets – Web-Subnet and DB-Subnet. There are 3 virtual machines in these subnets.
End customer has defined Network address of 192.168.0.0/16 for virtual network KNET1, 192.168.1.0/24 for Web-Subnet and 192.168.2.0/24 for DB-Subnet.

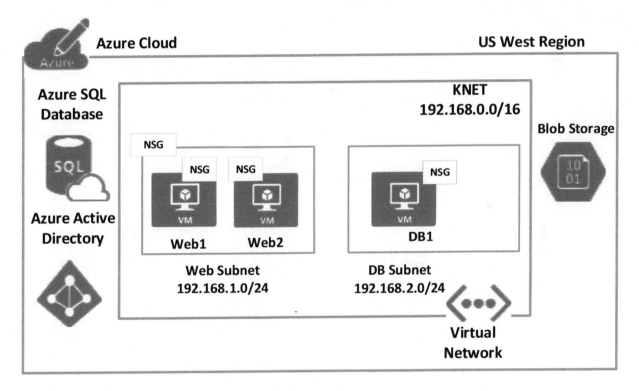

Virtual Network is created by the customer. Resources within Virtual Network are created and managed by end customers. Whereas Resources outside of VNET (Azure SQL, Azure AD etc) are Azure Managed Resources with Public IPs. Azure Managed Resources are not only accessed by VMs in VNET but are also accessed through internet.

Virtual Network Hybrid Connectivity

You can connect Virtual Network to on-premises Datacenter through virtual network gateway located in GatewaySubnet using either Internet VPN (P2S or S2S VPN) or ExpressRoute Private WAN connectivity.

For Internet VPN you deploy virtual network gateway of type VPN. For Private WAN connectivity you deploy virtual network gateway of type ExpressRoute.

Figure below shows Virtual Network Connected to on-premises Datacenter.

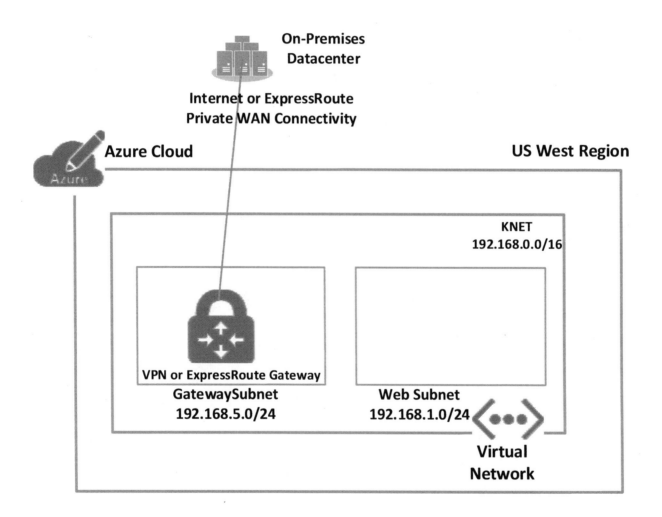

VNET Hybrid Connectivity with on-premises Data Center will be further discussed in Chapter 10.

Virtual Network Subnets

VNET is divided into subnets. Subnets are assigned IP addresses by subneting VNET network address space. Access to the subnet can be controlled through Network Security groups (NSG). User defined route (UDR) tables can also be assigned to subnets. Virtual Machines are created in Subnets.

Default Communication within and between Virtual Network Subnets

1. All VM to VM traffic within subnet or between subnets is allowed.
2. VM to internet traffic is allowed
3. Azure Load balancer to VM is allowed.
4. Inbound internet to VM is blocked

Note: Default rules can be overridden by new rules you create using NSG.

Private Address Range for Virtual Networks

You can use following class A, Class B and Class C address range for virtual networks.

10.0.0.0/8
172.16.0.0/12
192.168.0.0/16

Once the IP address range is decided, we can then divide this range into subnets. Virtual Machines NICs in the subnet are assigned private IP addresses via Azure DHCP from the subnet network address range.

There are 5 Reserved addresses within the subnet:: Within a virtual network subnet, the protocol reserves the first and last IP addresses of a subnet: a host ID of all 0s is used for the network address, and a host ID of all 1s is used for broadcast. In addition, Azure reserves the first three IP addresses in each subnet (binary 01, 10, and 11 in the host ID portion of the IP address) for internal purposes.

Exercise 1: Create Virtual Network with default subnet

In this exercise we will create Virtual Network using 192.168.0.0/16 address space. We will name default subnet as web-subnet with address 192.168.1.0/24. We will also create a Resource group name test.

1. In Azure Portal Click + Create a resource > Networking > Virtual Network> Create Virtual Network Blade opens> Use 192.168.0.0/16 Address space for Virtual Network. Name default Subnet as web-subnet and use Address space of 192.168.1.0/24. Create Resource Group test.> Click create.

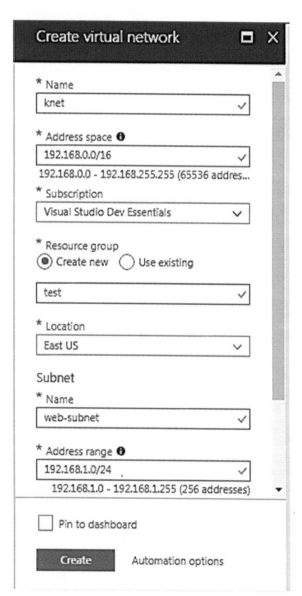

Exercise 2: Create additional Subnet (db-subnet 192.168.2.0/24)

1. Figure below shows VNET Dashboard. From VNET Dashboard you can create additional Subnets, add a custom DNS server, Tag your VNET etc.

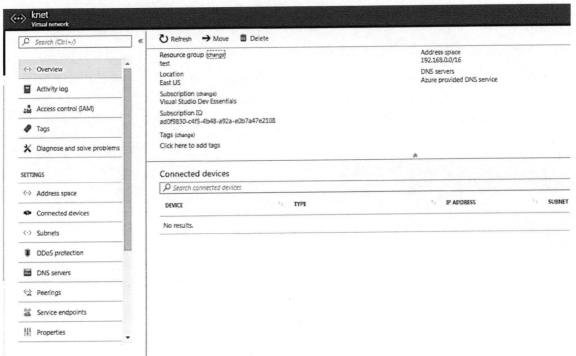

2. In VNET dashboard click Subnets in left pane>In right pane click +Subnet>Add Subnet blade opens>Enter required information and click ok.

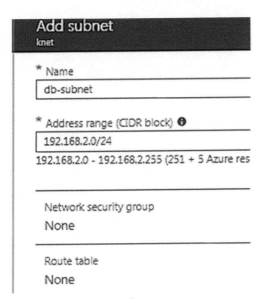

Virtual Networks Limits Pricing

Virtual Network in Azure is free of charge. Every subscription is allowed to create up to 50 Virtual Networks across all regions.

Public IP addresses used on services inside a virtual network are charged. Virtual Machines & Network appliances such as VPN Gateway and Application Gateway that are run inside a virtual network are also charged.

Traffic Filtering using Network security Groups (NSG)

Network Security Group (NSG) is a Virtual Firewall. NSGs control **inbound** and **outbound** access to network interfaces (NICs) and subnets. Each NSG contains one or more rules specifying whether or not traffic is approved or denied based on source IP address, source port, destination IP address, destination port and protocol.

NSGs can be associated with subnets and network interfaces of Virtual Machines within that subnet. When a NSG is associated with a subnet, the ACL rules apply to all the VM instances in that subnet. In addition, traffic to an individual VM can be further restricted by associating a NSG directly to that VM NIC.

Figure below Shows VNET with 2 Subnets. Virtual Machine in Web-Subnet is protected by 2 Levels of NSG – NSG at Subnet level and NSG at Virtual Machine Network Interface level. Whereas Virtual Machine in DB-Subnet is protected by one level of NSG applied at Virtual Machine Network Interface Level.

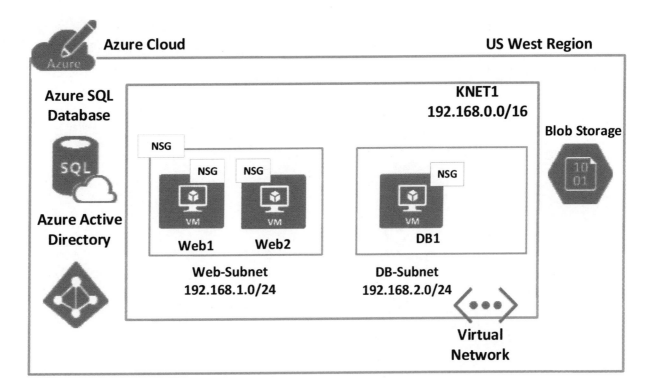

Design Nugget

1. By Default there is no NSG assigned to a subnet. But you have option of adding NSG during subnet creation or after subnet is created. To assign a NSG to a subnet you need to first create NSG.
2. By default when Virtual Machine is created a NSG is assigned to the network interfaces (NICs) of the Virtual Machine. Note that during VM installation you can deselect NSG option.
3. Associating NSG to subnet is recommended and not compulsory.

Design Nugget

1. You can apply only one NSG to a subnet or a VM NIC. But same NSG can be applied to multiple resources
2. Deploy each tier of your workload into different subnet and then apply NSG to the subnets.
3. When implementing a subnet for a VPN gateway, or ExpressRoute circuit, do not apply an NSG to that subnet. If you do so, your cross VNet or cross premises connectivity will not work.
4. Each NSG rules has a priority. Higher the priority number, lower the priority. You can override default NSG by creating new NSG rules with higher priority than default rules.

NSG Limits

1. Number of NSGs you can associate to a subnet or NIC: 1
2. You can associate Same NSG to Multiple Subnets or/and NICs.
3. NSGs per region per subscription: 100
4. NSG rules per NSG: 200

Default NSG rules

NSGs contain a set of default rules. The default rules cannot be deleted, but because they are assigned the lowest priority, they can be overridden by creating new rules with higher priority. **Higher the Number Lower the priority.**

Inbound default rules (check this again with Service Tags)

Name	Priority	Source IP	Src Port	Dest IP	Dest Port	Protocol	Access
ALLOW VNET INBOUND	65000	VIRTUAL_NETWORK	*	VIRTUAL_NETWORK	*	*	Allow
ALLOW AZURE LOAD BALANCER INBOUND	65001	AZURE_LOADBALANCER	*	*	*	*	Allow
DENY ALL INBOUND	65500	*	*	*	*	*	Deny

Outbound default rules

Name	Priority	Source IP	Src Port	Dest IP	Dest Port	Protocol	Access
ALLOW VNET OUTBOUND	65000	VIRTUAL_NETWORK	*	VIRTUAL_NETWORK	*	*	Allow
ALLOW INTERNET OUTBOUND	65001	*	*	Internet	*	*	Allow
DENY ALL OUTBOUND	65500	*	*	*	*	*	Deny

- * Represent all addresses, Ports & Protocols.

We can infer following from the above default rules:

1. All VM to VM traffic within subnet or between subnets is allowed.
2. VM to internet traffic is allowed.
3. Azure Load balancer to VM is allowed.
4. Inbound internet to VM is blocked.
5. Default rules can be overridden by creating new rules with higher priority.

Architecting Microsoft Azure Solutions Study & Lab Guide Part 1: Exam 70-535

Exercise 3: Create Network Security Group (NSG) and add inbound http and RDP allow rule

In this Exercise we will create Network Security Group knsg1. We will add inbound http and RDP allow rule in knsg1. This rule will allow http and RDP traffic to windows server VM in web-subnet. Windows VM will be created in compute chapter.

1. In Azure Portal Click + Create a resource>Networking>Network Security Group>Create Network Security Group opens> Fill as per your Requirement and Click create.

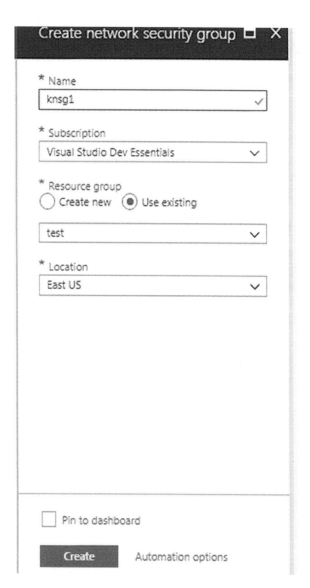

2. **Network Security Group Dashboard**: Figure below shows default inbound and outbound security rules.

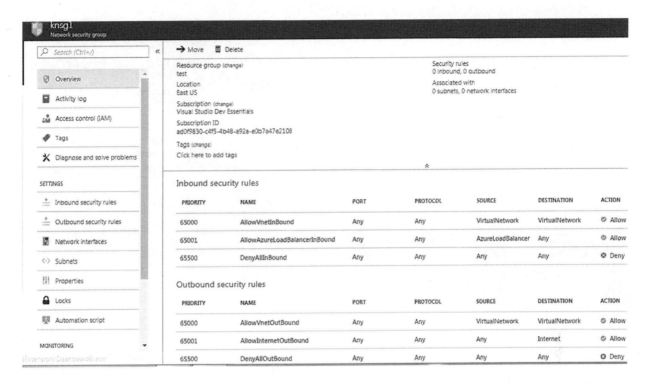

Note 1: In inbound security rules all inbound traffic is set to deny. This is rule number 3 with priority 65500 as shown in figure above.

Note 2: Best Practice is to create a new inbound rule and allow traffic which is needed. Do not make this rule allow for all the traffic.

Note 3: Override Default inbound rule by creating new rule with higher priority or lower number than the default inbound rule.

Note 3: In next step we will allow inbound RDP and http traffic to windows server VM in web-subnet. Windows Server VM will be created in compute chapter.

3. **Add inbound RDP rule**: In NSG dashboard click inbound security rules in left pane>In Right pane click +Add>Add inbound security rule blade opens> Enter RDP port 3389 in destination port range> Assign Priority of 100>Give a name to the rule and click Add.

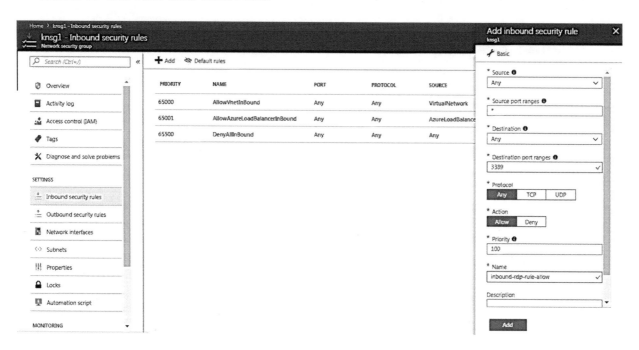

4. **Add inbound allow http rule**: Similarly add allow http rule. Enter http port 80 in destination port range> Assign Priority of 110>Give a name to the rule and click Add.

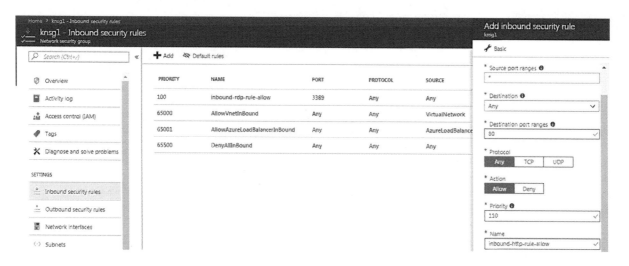

Exercise 4: Associate Network Security Group knsg1 with web-subnet

1. In NSG Dashboard click Subnets in left pane> In right pane click +Associate > Associate Subnet blade opens.

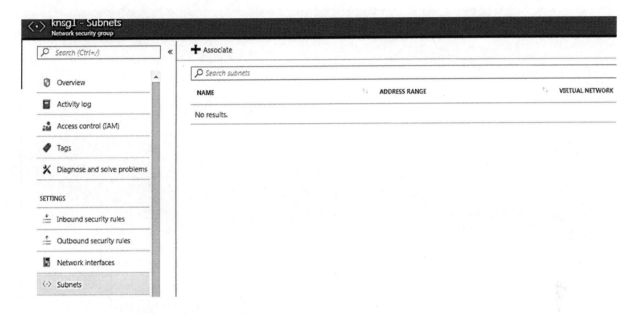

2. In Associate Subnet Blade select Virtual Network "knet" & Subnet "web-subnet" (Created in Exercise 1)

Service Tags for identification of category of IP Addresses in NSG Rules

Service tags are system-provided identifiers to address a category of IP addresses. Service tags are used in the **source address prefix** and **destination address prefix** properties of any NSG rule.

1. **VirtualNetwork**: This default tag denotes virtual network address space assigned to Azure Virtual Network.
2. **AzureLoadBalancer**: This default tag denotes Azure's Infrastructure load balancer. This will translate to an Azure datacenter IP where Azure's health probes originate.
3. **Internet**: This default tag denotes the IP address space that is outside the virtual network and reachable by public Internet. This range includes Azure owned public IP space as well.
4. **AzureTrafficManager**: This tag denotes the IP address space for the Azure Traffic Manager probe IPs.
5. **Storage**: This tag denotes the IP address space for the Azure Storage service. If you specify *Storage* for the value, traffic is allowed or denied to storage. If you only want to allow access to storage in a specific region, you can specify the region.
6. **Sql**: This tag denotes the address prefixes of the Azure SQL Database and Azure SQL Data Warehouse services. If you specify *Sql* for the value, traffic is allowed or denied to Sql.
7. **AzureCosmosDB** (Resource Manager only): This tag denotes the address prefixes of the Azure Cosmos Database service. If you specify AzureCosmosDB for the value, traffic is allowed or denied to AzureCosmosDB.
8. **AzureKeyVault** (Resource Manager only): This tag denotes the address prefixes of the Azure KeyVault service. If you specify *AzureKeyVault* for the value, traffic is allowed or denied to AzureKeyVault.

Case Study 1: Design Virtual Network and Network Security Groups

Design a virtual network (KNET) with 2 subnets (App & DB) using Class A address of 192.168.0.0/16. App subnet will have 2 application servers - Production Application Server (App-Prod) and Test Application Server (App-Test).

Design Network Security groups to satisfy following requirements:
Traffic allowed to Production Application Server (App-Prod) is https and RDP.
Traffic allowed to Test Application Server (App-Test) is http and RDP.

Solution

Subnet VNET network address space 192.168.0.0/16 into 192.168.1.0/24 and 192.168.2.0/24 and assign it to App and DB subnets respectively as shown below.

We will create 3 Network Security Groups – NSGSubnet, NSGProd & NSGTest.
- NSGSubnet will be associated with App Subnet and add 3 inbound allow rules - http, https & RDP.
- NSGProd will be associated with Network Interface of App-Prod Server and add 2 inbound allow rules - https & RDP
- NSGTest will be associated with Network Interface of App-Test Server and add 2 inbound allow rules - http & RDP

NSG Working: NSGSubnet will only allow inbound http, https and RDP traffic and will block any other traffic. NSGProd will allow https & RDP and will block http. NSGTest will allow http & RDP and will block https. From above you can infer that 2 levels of Firewalls (NSG) are Protecting Virtual Machines.

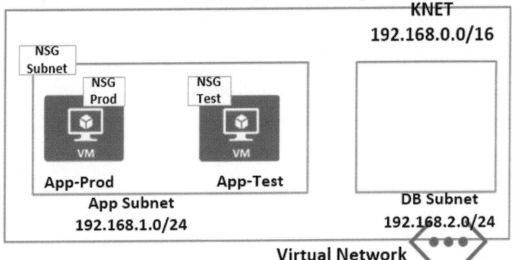

Public IP addresses in Azure

Public IP addresses allow Azure resources to communicate with Internet and to Azure public-facing services such as Azure Redis Cache, Azure Event Hubs, SQL databases, and Azure storage.

Types of Public IP Addresses: Basic & Standard (Preview). Standard is in Preview and is not being discussed here.

Public IP Address Allocation Methods

Dynamic Public IP: IP address is **not** allocated at the time of its creation. Instead, the Dynamic public IP address is allocated when you start or create the associated resource (like a VM or load balancer).
The IP address is released when you stop or delete the resource. This causes the IP address to change when you stop and start a resource.

Static Public IP: IP address for the associated resource remains the same when start or stop the resourse.
In this case an IP address is assigned immediately. It is released only when you delete the resource or change its allocation method to *dynamic*.

You can associate a public IP address resource with following resources:

VMs | Internet-facing load balancers | VPN gateways | Application gateways

Azure Resource	Dynamic	Static
Virtual Machine	Yes	Yes
Internet-facing load balancers	Yes	Yes
VPN gateways	Yes	No
Application gateways	Yes	No

DNS hostname resolution for Resources with Public IP

Resources with Public IP have Fully Qualified Domain Name in the format
resourcename.location.cloudapp.azure.com.
For Example, if you create a public IP resource with **test** as a resource name in
the West US Azure location, the fully qualified domain name (FQDN)
test.westus.cloudapp.azure.com resolves to the public IP address of the resource.

If you want use your own domain name (Test.com) with Azure Resource with
Public IP, you have 2 options depending upon IP Address allocation method.
Dynamic IP: Use cname record to point to Azure resource FQDN.
Static IP: You can either use A record name to point to Azure resource Public IP
or use cname record to point Azure Resource FQDN.

Public IP Address Pricing

Dynamic Public IP Address – Dynamic Public IP addresses in Azure are charged
at $0.004/hr (about $3/month).

Static Public IP address - First five static public IP addresses are charged for usage
at $0.004/hr. Additional static public IPs are charged for reservation at $0.004/hr
and usage at $0.004/hr for a total of $0.008/hr.

Important Note: There is no charge for "dynamic" public IP addresses when the
associated VM is "Stopped or Deallocated". However, you're charged for a "static"
public IP address irrespective of the state of associated resource (unless it is part
of the first five static ones in the region).

Private IP addresses

Private IP addresses allow Azure resources to communicate with other resources in a yvirtual network or an on-premises network through a VPN gateway or ExpressRoute circuit, without using an Internet-reachable IP address.

Private IP address is associated with following types of Azure resources:

1. VMs
2. Internal load balancers (ILBs)
3. Application gateways

Private IP Addresses are assigned from the subnet address range in which the resource is created. Private IP Address can be Static or Dynamic.

Private Dynamic IP Address: Azure assigns the next available unassigned or unreserved IP address in the subnet's address range. Once assigned, dynamic IP addresses are only released if a network interface is deleted, assigned to a different subnet within the same virtual network, or the allocation method is changed to static, and a different IP address is specified.
Dynamic is the default allocation method.

Private Static IP Address: You select and assign any unassigned or unreserved IP address in the subnet's address range. Static addresses are only released if a network interface is deleted.

Internal DNS hostname resolution for virtual machines with Private IP

When you create a virtual machine, a mapping for the hostname to its private IP address is added to the Azure-managed DNS servers by default.
These DNS servers provide name resolution for virtual machines that reside within the same virtual network.To resolve host names of virtual machines in different virtual networks, you must use a custom DNS server.

Private IP Address Pricing

There is no charge for Private IP Addressing.

Default System Routes

Azure automatically creates Default system routes and assigns the routes to each subnet in a virtual network. You can't create system routes, nor can you remove system routes, but you can override some system routes with Custom Routes which can be User Defined Routes (UDR) or BGP Routes or both.

For Example Virtual machines (VMs) in virtual networks can communicate with each other and to the public internet, automatically. You do not need to specify a gateway, even though the VMs are in different subnets.

This happens because every subnet created in a virtual network is automatically associated with a system routes that contains the following system route rules:

- **Local VNET Rule**: This rule is automatically created for every subnet in a virtual network. It specifies that there is a direct link between the VMs in the VNET and there is no intermediate next hop.
- **Internet Rule**: This rule handles all traffic destined to the public Internet (address prefix 0.0.0.0/0) and uses the infrastructure internet gateway as the next hop for all traffic destined to the Internet.
- **On-premises Rule**: This rule applies to all traffic destined to the on-premises address range and uses VPN gateway as the next hop destination.

Azure automatically creates the following default system routes for each subnet:

Source	Address Prefix	Next Hop Type
Default	Unique to the virtual network	Virtual network
Default	0.0.0.0/0	Internet
Default	10.0.0.0/8	None
Default	172.16.0.0/12	None
Default	192.168.0.0/16	None
Default	100.64.0.0/10	None

Traffic routed to the **None** next hop type is dropped, rather than routed outside the subnet. But for these Addresses (10.0.0.0/8, 172.16.0.0/12, 192.168.0.0/16, 100.64.0.0/10) Azure automatically changes the next hop type for the route from None to **Virtual network** (Local VNET Rule)

Optional Default System Routes

Azure creates default system routes for each subnet, and adds additional optional default routes to specific subnets, or every subnet, when you enable specific Azure capabilities.

Source	Address Prefix	Next Hop Type	Subnet within virtual network that route is added to
Default	Unique to the virtual network	VNET peering	All
Virtual network gateway	Prefixes advertised from on-premises via BGP, or configured in the local network gateway	Virtual Network Gateway	All
Default	Multiple	VirtualNetworkServiceEndpoint	Only the subnet a service endpoint is enabled for.

System routes control the flow of communication in the following scenarios:

- From within the same subnet.
- From a subnet to another within a VNET.
- From VMs to the Internet.
- From a VNET to another VNET through a VPN gateway.
- From a VNET to another VNET through VNet Peering.
- From a VNET to your on-premises network through a VPN gateway.
- From a Subnet to Azure Services through VirtualNetworkServiceEndpoint.

Figure Below shows Default System Route associated with Subnets.

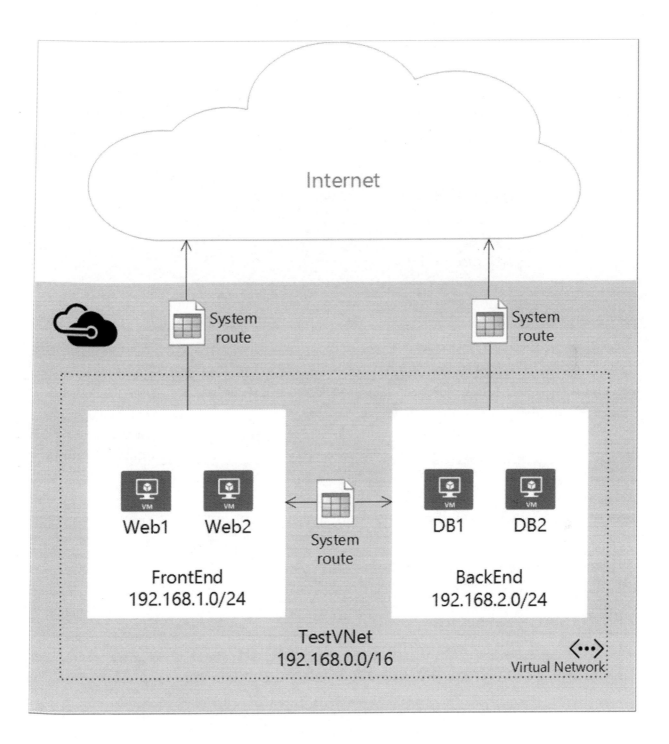

User-defined routes (UDR)

With user-defined routes you not only override Azure's default system routes but can also add additional routes to a subnet's route table.

With User Defined routes, Virtual Machine traffic in a Subnet goes through a **Network virtual appliance (NVA)** located in another subnet. This is done by creating Route table (Consisting User Defined Routes) and associating Route Table with the Subnets where traffic originates and terminates.

With UDR, NVA VM acts the gateway for other VMs in your virtual network.

In Figure below a Custom route table consisting of UDR is created and Associated with Web-Subnet and DB-Subnet. Traffic from Web-Subnet to DB-subnet and Vice versa goes through network virtual appliance (NVA) located in DMZ subnet **as UDR Route is preferred over Default System Route.**

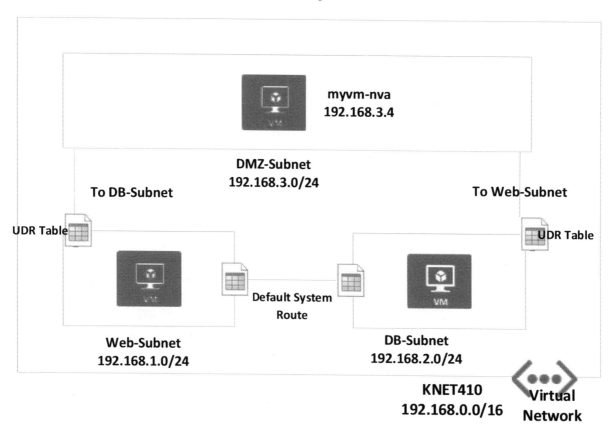

Network virtual appliance (NVA) VM: NVA VM is a Windows Server VM with Private IP and with IP forwarding enabled on Network Interface of the VM.

How Azure selects a route

Subnets rely on Default system routes until a route table is associated to the subnet. Once an association exists, routing is done based on Longest Prefix Match (LPM) among both user defined routes and system routes. If multiple routes contain the same address prefix, Azure selects the route type, based on the following priority:

1. User defined route
2. BGP route (when ExpressRoute is used)
3. System route

Route Table

A route table is a collection of individual routes used to decide where to forward packets based on the destination IP address. Route table is associated with Subnet. A route consists of the following:

Address prefix: The destination address in CIDR format.
Next hop type: Next hop type can be Virtual Network, Virtual Network gateway, Internet, virtual appliance (NVA) or none.
Next hop Address: It is the Address of the Virtual Appliance VM. Next hop values are only allowed in routes where the next hop type is *Virtual Appliance*.

IP Forwarding

To allow Virtual Machine (NVA) to receive traffic addressed to other destinations, enable IP Forwarding for the NVA VM.

Design Nugget UDR

Design Nugget 1: User defined routes are only applied to traffic leaving a subnet. You cannot create routes to specify how traffic comes into a subnet.
Design Nugget 2: The appliance you are forwarding traffic to cannot be in the same subnet where the traffic originates. Always create a separate subnet for your appliances.
Design Nugget 3: Each subnet can be associated with one or zero route table apart from system routes. But the same route table can be associated to one or more subnets. All VMs in a subnet use the route table associated to that subnet.

Case Study 2 UDR: Routing Traffic between 2 Subnets to pass through another Subnet.

Route traffic between Web-Subnet and DB-Subnet to pass-through a network virtual appliance located in another Subnet. The idea behind this exercise to clear UDR concepts and this is not a step by step Exercise.

Solution

1. Create DMZ Subnet.
2. Deploy Windows Server 2016 NVA VM (myvm-nva) in DMZ subnet with Private IP (192.168.3.4) only.

Figure below shows the architecture of the solution.

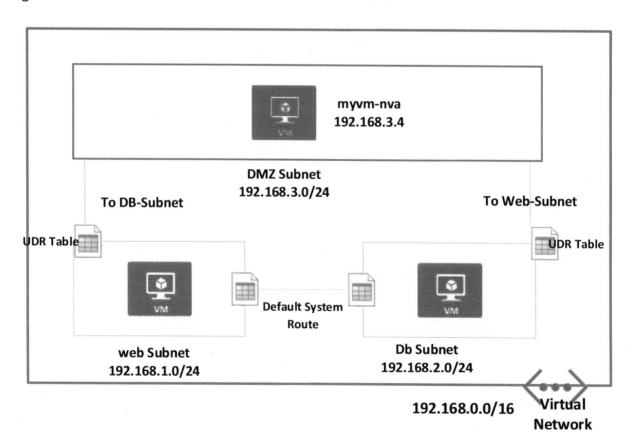

Step 1: To allow NVA Virtual Machine in DMZ subnet to receive traffic addressed to other destinations, enable IP Forwarding for the NVA VM.

Enable IP Forwarding in NVA Virtual Machine in DMZ subnet: Go to NVA VM Dashboard> Click Networking under settings> In Right pane click Private Network Interface attached to NVA VM>Network Interface Dashboard opens>Click IP Configuration in left Pane>In Right Pane Click Enabled.

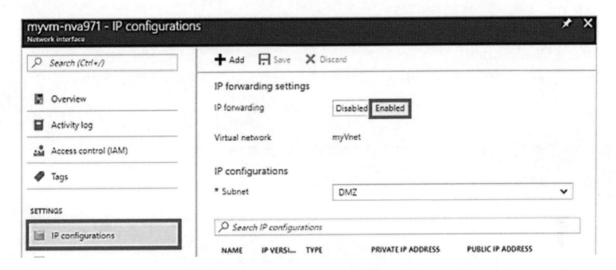

Step 2 Create Route Table: Click + Create a Resource> Networking> Route Table> Create Route Table Blade opens>Enter Information and click create.

Step 3 Add a route in Route Table (ToDBSubnet): Go to ToDBSubnet Route table Dashboard> Click Routes in left Pane>Click +Add> Add Route Blade opens > Enter information and click ok.

Address Prefix: Network Address of DB-Subnet 192.168.2.0/24

Next Hop Address: IP Address of NVA VM (myvm-nva) 192.168.3.4

Step 4 Associate Route Table (ToDBSubnet) with Web Subnet: Go to Virtual Network knet Dashboard>click Subnets in left pane>In Right pane click Web-Subnet>Web-Subnet Blade opens>Click Route table>In Right Pane select ToDBSubnet>Click Save in Top left.

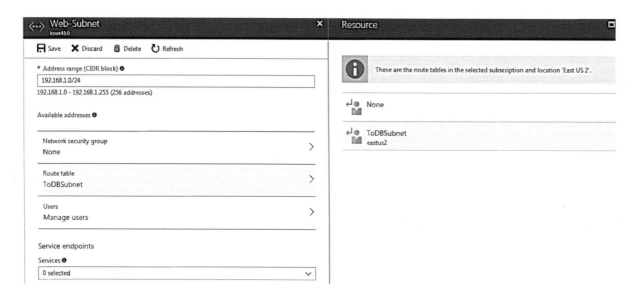

Step 5, 6 & 7: Similarly create Route table ToWebSubnet, add a route to Route Table and associate Route Table with DB Subnet.

Result 1 of above actions: We have both default routes and User defined Routes associated with Web Subnet & DB Subnet.

Result 2 of above actions: Network traffic between any resources in the Web-Subnet and DB- Subnets flows through the network virtual appliance. Though system route specify that Traffic can flow directly between Web and DB subnet but Traffic flows through NVA **as UDR is preferred over System Route.**

Virtual Networks Peering

Virtual network (VNET) peering connects two VNETs in the same region through the Azure backbone network. Once peered, the two VNETs appear as one for connectivity purposes. Virtual machines (VM) in the peered VNETs can communicate with each other directly by using private IP addresses.

You no longer have to configure Site-to-Site (S2S) VPN between Virtual Networks using Virtual Network gateway. The disadvantage of this option is that connectivity between VNET is over the internet backbone.

Figure Below shows VNET peering between 2 Virtual Networks (VNET1 & VNET2). VMs in both VNETs can now communicate with each other using their Private IPs.

VNET1   VNET2

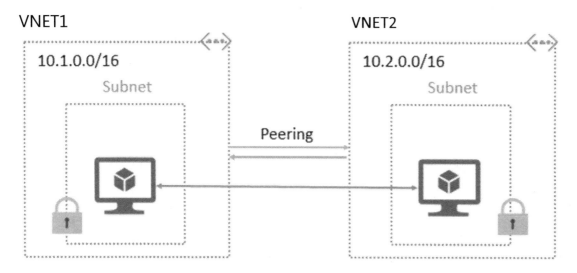

Advantages of VNET Peering

1. VNET-VNET connectivity happens over a low-latency, high-bandwidth connection.
2. You no longer have to configure Site-to-Site (S2S) VPN between Virtual Networks using Virtual Network gateway. This results in operational simplicity as Installing and Configuring VPN Gateway is a complex operation. Installation of VPN Gateway takes around 45 Minutes.

Pre-requisite for VNET-VNET Connectivity

1. The peered VNET must exist in the same Azure region.
2. The peered VNETs must have non-overlapping IP address spaces.

VNET Peering Pricing

Inbound and outbound Data transfer in the VNET is charged at both ends of the peered networks.

Data Transfer	Price
Inbound data transfer	$0.01 per GB
Outbound data transfer	$0.01 per GB

Exercise 5: Configuring Peering between Virtual Networks (VNET1 & VNET2)

1. Create 2 VNETS- VNET1 (10.1.0.0/16) & VNET2 (10.2.0.0/16) in the same region. Procedure to create VNET was shown in Exercise 1.

2. Go to VNET1 Dashboard>Click Peering in left pane> In Right Pane Click +Add > Add Peering blade opens > Select VNET2 in Virtual Network and click ok.

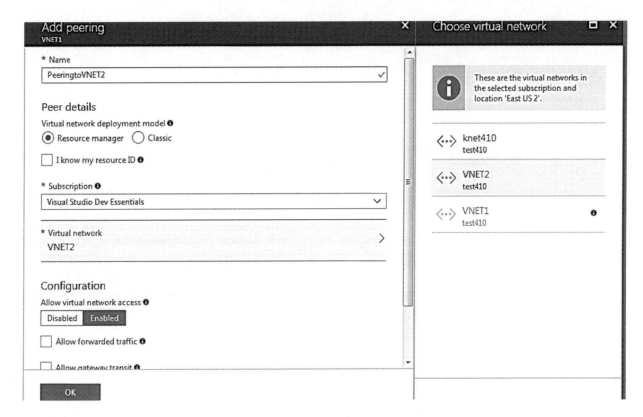

3. Repeat the above steps in VNET2.
4. The 2 VNETs are now peered and connected. You can check the peering status by clicking peering in Virtual Network (VNET1 or VNET2) dashboard as shown below.

You can see in above configuration how easily VNET peering was done in just 2 steps. Secondly there was no complex configuration to be completed as we do in S2S VPN using Virtual Network gateway.

Case Study 3: Workload Isolation with Hub and Spoke VNETs using VNET Peering

Spoke VNETs will be used to isolate workloads such as Production & Dev & Test.

Hub VNET will run shared workloads such as DNS, AD DS & Security Appliances.

Spoke VNETs will peer with Hub VNET. Hub VNET will also provide hybrid connectivity to on-premises Data center over internet using Virtual Network Gateway.

Hub VNET acts as a central point of connectivity for on-premises network and spoke VNETs.

Figure below shows Spoke 1 and Spoke 2 VNETs are peered with Hub VNET. Hub VNET is also connected to on-premises network using VPN Gateway.

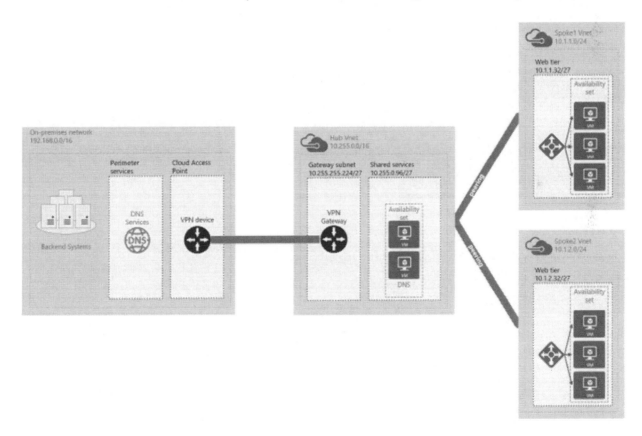

Spoke VNET to Spoke VNET Connectivity (Optional)

If Spoke to Spoke connectivity is required then User Defined Route (UDR) and Network Virtual Appliances (NVA) will be used.

UDR attached to Subnet in the Spoke VNET will forward traffic to NVA VM in Hub VNET. NVA VM will route traffic to other spoke VNET.

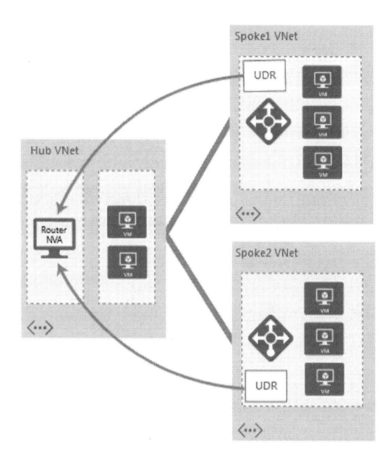

Enterprise use case for this architecture include following:

1. Workloads requiring isolation such as development, testing, and production, but require shared services such as DNS, IDS, NTP, or AD DS. Shared services are placed in the Hub VNET, while each environment is deployed to a spoke VNET to maintain isolation.
2. Enterprises that require central control over security aspects, such as a firewall in the hub as a DMZ, and segregated management for the workloads in each spoke.
3. Require secure Hybrid connectivity to on-premises Data Center.

Architecting Microsoft Azure Solutions Study & Lab Guide Part 1: Exam 70-535

Benefits of this Architecture include following:

1. **Cost savings** by centralizing services such as network virtual appliances (NVAs) and DNS servers in Hub VNET, that can be shared by multiple workloads in Spoke VNETs.

2. **Separation of operations** between central IT (SecOps, InfraOps) and workloads (DevOps). Central IT Managing Hub VNET and Application owners managing Spoke VNETs.

Global VNET Peering

Global VNET peering concepts are similar to VNET Peering except for one difference which is that you connect Virtual Networks in 2 different regions.

Global VNET peering connects two VNETs in the different region through the Azure backbone network. Once peered, the two VNETs appear as one for connectivity purposes. Virtual machines (VM) in the peered VNETs can communicate with each other directly by using private IP addresses.

You no longer have to configure Site-to-Site (S2S) VPN between Virtual Networks using Virtual Network gateway.

Figure below shows Global VNET peering between 2 Virtual Networks (VNET1 & VNET2). VMs in both VNETs can now communicate with each other using their Private IPs.

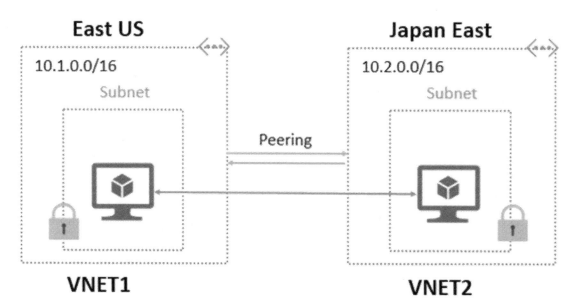

Features of Global VNET Peering

1. You can peer across VNETs in any Azure public regions with non-overlapping address spaces.
2. You can globally peer across subscriptions.
3. Traffic across globally peered links is completely private and stays on the Microsoft Backbone.

Configuring Global VNET Peering

Configuration of Global VNET Peering is similar to configuration of VNET Peering.

Global VNET Peering Pricing

Global VNET Peering Pricing will differ based on the zone your VNETs are in.

	ZONE 1	ZONE 2	ZONE 3
Inbound data transfer	$0.035 per GB	$0.09 per GB	$0.16 per GB
Outbound data transfer	$0.035 per GB	$0.09 per GB	$0.16 per GB

Zone 1—East US, East US 2, Central US, North Central US, South Central US, West Central US, West US, West US 2, Canada East, Canada Central, North Europe, West Europe, UK West, UK South, France Central, France South.

Zone 2—Southeast Asia, East Asia, Australia East, Australia Southeast, Central India, West India, South India, Japan East, Japan West, Korea Central, Korea South, Australia Central, Australia Central 2, South Africa North, South Africa West.

Zone 3—Brazil South.

Virtual Network Service Endpoint

By default Azure Managed Resources or Azure Services such as Azure Storage and Azure SQL Database with Public IP are accessed over internet connection from outside Azure and by VMs in Virtual Network over internet connection.

With Azure Virtual Network Endpoints, traffic between Azure Virtual Network and Azure Managed Resources remains on the Microsoft Azure backbone network and not on Public Internet. Virtual Network Endpoints feature is currently available for the following Azure services:

Azure Storage
Azure SQL Database
Azure Cosmos DB
Azure SQL Data Warehouse (In Preview)

Figure below shows the **Architecture of VNET Service Endpoints**.

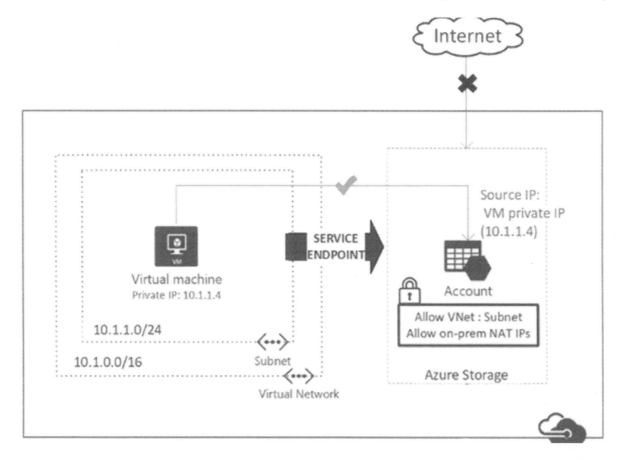

Woking of VNET Service Endpoints

Virtual Network Service Endpoints are created in Virtual Network and are attached to Subnets. They extend Azure Virtual Network private address space to Azure Managed services. You can also restrict Azure resources to only be accessed from your VNET and not via the Internet. You also have the option to allow access from internet from particular IP range only.

Why we need Azure Virtual Network Endpoints

Azures Managed Resources such as Azure Storage and Azure SQL have Internet facing IP addresses. Because of security reasons many customers prefer that their Azure Managed Services not be exposed directly to the Internet.

Exercise 6: Setting up Virtual Network Service Endpoints

For these Exercise we will create VNET Service Endpoints for Azure Storage. We have file Hello World.Txt in Blob Storage which can be opened from following link https://sa535.blob.core.windows.net/c535/Hello World.txt. After setting up Service Endpoint and blocking access of Azure storage from internet we will check whether we can still open the file. We will then open the file from Azure VM wvm535 located in Web-Subnet.

Note for the Readers: **Attempt this exercise after you have completed Storage chapter.** In Compute, Storage Account and Storage chapters we will add VM wvm535, Storage Account sa535 and upload a file to Blob Storage respectively.

Step 1 Check whether you can access Hello World.txt from internet or not: open Hello World.Txt from https://sa535.blob.core.windows.net/c535/Hello World.txt. Yes this opens from internet.

Step 2: Go the Virtual Network knet Dashboard> click Service endpoints in left pane> Click +Add> Add service endpoints blade opens> Select Storage and Web-subnet from dropdown boxes>click Add.

Step 3: Go Storage Account sa535 dashboard>Click Firewalls and Virtual Networks in left pane>Click selected Networks Radio Button in right pane>click +Add Existing Virtual Network> Add Network blade opens>Select knet from dropdown box>Select web-subnet from dropdown box and click Add>click save.

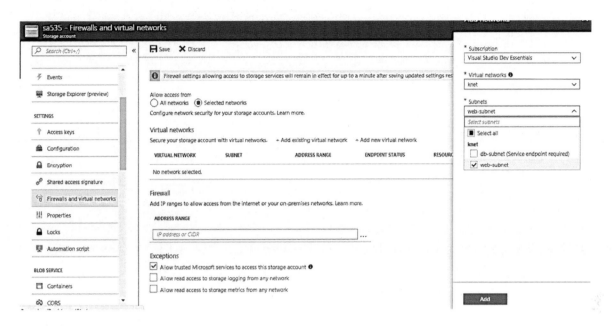

Note Firewall option: Here you can add IP address range which can access Azure storage from internet. Note also the 3 Exception options.

Step 4: Check whether you can download Hello World.txt file from internet or not. Open a different browser and enter
https://sa535.blob.core.windows.net/c535/Hello World.txt
Note: we are using different browser because Hello World.Txt might be in cache of browser when we opened the file in step 1.

It shows "This request is not authorized to perform this operation".

Step 5: RDP to Virtual Machine wvm535>open internet explorer and log on Azure Portal>Go to sa535 Dashboard>Click Blobs>Click container c535>Click Hello World.txt>Click download button at top>Hello World.txt file opens in Internet Explorer.

As an exercise to the readers edit the Service Endpoint Connection by allowing connection from internet from your IP only. Check whether you can download or not. Under Firewall add your IP assigned by ISP.

Step 6 Enable back Storage Account access from all Networks: In Storage Network sa535 Dashboard click Firewall and Virtual Networks in left pane>Select the radio button All Networks>Click save.

Note: We need access to Storage Account from internet for other exercises.

Chapter 2 Azure Compute

This Chapter covers following Topic Lessons

- Azure Virtual Machine
- Virtual Machine Series
- Virtual Machine Storage Architecture
- Virtual Machine Disk Types (OS, Data & Temporary)
- Managed & Unmanaged Disks
- Virtual Machine Standard Storage (HDD) & Premium Storage (SSD)
- Virtual Machine Networking & IP Addressing
- Virtual Machine Availability Set
- Virtual Machine Limits
- Virtual Machine Storage Pricing
- Virtual Machine Compute Pricing

This Chapter Covers following Case Studies

- Availability Set
- Choosing VM size and Designing IOPs

This Chapter Covers following Lab Exercises to build below topology

- Creating Virtual Machine wvm535
- Logging on to VM using RDP
- Installing IIS Web Server on Virtual Machine
- Virtual Machine Host Level Monitoring
- Virtual Machine Guest Level Monitoring
- Demonstrating additional functionalities of the Virtual Machine

Chapter Topology

In this chapter we will add Virtual Machine **wvm535** to the topology.

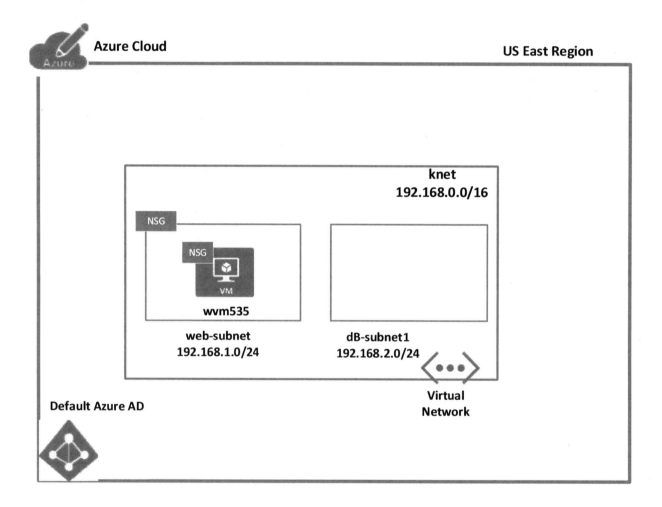

Azure Virtual Machine

Azure Virtual Machine is on-demand, resizable computing resource in the cloud that can be used to host variety of applications. Azure Virtual Machine runs on a Hyper-V host which also runs other Virtual Machines.

You can scale up computing/Memory resource by using bigger size VM or scale out using additional instance of the virtual machine and then Load Balancing them.

Azure VM can be Windows or Linux based.

Virtual Machine (VM) Sizes

Virtual Machines are available in various sizes and categorized under series. Under each series various virtual machine sizes are available with options for memory, CPU family, Number of CPU cores, Standard or Premium Storage, Number of Data Disks, Number of NIC's and Temporary Storage.

Various Virtual Machine Series are available either with Standard Storage or both Standard & Premium Storage.

Virtual Machines with standard storage are available under A-series, Av2-series, D-series, Dv2-series, Dv3, F-series, G-Series, H-series and N-series. These VMs use magnetic HDD to host a virtual machine disks (OS and Data Disk). Temporary storage is on SSD except for A series which are on magnetic HDD.

Virtual Machines with premium Storage are available under DS-series, DSv2-series, DSv3, ESv3, FS-series, GS-series etc. These VMs can use solid-state drives (SSDs) or HDD to host a virtual machine disks (OS and Data Disk) and also provide a local SSD disk cache. Temporary storage is on SSD.

Note: Virtual Machines with letter **s** in its size designation support both Standard Storage and Premium Storage.

Virtual Machines Series

Virtual Machines series in Azure can be categorized under General purpose, Compute optimized, Memory optimized, Storage Optimized, GPU and High Performance Compute.

Type	Series	Description
General purpose	DSv3, Dv3, DSv2, Dv2, DS, D, Av2, A0-4 Basic, A0-A7 Standard	Balanced CPU-to-memory ratio. Ideal for testing and development, General Purpose Production workloads, small to medium databases, and low to medium traffic web servers.
Compute optimized	Fs, F, Fv2 & FSv2	High CPU-to-memory ratio. Good for medium traffic web servers, network appliances, batch processes, and application servers.
Memory optimized	ESv3, Ev3, M, GS, G, DSv2, Dv2, DS & D	High memory-to-core ratio. Great for relational database servers, medium to large caches, and in-memory analytics.
Storage optimized	Ls	High disk throughput and IO. Ideal for Big Data, SQL, and NoSQL databases.
GPU	NC, NCv2, NCv3, NV & ND	Specialized virtual machines targeted for heavy graphic rendering and video editing. Available with single or multiple GPUs.
High performance compute	H, A8-11	High Performance Computing VMs are good for high performance & parallel computing workloads such as financial risk modeling, seismic and reservoir simulation, molecular modeling and genomic research.

Note 1: D, DS and A0-A7 Standard are being phased out.
Note 2: Virtual Machines with letter **s** in its size designation support both Standard Storage and Premium Storage.
Note 2: Dv2 & DSv2 machines are included in both General Purpose & Memory. General Purpose includes following sizes: D1v2, D2v2, D3v2, D4v2 and D5v2. Memory Optimised includes following: D11v2, D12v2, D13v2, D14v2 & D15v2.
Note 3: Microsoft recommends that to get the best performance for price, use the latest generation VMs where possible.

Azure Compute Unit (ACU)

With Azure Compute Unit (ACU) you can compare CPU performance across various Virtual Machine sizes. ACU is currently standardized on a Small (Standard_A1) VM being 100 and all other VM sizes then represent approximately how much faster that SKU can run a standard benchmark with respect to A1.

Virtual Machine	ACU/Core
A1	100
AV2 & AMV2	100
A8-A11	225
D1	160
DS1	160
Dv2	210-250
DSv2	210-250
Dv3	160-190
DSv3	160-190
Ev3	160-190
ESv3	160-190
F	210-250
Fs	210-250
G	180-240
GS	180-240
H	290-300
LS	180-240
M	160-180

Virtual Machine Storage Architecture

Storage for Virtual Machines is provided by Virtual Machine Disks. Azure Virtual Machine Disks (OS & Data) are stored in Page Blob and are accessed over the network.

You can also mount Azure File shares to Virtual Machine disks for additional Storage. File shares will be further discussed in Storage chapter.

Figure bellows shows Storage options for Azure Virtual Machines.

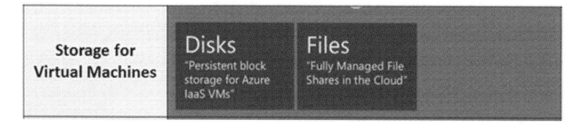

Figure below shows OS and Data Disks are stored in Azure Blob (Page) Storage and are accessed over the network. Temporary disk is located on the physical host where the virtual machine is running.

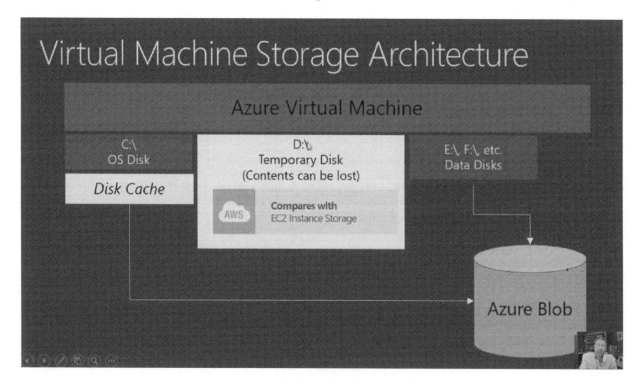

Virtual Machine Storage Disk Types

Azure Virtual Machine Disks are stored in Page Blob storage. Page Blob storage can use Standard Storage or Premium Storage. Standard Storage is backed by Magnetic HDD and Premium Storage is backed by SSD.

Azure Virtual Machines have minimum of 2 disks: OS Disk and Temporary Disk. You can also attach additional Data Disks. Number of Data Disks depend upon the series and the size of the VM choosen.

Virtual Machine Disks (OS and Data disk) are accessed over the network. Temporary disk is located on the physical host where the virtual machine is running. Virtual machines use virtual hard disks (VHDs) to store their operating system (OS) and data. Virtual Machine disks (VHDs) are stored in page blobs.

Operating System Disks

Every virtual machine has one **network attached** operating system disk and is **accessed over the network**. It's labeled as the C: drive. This disk has a maximum capacity of 4095 gigabytes (GB). Data is persisted in the event virtual machine is rebooted, started or stopped. It is registered as SATA Drive.

Temporary Disk

The temporary disk is automatically created on physical host where virtual machine is running. The temporary disk is labeled as the D: drive and it is used for storing page or swap files. Data is lost in the event virtual machine is rebooted or stopped. The size of the temporary disk is based on the size of the VM.

Data Disk

A data disk is a VHD that's attached to a virtual machine to store application data and is **accessed over the network**. The size of the virtual machine determines how many data disks you can attach to it. Data is persisted in the event virtual machine is rebooted, started or stopped. Data disks are registered as SCSI drives and are labeled with a letter that you choose.

Managed and Unmanaged Disk

Azure Virtual Machine disk types (OS & Data Disk) can be Unmanaged or Managed.

Disks are associated with storage accounts. Maximum IOPS of storage account is 20000 IOPS. We have to make sure that IOPS of all disks in the storage account should not exceed 20000 IOPS otherwise throttling happens.

Unmanaged Disks

With unmanaged disks we have to create and specify the storage account when we create unmanaged disk. We have to make sure that the combined IOPS of disks in the storage account do not exceed 20000 IOPS. We have to also plan number of storage accounts needed to accommodate our disks.

Managed Disks

Managed Disk option takes care of storage account creation and management and also ensures that users do not have to worry about 20000 IOPS limit in the storage account.

Managed Disks allow you to create up to 10,000 VM **disks** in a subscription.

When using availability set (AS) managed disk option ensures that disks of VMs in AS are isolated from each other to avoid SPOF.

The advantage of Managed Disk option is that it eliminates the operational overhead of planning, creating and managing Storage Accounts.

MS recommends that Managed Disk option to be used for all new VMs and convert previously created unmanaged disks to managed disks to take advantage of new features in managed disks.

Note : Unmanaged or Managed OS Disk is chosen during Virtual Machine creation.

Virtual Machine Disk Performance Tiers

There are two types of Performance tiers for virtual machine disk storage – Standard Storage & Premium Storage. Virtual Machines disks are stored in Page Blobs. Page blobs can be created under General Purpose Standard Storage account or General purpose premium Storage account.

Standard Storage

With Standard Storage, OS and Data disks are stored in page blob backed by Magnetic HDD. You can use standard storage disks for Dev/Test scenarios and less critical workloads.

Standard Storage disks can be created in 2 ways – Unmanaged disks or Managed Disks. With Unmanaged disk you need to create storage account. Whereas Managed Disk option takes care of storage account creation.

Standard disks limits (unmanaged) This has gone to 8 TB

VM Tier	Basic Tier	Standard Tier
Max Disk size	4095 GB	4095 GB
Max 8 KB IOPS per disk	300	500
Max throughput per disk	60 MB/s	60 MB/s

Maximum Disk Size in Standard Unmanaged disk is 4095 GB. You pay only for the capacity used. It is therefore recommended you create the disk with Max size as you are paying only for the capacity used.

Standard Managed disk Sizes

Standard Managed Disk Type	S4	S6	S10	S20	S30	S40	S50
Disk Size (GB)	32	64	128	512	1024	2048	4095
Max IOPS per disk	500	500	500	500	500	500	500
Max throughput per disk	60 MB/s	60 MB/s	60 MB/s	60 MB/s	60 MB/s	60 MB/s	60 MB/s

Premium Storage

Premium Storage disks are backed by solid-state drives (SSDs). With Premium Storage, OS and Data disks are stored in page blob backed by SSD.

Azure Premium Storage delivers high-performance, low-latency disk support for virtual machines (VMs) with input/output (I/O)-intensive workloads. You can use Premium storage disks for I/O intensive and mission-critical production applications.

Requirements for Premium Storage

1. You can use Premium Storage disks only with VMs that are compatible with Premium Storage Disks. Premium Storage supports DS-series, DSv2-series, DSv3 Series, GS-series, Ls-series, and Fs-series, ESv3 VMs etc only.

2. You will require Premium storage account to create Premium Storage Disks. A premium storage account supports only locally redundant storage (LRS) as the replication option. Locally redundant storage keeps three copies of the data within a single region.

Features of Virtual Machines (DS-series, DSv2-series, DSv3, ESv3GS-series, Ls-series, and Fs-series, M etc) backed by Premium Storage

1. **Virtual Machine OS Disk:** Premium Storage VM can use either a premium or a standard operating system disk.

2. **Virtual Machine Data Disk:** Premium Storage VM can use both Premium and Standard Storage Disks.

3. **Cache:** VMs with Premium Storage have a unique caching capability for high levels of throughput and latency. The caching capability exceeds underlying premium storage disk performance. You can set the disk caching policy on premium storage disks to **ReadOnly**, **ReadWrite**, or **None**. The default disk caching policy is **ReadOnly** for all premium data disks and **ReadWrite** for operating system disks.

Architecting Microsoft Azure Solutions Study & Lab Guide Part 1: Exam 70-535

4. **VM scale limits and performance:** Premium Storage-supported VMs have scale limits and performance specifications for IOPS, bandwidth, and the number of disks that can be attached per VM.

For example, a STANDARD_DS1 VM has a dedicated bandwidth of 32 MB/s for premium storage disk traffic. A P10 premium storage disk can provide a bandwidth of 100 MB/s. If a P10 premium storage disk is attached to this VM, it can only go up to 32 MB/s. It cannot use the maximum 100 MB/s that the P10 disk can provide.

Premium Storage disk Sizes and limits (Unmanaged)

Premium storage disk type	P10	P20	P30	P40	P50
Disk Size (GB)	128	512	1024	2048	4095
Max Throughput per Disk	100 MB/s	150 MB/s	200 MB/s	250 MB/s	250 MB/s
Max IOPS per Disk	500 IOPS	2300 IOPS	5000 IOPS	7500 IOPS	7500 IOPS

Premium Storage Managed disk Sizes and limits

Premium storage disk type	P4	P6	P10	P20	P30	P40	P50
Disk Size (GB)	32	64	128	512	1024	2048	4095
Max Throughput per Disk	25 MB/s	50 MB/s	100 MB/s	150 MB/s	200 MB/s	250 MB/s	250 MB/s
Max IOPS per Disk	120 IOPS	240 IOPS	500 IOPS	2300 IOPS	5000 IOPS	7500 IOPS	7500 IOPS

Premium vs Standard Storage Comparison Chart

Feature	Premium Storage	Standard Storage
Storage Account Supported	General Purpose Premium storage account	General Purpose Standard storage account
Disk Type	SSD	Magnetic HDD
Use case	Production and I/O Intensive workloads.	Dev/Test, low end and non critical applications.
Unmanaged Disk Size	P10: 128 GB; P20: 512 GB; P30: 1024 GB; P40: 2048 GB; P50: 4095 GB	1 GB – 4 TB (4095 GB)
Managed Disk Size	P4: 32 GB; P6: 64 GB; P10: 128 GB; P20: 512 GB; P30: 1024 GB; P40: 2048 GB; P50: 4095 GB	S4: 32 GB, S6: 64 GB, S10: 128 GB, S20: 512 GB, S30: 1024 GB, S40: 2048 GB, S50: 4095 GB
Max Throughput per Disk	200 MB/s	60 MB/s
Max IOPS per Disk	7500	500

Design Nuggets

1. Throughput is the bandwidth available to access the disk over the network.
2. **IOPS** refers to performance in solid-state drives (SSD) or hard disk drives (HDD).To increase the capacity and performance of the volume combine multiple disks and stripe across the disks.
3. Make sure sufficient Bandwidth is available on your VM to drive disk traffic, as described in Premium Storage supported VMs, otherwise your disk throughput and IOPS are constrained to lower values. <u>Maximum throughput and IOPS are based on VM limits and not on disk limits described in the preceding table.</u>
   For example, a STANDARD_DS1 VM has a dedicated bandwidth of 32 MB/s for premium storage disk traffic. A P10 premium storage disk can provide a bandwidth of 100 MB/s. If a P10 premium storage disk is attached to this VM, it can only go up to 32 MB/s. It cannot use the maximum 100 MB/s that the P10 disk can provide.

Virtual Machine Disk Encryption

Azure Disk Encryption encrypts your Azure Windows and Linux Virtual Machine disks. Azure Disk Encryption leverages the industry standard **BitLocker** feature of Windows and the **DM-Crypt** feature of Linux to provide volume encryption for the OS and the data disks.

BitLocker is an industry-recognized Windows volume encryption technology that's used to enable disk encryption on Windows IaaS VMs.

DM-Crypt is the Linux-based, transparent disk-encryption subsystem that's used to enable disk encryption on Linux IaaS VMs.

The solution is integrated with Azure Key Vault to help you Protect and manage the disk encryption keys (windows VM) and secrets (Linux VM) in your key vault subscription.

You can use Azure Command Line interface (CLI), Azure PowerShell or Azure Resource Manager templates to encrypt an Azure VM Disks.

Figure below shows step by step configuration of Disk Encryption.

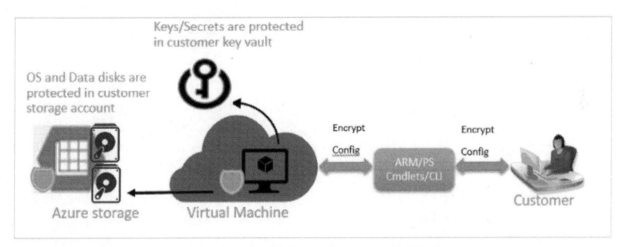

Design Nugget: VM Disk encryption feature encrypts data at rest using Customer managed keys for particular VM disk.
Design Nugget: By default Storage Service encryption (SSE) feature encrypts data at rest for all VM disks stored in Storage Account using Azure Managed keys. You have the option of using your own keys.

Virtual Machine Networking

Azure Virtual Machines are created in Virtual Networks. An Azure virtual network (VNET) is Virtual Data Center in the cloud. You can further segment virtual network (VNET) into subnets. Access to the subnets can be controlled using Network Security groups. You can define the IP address blocks, security policies, and route tables within this network.

In the below diagram you have Virtual Network KNET1 with network address 192.168.0.0/16 divided into two Subnets- Web-Subnet1 and DB-Subnet1 with network addresses 192.168.1.0/24 and 192.168.2.0/24 respectively.

These Network Addresses are defined by the user and not by Azure Cloud.

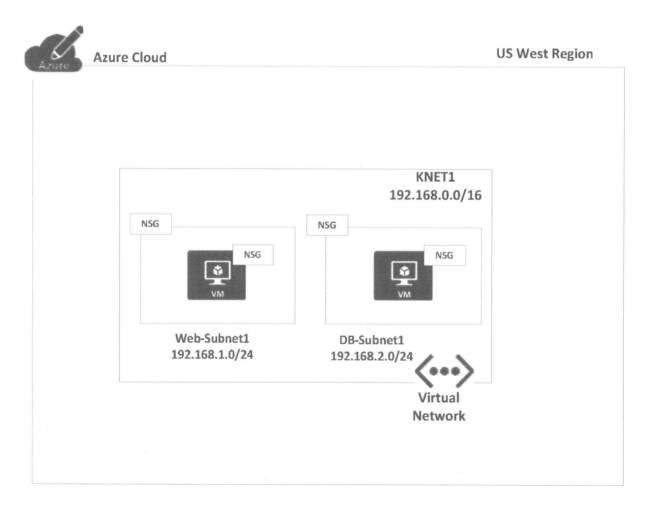

Azure Virtual Machines private address is derived from subnet address. In the above figure Virtual Machines in Web-Subnet1 will get **private address** of 192.168.1.x/24 and Virtual Machines in DB-Subnet1 will get private address of 192.168.2.x/24. Private IP Address is used for communication within a Virtual Network, your on-premises network and the Internet (with NAT).

You can use following class A, Class B and Class C address range for virtual networks.

10.0.0.0/8
172.16.0.0/12
192.168.0.0/16

Once the IP address range is decided, we can then divide this range into subnets. Azure Virtual Machines private address is derived from subnet address.

Virtual Machine Public address will be assigned by Azure. Public Address can be Static or Dynamic. Dynamic Public IP will change every time you stop or reboot your Virtual Machine. To ensure the IP address for the VM remains the same, set the allocation method to static.
Public IP address is used for communication with internet and Public facing Azure resources which are not part of Virtual Network.

Network Security Group (NSG) acts as a Firewall. Network Security Group (NSG) contains a list of rules that allow or deny network traffic to subnets, VM NICs, or both. NSGs can be associated with subnets and/or individual VM NICs connected to a subnet. When an NSG is associated with a subnet, the rules apply to all the VMs in that subnet. In addition, traffic to an individual VM NIC can be restricted by associating an NSG directly to a VM NIC.

Virtual Machine Accelerated Networking (AN)

Accelerated Networking (AN) provides ultra-low network latency for Virtual Machine Network Traffic. AN provides up to 30Gbps in networking throughput.

With AN much of Azure's software-defined networking stack is moved into FPGA-based SmartNICs. Accelerated networking enables single root I/O virtualization (SR-IOV) to a VM, greatly improving its networking performance.
The SR-IOV allows different virtual machines (VMs) in a virtual environment to share a single PCI Express hardware interface.

With AN, Virtual Machine Networking Traffic bypasses Virtual switch on the host and directly connects to Host SmartNIC, reducing latency, jitter, and CPU utilization. All network policies that the virtual switch applies are now offloaded and applied in hardware.

Figure below shows communication between two VMs with and without accelerated networking.

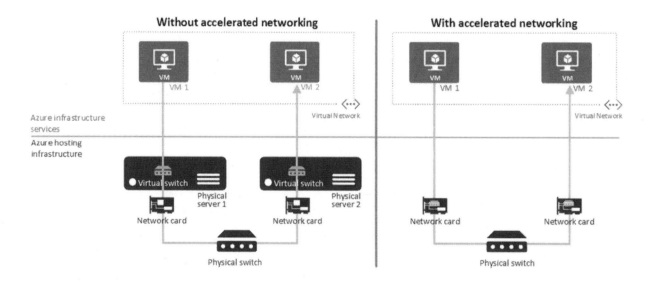

AN features has best results when enabled on VMs which are connected to same Virtual Network (VNET). When communicating across VNETs or connecting on-premises, this feature has minimal impact to overall latency.

Benefits of Accelerated Networking (AN)

Lower Latency / Higher packets per second (pps): Removing the virtual switch from the datapath removes the time packets spend in the host for policy processing and increases the number of packets that can be processed inside the VM.

Reduced jitter: Virtual switch processing depends on the amount of policy that needs to be applied and the workload of the CPU that is doing the processing. Offloading the policy enforcement to the hardware removes that variability by delivering packets directly to the VM, removing the host to VM communication and all software interrupts and context switches.

Decreased CPU utilization: Bypassing the virtual switch in the host leads to less CPU utilization for processing network traffic.

Operating System supported by Accelerated Networking

Windows	Linux
Windows Server 2016 Datacenter	Ubuntu 16.04
Windows Server 2012 R2 Datacenter	SLES 12 SP3
	RHEL 7.4
	CentOS 7.4
	CoreOS Linux
	Debian "Stretch" with backports kernel
	Oracle Linux 7.4

Supported VM instances

Accelerated Networking is supported on most general purpose and compute-optimized instance sizes with 2 or more vCPUs. These supported series are: D/DSv2 and F/Fs.

On instances that support hyperthreading, Accelerated Networking is supported on VM instances with 4 or more vCPUs. Supported series are: D/DSv3, E/ESv3, Fsv2, and Ms/Mms.

Availability Set (AS)

Availability Set (AS) Provides high Availability against hardware failure in Azure Cloud by eliminating single point of failure. Availability Set (AS) in itself is not a full high availability solution. To provide application HA, Availability Set (AS) has to be combined with Azure Load Balancer.

Before going into details of Availability Set, let's discuss why we need it in first place. Consider a scenario where there are 2 applications and each application is running 2 instances - Application A (VMA-1 & VMA-2) & Application B (VMB-1 & VMB-2). Application Instances are load balanced.

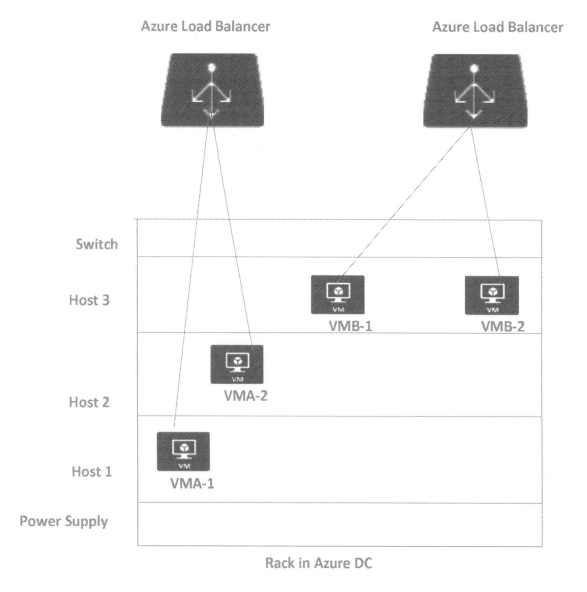

Application A has 2 single point of failure – Power Supply & TOR Switch.
Application B has 3 single point of failure - Host, Power Supply & TOR Switch.

With Availability Set we can eliminate above single point of failures.
By creating an **Availability Set** and adding virtual machines to the Availability Set, Azure will ensure that the virtual machines in the set get distributed across the physical hosts, Network switch & Rack that run them in such a way that a hardware failure will not bring down all the machines in the set.
Each virtual machine in the Availability Set is assigned an update domain and a fault domain by Azure.

An **Update Domain (UD)** is used to determine the sets of virtual machines and the underlying hardware that can be rebooted together. For each Availability Set created, five Update Domains will be created by default, but can be changed. You can configure Maximum of 20 Update Domains. When Microsoft is updating physical host it will reboot only one update domains at a time.

Fault domains (FD) define the group of virtual machines that share a common power source and network switch. For each Availability Set, two Fault Domains will be created by default, but can be changed. You can configure Maximum of 3 Fault Domains.

Design Nuggets

1. Update Domains helps with Planned Maintenance events like host reboot by Azure.
2. Fault Domain helps with unplanned Maintenance events like hardware (Host, TOR Switch or Rack Power Supply) failure.
3. Configure each application tier into separate availability sets.
4. Assign different storage accounts to virtual machines in the availability set. If there is an outage in the storage account it will not affect all the virtual machines in the set.
5. Use Azure Load Balancer to distribute traffic to virtual machines in the Availability Set. If there is a Hardware failure (Host, TOR Switch, Rack Power Supply) then it will not affect traffic to other virtual machines in the Availability Set.

Azure Availability Zones (AZ)

Azure Availability Zone protects your applications and data from Complete Location Breakdown or Datacenter wide outage which affects the entire Azure Data Center.

With Azure Availability Zones (AZ), **Azure Region will have 3 or more physically separate Data Centre's within Metro distance connected by High Speed Fibre Optic cables.** This distance can be 500M, 1 KM, 5 KM or 10 KM etc. The important point here is that Availability Zones (AZ) will not be sharing any infrastructure like Networking, Grid Power Supply and Cooling etc. The figure below shows three Availability Zones in a Region connected by High speed Fibre Optic Cables. These AZs are separate Azure Data Centers.

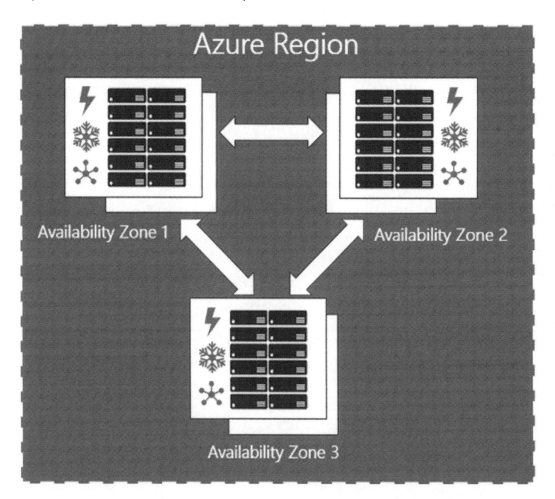

Azure services that support Availability Zones fall into two categories:
Zonal services – you pin the resource to a specific zone (for example, virtual machines, managed disks, IP addresses), or
Zone-redundant services – platform replicates automatically across zones (for example, zone-redundant storage, SQL Database).

STEP BY STEP PROVIDING HIGH AVAILABILITY TO LOAD BALANCED WEB 1, WEB2 & WEB3 VIRTUAL SERVERS USING AZURE AVAILABILITY ZONES

1. Virtual Network & Subnet created will span Availability Zone 1 (AZ1), Availability Zone 2 (AZ2) and Availability Zone 3 (AZ3) in the region.
2. Create Web1 VM with Managed disk in Subnet1 in AZ1.
3. Create Web2 VM with Managed disk in Subnet1 in AZ2.
4. Create Web3 VM with Managed disk in Subnet1 in AZ3.
5. Use Azure Standard Load Balancer (Zone Redundant) with Standard IP (Zone Redundant) to Load Balance Traffic to Web1, Web2 & Web3 Virtual Server.

Figure below shows Azure Standard Load Balancer providing cross-zone Load Balancing to 3 VMs located in AZ1, AZ2 and AZ3 respectively.

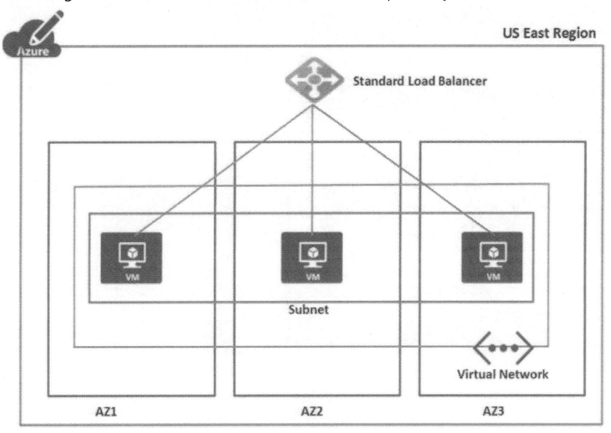

Azure Services that support Availability Zones

Azure Availability Zones preview supports following Azure Services:

Windows Virtual Machine
Linux Virtual Machine
Zonal Virtual Machine Scale Sets
Managed Disks
Load Balancer
Public IP address
Zone-redundant storage
SQL Database

Regions that support Availability Zones

Azure Availability Zones is now GA in select regions in the United States and Europe.

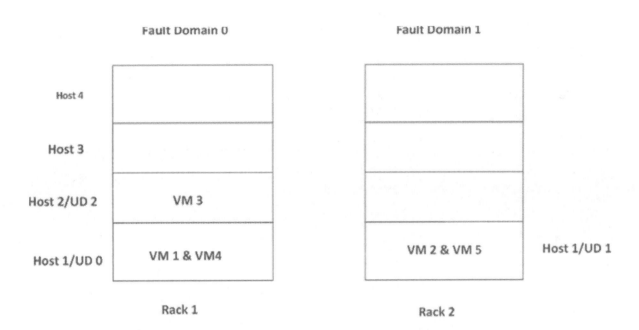

Case Study 4: Placement of Virtual Machines in Availability Set

Consider a scenario where we have 5 Virtual Machines in Availability Set with 3 Update Domains (UD) and 2 Fault Domains (FD) are configured. Show the possible placement of Virtual Machines.

AS is configured with 2 Fault Domains which means VMs will be spread across 2 racks. AS is configured with 3 Update Domains which means VMs will be placed across 3 hosts.

VM1, VM2 & VM3 will be placed in UD 0, UD 1 and UD 2 respectively. VM4 will be placed in UD 0 and VM5 will be placed in UD1.

VM1, VM3 & VM4 will share FD 0 and VM2 & VM5 will share FD 1.

In case of host failure, maximum of 2 VMs out of 5 VMs will be affected. In case of Rack Failure (PS/TOR Switch) maximum of 3 VMs out of 5 VMs will be affected.

Case Study 5: Choosing VM size and Designing IOPs

A company is shifting test & Dev app to cloud. It's a 2 Tier application – Web/App & Database tier. Application & Database owner have specified following requirements for the Virtual Machines.

Feature	Application	Database
vCPU	8	4
Memory	16 GB	64 GB
IOPS		1200
Database Size		100 GB

They want to use latest Generation Dv3 VM. To save on cost they want use Magnetic HDD for storage. They want Database Data to be on separate Data Disks and not on OS Disk.

Suggest size and configuration for Dv3 VM for Application and Database server.

Solution

Following Sizes are available in Dv3 series.

Size	vCPU	Memory	Max NICs	Temp Storage SSD	Max Data Disks	Max IOPS	Price/ hour
D2 v3	2	8	2	50 GB	4	4X500	$0.188
D4 v3	4	16	2	100 GB	8	8X500	$0.376
D8 v3	8	32	4	200 GB	16	16X500	$0.752
D16 v3	16	64	8	400 GB	32	32X500	$1.504
D32 v3	32	128	8	800 GB	32	32X500	$3.008
D64 v3	64	256	8	1600 GB	32	32X500	$6.016

For App Server We will choose D8v3 to satisfy both vCPU and Memory Req.

For DB Server we will choose D16v3 to satisfy both vCPU and Memory Req.

We need to add 3 Data disks to the instance to satisfy IOPS requirement of 1200. 3 Data Disks will give an IOPS of 1500 (3X500). Note 2 Data disks will give an IOPS of 1000 only. Data will be stripped across 3 Hard Disk to achieve the required IOPS.

Exercise 7: Create Availability Set

In Azure Portal Click Create a Resource> In search type enter Availability Set and press enter> In search result select Availability Set >Click create> Create availability set blade opens>enter as per your requirement and click create.

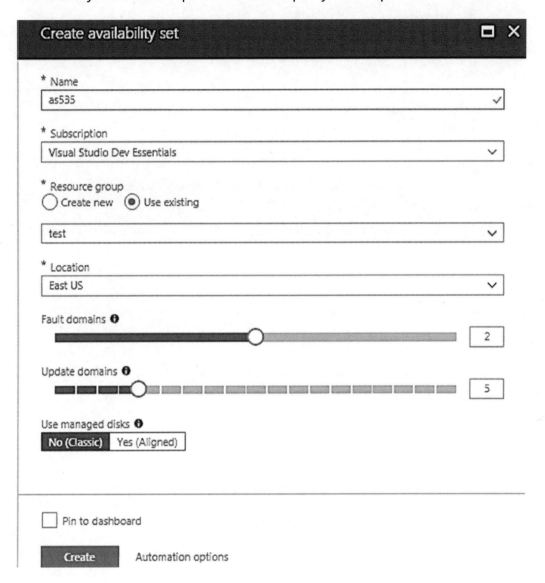

Note 1: Default values for Fault and update domains is 2 & 5 respectively.
Note 2: Max Values for Fault and update domains is 3 & 20 respectively.
Note 3: you can change the default values as per your requirement.

Exercise 8: Creating Virtual Machine

1. In Azure Portal Click Create a Resource> Compute> Windows Server 2016 Datacenter> Create Virtual Machine Blade opens>Choose parameters as per your requirement and click create.

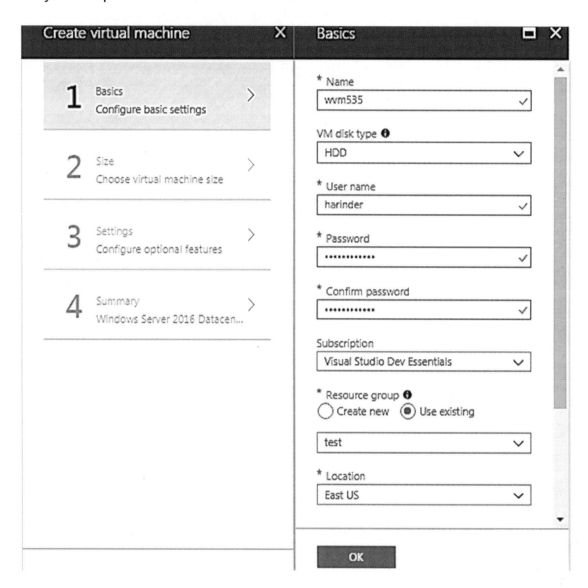

Note 1: VM Size selected is A2_v2

Note 2: In settings we have Selected Availability Set as535 created in Exercise 6, for Virtual Network & Subnet we have selected knet and web-subnet created in Exercise 1 and for Network Security Group we selected Basic option and selected http and RDP port options (This will open inbound http and RDP Ports on VM).

Exercise 9: log on to Virtual Machine using RDP

1. In Azure Portal go to Virtual Machine Dashboard>click connect in top pane>Connect to Virtual Machine Blade opens>Select IP address options>Click download RDP file> It will download RDP file with IP address of the Virtual Machine on your desktop> Open RDP file from your desktop> Enter username & password>This will RDP to wvm535 from your desktop.

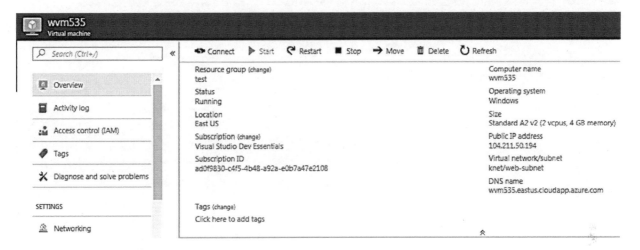

2. Open RDP file from your desktop> Enter username & password>This will RDP to wvm535 from your desktop as shown below.

Exercise 10: Installing and connecting to IIS Web Server in wvm535

1. Open RDP file from your desktop> Enter username & password>This will RDP to wvm535 from your desktop.
2. Open Server Manager>Click add roles and Feature>Next>Select Role-based or feature-based installation and click next>Select wvm535 from server pool and click next>On the Server Roles page, select Web Server (IIS) and click next>In the pop-up about adding features required for IIS, make sure that Include management tools is selected and then click Add Features. When the pop-up closes, click Next in the wizard>Click next, next, next>Install> It will take around 1-2 minute to install the IIS. After Installation is complete click close.
3. **Connect to Default IIS website in wvm535**: Go to wvm535 dashboard> Note down wvm535 IP address which is 104.211.50.194>Open a browser and type http:// 104.211.50.194. Default website opens as shown in figure below.

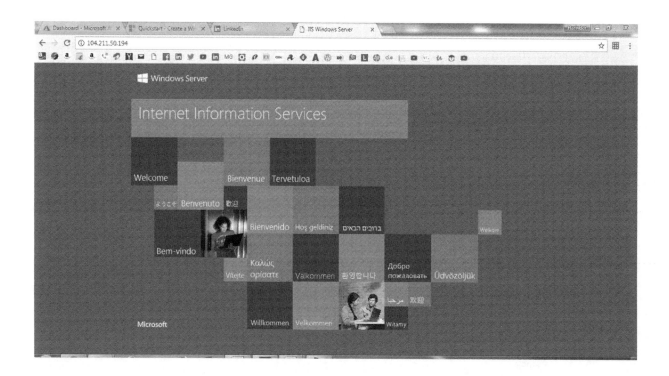

Exercise 11: Virtual Machine Host Level Monitoring

Azure Monitoring collects host-level metrics – like CPU utilization, disk and network usage – for all VMs without installing any additional agent on the VM.

You can see VM Host level monitoring through VM Dashboard or through Monitor Dashboard by clicking Metrics in left pane.

1. In Azure Portal go to Virtual Machine Dashboard or Monitor Dashboard>click Metrics in left pane>In Right Pane select Subscription, Resource group and Virtual Machine wvm535> Select a Metric. For this exercise I selected Host Percentage CPU.

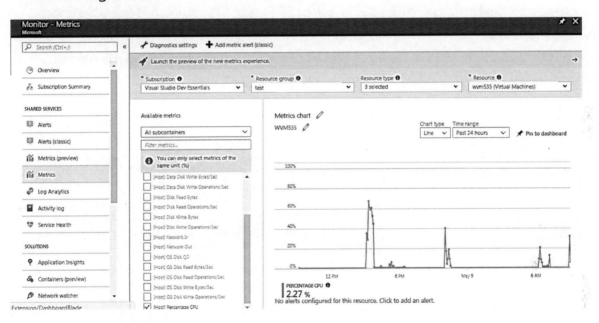

Readers are advised to go through other metrics.

Exercise 12: Virtual Machine Guest Level Monitoring using Diagnostic Agent.

By installing Diagnostic Agent on the Virtual Machine you can collect guest-level metrics aka Performance Counters, Event logs, and other diagnostic data. Performance counter captures enhanced data for CPU, Memory, Disk & Network. Event Logs Capture data for Applications, Security and Systems.

You can install Diagnostic Agent during VM creation or after VM creation from VM dashboard.

You can view VM diagnostic Data by clicking in Diagnostic Settings in VM Dashboard.

Enable Guest Level Monitoring through VM Dashboard

1. Log on to Azure Portal and go to wvm535 dashboard>Click diagnostic settings in left pane>In Right click enable guest level monitoring.

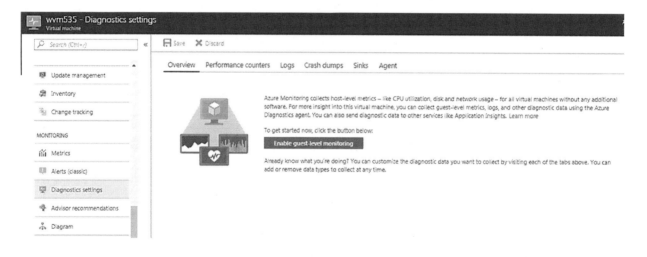

Exercise 13: Demonstrating functionalities of Azure VM Dashboard

1. **Resizing Virtual Machine**: You can resize Virtual Machine to a different or same series with a changed configuration.

In Azure Portal go to Virtual Machine Dashboard>**click size** in left pane>choose a size blade opens>It will show available size>Select a size as per your requirement and click select.

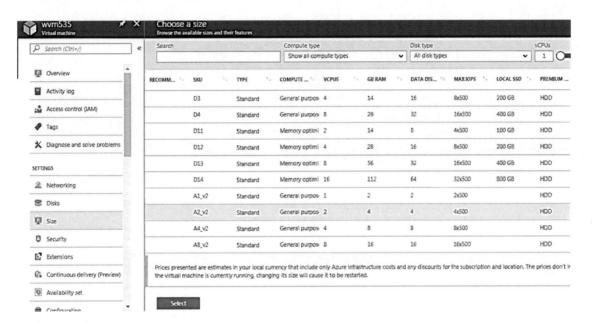

2. **Adding Data Disk to VM**

In Virtual Machine Dashboard>click **Disks** in left pane> In right pane Click + Add Data Disk> Attach Disk Blade opens.

3. **Virtual Machine Extensions**: Azure virtual machine extensions are small applications that provide post-deployment configuration and automation tasks on Azure virtual machines.

Azure virtual machine extensions can be installed during Virtual Machine Creation or Post Installation using Azure Portal, PowerShell or Azure CLI.

In Azure Portal go to Virtual Machine Dashboard>click **Extension** in left pane> In Right pane click + Add>Add New Resource blade opens>Select your extension and click create. Readers are advised to go through all extensions in Right Pane.

Partial use cases

1. Apply PowerShell Desired State configurations to a virtual machine by using the DSC extension for Windows.
2. Apply Microsoft Antimalware for Azure Virtual Machines for real-time protection capability that helps identify and remove viruses, spyware, and other malicious software, with configurable alerts when known malicious or unwanted software attempts to install itself or run on your system.
3. Apply Network Watcher agent extension to enable capture of network traffic and leverage other advanced functionality provided by the Network Watcher.

Virtual Machine Limits

Resource	Default Limit	Max Limit
Reserved IPs per subscription	20	100
VMs per subscription	10000 Per Region	10000 Per Region
VM total cores per subscription	20/Region	Contact Support
VM per series (Dv2, F, etc.) cores per subscription	20/Region	Contact Support
Virtual machines per availability set	200	200
Maximum number of VMs in a scale set	1000	1000
Maximum number of VMs based on a custom VM image in a scale set	300	300
Storage Account Per Subscription	200	250

Design Nugget: If you want to get the best performance for your VMs, you should limit the number of data disks to 2 disks per vCPU.

Note 1: Virtual Machines with letter **s** in its size designation support both Standard Storage and Premium Storage.
Note 2: MS recommends the latest generation VMs be used where possible.
Design Nugget:

Virtual Machine Storage Pricing

Virtual Machine Disks are stored in Page Blobs. Virtual Machine Disks (OS & Data) can be Managed or Unmanaged. Virtual Machine Disks can use Standard Storage (HDD) or Premium Storage (SSD).

Standard Storage (Unmanaged) Page Blobs Pricing (GP v2 Storage Account)

LRS	ZRS (Preview)	GRS	RA-GRS
$0.045 per GB	NA	$0.06 per GB	$0.075 per GB

Replication prices for Disks and Page Blobs

LRS/ZRS	GRS/RA-GRS
NA	$0.02

Managed Standard Storage Disk (HDD) Pricing

	S4	S6	S10	S15	S20	S30	S40	S50
Disk Size	32 GB	64 GB	128 GB	256 GB	512 GB	1 TB	2 TB	4 TB
Price/Month	$1.54	$3.01	$5.89	$11.33	$21.76	$40.96	$77.83	$143.36

Managed & Unmanaged Premium Storage Disk (SSD) Pricing

	P4	P6	P10	P15	P20	P30	P40	P50
Disk Size	32 GB	64 GB	128 GB	256 GB	512 GB	1 TB	2 TB	4 TB
IOPS	120	240	500	1100	2300	5000	7500	7500
Throughput Per Disk	25	50	100	125	150	200	250	250
Price/Month	$5.28	$10.21	$19.71	$38.02	$73.22	$135.17	$259.05	$495.57

Note 1: Throughput per disk is in MB/second.
Note 2: Outbound Data Transfer price is separate.
Note 3: There is a charge of $0.0005 per 10,000 transactions for Standard Storage (Managed & Unmanaged Disks). Any type of operation against the storage is counted as a transaction, including reads, writes and deletes.

Virtual Machine Compute Pricing

Virtual Machine Compute pricing includes cost of compute instance, Operating System & Temporary Storage on the host. OS Disk Storage and Data Disk Storage cost is separate. IP addressing Cost is separate.

Payment options for Virtual Machines

Pay as you go (PAYG): Pay for compute capacity by the second, with no long-term commitment or upfront payments. Increase or decrease compute capacity on demand. Start or stop at any time and only pay for what you use.

Reserved Virtual Machine Instances: An Azure Reserved Virtual Machine Instance is an advanced purchase of a Virtual Machine for one or three years in a specified region. The commitment is made up front, and in return, you get up to 72% price savings compared to pay as you go pricing. Reserved VM Instances are flexible and can easily be exchanged or returned.

Pay as you go	Reserved Virtual Machine Instances
Users who prefer the low cost and flexibility of Azure Virtual Machines.	Applications with steady-state usage.
Applications with short-term, spiky, or unpredictable workloads that cannot be interrupted.	Customers who want budget predictability.
Applications being developed or tested on Azure Virtual Machines for the first time.	Customers who can commit to using a Virtual Machine over a one or three-year term to reduce computing costs.

Azure Hybrid Benefit

PAYG and Reserved Virtual Machine payment options can be combined with Azure Hybrid Benefit for additional saving. Use your on-premises Windows Server licenses with Software Assurance to cover the cost of the OS (on up to two virtual machines!), while you just pay for base compute costs.

<u>**Note 1**</u> : All Pricing for Azure VMs shown in following pages are with Windows OS and PAYG Model.
<u>**Note 2**</u>: MS recommends the latest generation VMs be used where possible.

General Purpose workload Series

General purpose VMs have Balanced CPU-to-memory ratio. **Example use cases include** test & development servers, General Purpose Production workloads, low traffic web servers, small to medium databases servers, servers for proof-of-concepts and code repositories.

General purpose virtual machines include B, AV2, Dv2, DSv2, Dv3 & DSv3 Series. **Note**: Dv2 & DSv2 machines are also included in Memory Optimised Series. General Purpose includes following sizes: D1v2, D2v2, D3v2, D4v2 and D5v2. Memory Optimised includes following sizes: D11v2, D12v2, D13v2, D14v2, D15v2.

B Series does not use full vCPU assigned to it but is allowed to burst up to 100% of the CPU (based on accumulated CPU credit) when your application requires the higher CPU performance. The B-series burstable VMs are ideal for workloads that do not need the full performance of the CPU continuously like web servers, small databases and development and test environments. These workloads typically have burstable performance requirements. B series is priced very economically.

AV2 Standard is priced economically and is suitable for development workloads, build servers, code repositories, low-traffic websites and web applications, micro services, early product experiments and small databases. AV2 does not support Premium storage.

Dv2 & DSv2 series instances are based on the 2.4 GHz Intel Xeon E5-2673 v3 (Haswell) processor and can achieve 3.1 GHz with Turbo Boost. Dv2 instances offer a combination of CPU, memory and disk for most production applications.

Dv3 & DSv3 Series is hyper-threaded and is based on the 2.3 GHz Intel XEON E5-2673 v4 (Broadwell) processor and can achieve 3.5 GHz with Intel Turbo Boost. Dv3 & DSv3 instances offer the combination of CPU, memory, and local disk for most production workloads.
In Dv3 and DSv3 VMs there is shift from physical cores to Virtual CPU. These latest series VMs allow nested virtualization when running Windows Server 2016.

General Purpose B Series

Instance	vCPU	Memory	Temporary Storage (SSD) (GB)	Base Perf of a Core	Max Data Disks	Max Disk IOPS/MBps	Price/hour (PAYG)
B1S	1	1	2	10	2	400/10	$0.017/hour
B2S	2	4	8	20	2	800/10	$0.065/hour
B1MS	1	2	4	40	4	1600/15	$0.032/hour
B2MS	2	8	16	60	4	2400/22.5	$0.122/hour
B4MS	4	16	32	90	8	3600/35	$0.229/hour
B8MS	8	32	64	135	16	4320/50	$0.438/hour

General Purpose Standard Av2 Series

Size	Cores	Memory	Max NICs	Temp Storage SSD (GB)	Max Data Disks	Max IOPS	Price/ hour
A1 v2	1	2	10	10	2	2x500	$0.043
A2 v2	2	4	20	20	4	4x500	$0.091
A4 v2	4	8	40	40	8	8x500	$0.191
A8 v2	8	16	80	80	16	16x500	$0.40
A2m v2	2	16	20	20	4	4x500	$0.119
A4m v2	4	32	40	40	8	8x500	$0.249
A8m v2	8	64	80	80	16	16x500	$0.524

Note 1: Av2 Series VMs do not support Premium storage (SSD).

Note 2: Reserved VM Instances are not available for the Av2 series.

Note 3 : All Pricing for Azure VMs shown in following pages are with Windows OS and PAYG Model.

General Purpose Dv3 and DSv3 Series

Dv3 and DSv3 are latest generation of virtual Machines which offer hyper threading technology. In Dv3 and DSv3 VMs there is shift from physical cores to Virtual CPU. These latest series VMs allow nested virtualization when running Windows Server 2016.

The new Hyper-Threaded VM sizes will be priced up to 28% lower than the previous Dv2 sizes.

Dv3 VM sizes offer a good balance of memory to vCPU performance, with up to 64 vCPU's and 256GB of RAM.

Dsv3-series sizes are based on the 2.3 GHz Intel XEON E5-2673 **v4 (Broadwell) processor** and can achieve 3.5GHz with Intel Turbo Boost Technology 2.0.

Dv3 Series Sizes

Size	vCPU	Memory	Max NICs	Temp Storage SSD	Max Data Disks	Max IOPS	Price/ hour
D2 v3	2	8	2	50 GB	4	4X500	$0.188
D4 v3	4	16	2	100 GB	8	8X500	$0.376
D8 v3	8	32	4	200 GB	16	16X500	$0.752
D16 v3	16	64	8	400 GB	32	32X500	$1.504
D32 v3	32	128	8	800 GB	32	32X500	$3.008
D64 v3	64	256	8	1600 GB	32	32X500	$6.016

DSv3 Series (Premium SSD Support)

Size	vCPU	Memory	Max NICs	Temp Storage SSD	Max Data Disks	Max IOPS/MBps Supported	Price/ hour
D2s v3	2	8	2	50 GB	4	3200/48	$0.188
D4s v3	4	16	2	100 GB	8	6400/96	$0.376
D8s v3	8	32	4	200 GB	16	12800/192	$0.752
D16s v3	16	64	8	400 GB	32	25600/384	$1.504
D32s v3	32	128	8	800 GB	32	51200/768	$3.008
D64s v3	64	256	8	1600 GB	32	80000/1200	$6.016

Compute Optimized

Compute Optimized VMs have High CPU-to-memory ratio. They are good for application servers, medium traffic web servers, network appliances, gaming, analytics & batch processes.

Compute optimized Virtual Machines include Fv2 and F Series VM.

The **Fv2 & FSv2-Series** are latest generation of virtual Machines which offer hyper threading technology and are based on the 2.7 GHz Intel Xeon® Platinum 8168 (SkyLake) processor, which can achieve clock speeds as high as 3.7 GHz with the Intel Turbo Boost Technology 2.0. In Fv2 & FSv2 VMs there is shift from physical cores to Virtual CPU.

The **F-series** is based on the 2.4 GHz Intel Xeon® E5-2673 v3 (Haswell) processor, which can achieve clock speeds as high as 3.2 GHz with the Intel Turbo Boost Technology 2.0.

Fv2 & FSv2 Series

Instance	vCPU	RAM (GB)	Temporary Storage (SSD)	Price/hour
F2 v2	2	4	16 GB	$0.163/hour
F4 v2	4	8	32 GB	$0.326/hour
F8 v2	8	16	64 GB	$0.651/hour
F16 v2	16	32	128 GB	$1.302/hour
F32 v2	32	64	256 GB	$2.604/hour
F64 v2	64	128	512 GB	$5.209/hour
F72 v2	72	144	576 GB	$5.86/hour

F & FS Series

Instance	Core	RAM (GB)	Temporary Storage (SSD)	Price/hour
F1	1	2	16 GB	$0.096/hour
F2	2	4	32 GB	$0.192/hour
F4	4	8	64 GB	$0.383/hour
F8	8	16	128 GB	$0.766/hour
F16	16	32	256 GB	$1.532/hour

Memory Optimised

Memory Optimised VMs have High memory-to-core ratio. They are good for relational database servers, medium to large caches and in-memory analytics.

Memory optimized Virtual Machines include Ev3, ESv3, Dv2, DSv2, G, GS & M Series.
Note: Dv2 & DSv2 machines are also included in General Purpose Series.
General Purpose includes following sizes: D1v2, D2v2, D3v2, D4v2 and D5v2.
Memory Optimised includes following sizes: D11v2, D12v2, D13v2, D14v2, D15v2.

Ev3 & ESv3 are latest generation of virtual Machines which offer hyper threading technology. E2-64 v3 instances are based on the 2.3 GHz Intel XEON® E5-2673 v4 (Broadwell) processor and can achieve speed of 3.5 GHz with Intel Turbo Boost Technology 2.0. In Ev3 and ESv3 VMs there is shift from physical cores to Virtual CPU. These latest series VMs allow nested virtualization when running Windows Server 2016.

G & GS series virtual machines are based on Intel® Xeon® processor E5 v3 family and provide unparalleled computational performance to support large database workloads, specifically SAP HANA, SQL Server, Hadoop, DataZen, and Hortonworks.
G5 instance is isolated to hardware dedicated to a single customer.

M & Ms series virtual machines are hyper-threaded and feature Intel® Xeon® E7-8890 v3 2.5GHz (Haswell) processor. The M-series provides up to 128 cores and 3.8 TiB of memory, providing unparalleled computational performance to support large in-memory workloads.

Instance	vCPU	RAM (GB)	Temporary Storage (SSD) (GB)	Price/hour
M64ms	64	1750	2000	$14.90/hour
M128ms	128	3800	4000	$35.82/hour
M64s	64	1000	2000	$9.613/hour
M128s	128	2000	4000	$19.23/hour

Storage Optimised

Storage Optimised VMs have High disk throughput and IO. They are good for low latency workloads such as Big Data, SQL and NoSQL databases.

Storage Optimised Virtual Machines include L Series Virtual Machines.

L series VMs offer up to 32 CPU cores, using the Intel® Xeon® processor E5 v3 family with 8-GiB random-access memory (RAM) per core and from 678 GB to 6 TB of local solid state drive (SSD) disk. Supports Premium Storage.

Instance	Core	RAM (GB)	Temporary Storage (SSD) (GB)	Price/hour
L4	4	32	678	$0.496/hour
L8	8	64	1388	$0.992/hour
L16	16	128	2807	$1.984/hour
L32	32	256	5630	$3.968/hour

High Performance Computing

High Performance Computing VMs are good for high performance & parallel computing workloads such as financial risk modeling, seismic and reservoir simulation, molecular modeling and genomic research.

High Performance Computing Virtual Machines include H Series Virtual Machines. **H Series** Virtual Machines are based on the Intel Xeon E5-2667 v3 Haswell 3.2 GHz (3.6 GHz with turbo) with DDR 4 memory.

Instance	Core	RAM (GB)	Temporary Storage (SSD) (GB)	Price/hour
H8	8	56	1000	$1.129/hour
H16	16	112	2000	$2.258/hour
H8m	8	112	1000	$1.399/hour
H16m	16	224	2000	$2.799/hour
H16mr	16	224	2000	$3.012/hour
H16r	16	112	2000	$2.417/hour

H16r, H16mr also carry a second low latency, high-throughput network interface (RDMA) optimised and tuned for parallel computing workloads such as MPI applications.

GPU Based

GPU based VMs have Single or Multiple GPU. They are targeted for heavy graphic rendering and video editing workloads and also include some High performance computing workloads including AI & Machine learning.

GPU based Virtual Machines include NC, NCv2, NCv3, NV & ND Series Virtual Machines.

NC-series machines are powered by NVIDIA Tesla K80 GPUs.

NCv2-series machines are powered by NVIDIA Tesla P100 GPUs.

NCv3-series machines are powered by NVIDIA Tesla V100 GPUs.

NV-series virtual machines are powered by NVIDIA Tesla M60 GPUs.

ND-series virtual machines are powered by NVIDIA Tesla P40 GPUs.

ND Series

Instance	Core	RAM (GB)	Temporary Storage (SSD) (GB)	GPU	Price/hour
ND6	6	112	336	1 X P40	$2.493/hour
ND12	12	224	672	2 X P40	$4.986/hour
ND24	24	448	1344	4 X P40	$9.973/hour
ND24r	24	448	1344	4 X P40	$10.98/hour

Chapter 3 Storage Accounts

This Chapter covers following Topic Lessons

- Storage Account
- Storage Account Types
- Storage Account Performance Tiers
- Comparing Storage Accounts
- Storage Account Replication
- Storage Account endpoints

This Chapter Covers following Lab Exercises to build below topology

- Creating Storage Account Gpv2
- Demonstrating Functionalities of Storage Account

Azure Storage Account

An Azure storage account provides a unique namespace to store and access your Azure Storage data objects.

Azure Storage (Blob, Table, Queue and Files) is created under Storage Accounts. Storage Account is prerequisite for creating Azure Storage.

The image below shows the dashboard of General Purpose Storage Account. From here you will create Blob, File, table or Queue Storage.

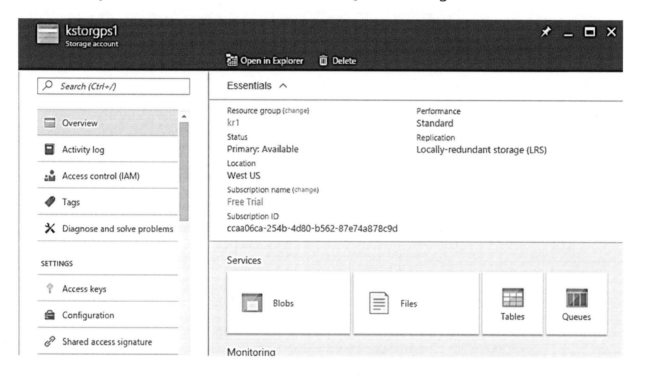

Figure below shows components of Blob, Table, Queue and File Storage.

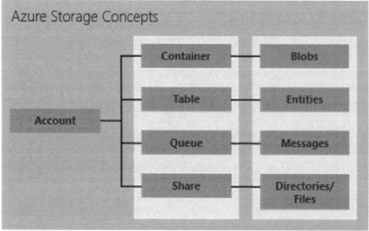

Storage Account Types

There are three types of storage accounts - General-purpose v2 (GPv2) Storage Account, General-purpose v1 (GPv1) Storage Account & Blob Storage Account.

General-purpose v2 (GPv2) Storage Account

General-purpose v2 (GPv2) storage accounts support storage services including blobs, files, queues, and tables. It supports all latest features for storage services.

For block blobs in a GPv2 storage account, you can choose between hot and cool storage tiers at the account level, or hot, cool, and archive tiers at the blob level.

General-purpose v1 (GPv1) Storage Account

General-purpose v1 (GPv1) storage account supports storage services including blobs, files, queues, and tables. It does not support latest features for storage services. It does not support blob storage tiering.

Blob Storage Account

Blob Storage accounts are specialized for storing blob data and support choosing an access tier – Hot or cool at account level.
Blob storage accounts support only block and append blobs and not page blobs.

Storage Account Performance Tiers

1. A **standard storage performance tier** which allows you to create Blobs, Tables, Queues, Files and Azure virtual machine disks. It is backed by magnetic disk HDD. Supports GPv1, GPv2 and Blob Storage Account.

2. A **premium storage performance tier** which allows you to create Page Blobs only. Page Blobs support Azure virtual machine disks. It is backed by SSD. Supports GPv1 & GPv2 Storage Account.

Comparing Storage Accounts

Description	GPv2	GPv1	Blob Storage Account
Storage Type Supported	Blob, File, Table and Queue	Blob, File, Table and Queue	Blob (block and append blob)
Types of Blob supported	page, block and append blob	page, block and append blob	block and append blob
Disk Type	HDD & SSD	HDD & SSD	HDD
Replication Options (Standard Storage	LRS, ZRS, GRS and RA-GRS	LRS, GRS and RA-GRS	LRS, GRS, RA-GRS
Replication Options (Premium Storage)	LRS	LRS	NA
Can be used for Virtual Machine Disks	Yes through page blobs	Yes through page blobs	No
Blob Storage Tiering	Yes	No	Yes
Use Case	It has wide and large use cases including VM disk.	It has wide and large use cases including VM disk.	Object Storage and Archiving

Azure Storage Account Replication

The data in the Microsoft Azure storage account is always replicated to ensure high availability. Replication copies data, either within the same data center, or to a second data center, depending on the replication option chosen. Azure Storage Accounts offer 4 Replication options – LRS, ZRS, GRS, RA-GRS.

Comparing Storage Account Replication Options

Features	LRS	ZRS	GRS	RA-GRS
Data is replicated across multiple datacenters.	No	Yes	Yes	Yes
Data can be read from a secondary location as well as the primary location.	No	No	No	Yes
Data Availability if Node becomes unavailable within Data Center	Yes	Yes	Yes	Yes
Data Availability if Data Center goes down	No	Yes	Yes	Yes
Data Availability if there is Region wide outage	No	No	Yes	Yes
SLA	11 9's	12 9's	16 9's	16 9's
Storage Account Supported	GPv1, GPv2, Blob	GPv2	GPv1, GPv2, Blob	GPv1, GPv2, Blob

Locally redundant storage (LRS)

Locally redundant storage (LRS) replicates your data three times in a datacenter in the region in which you created your storage account. A write request returns successfully only once it has been written to all three replicas.

The three replicas each reside in separate fault domains and upgrade domains within one storage scale unit.

LRS is the lowest cost option. LRS can protect your data from underlying storage node failure but not from Data Center wide outage.

Following are some of the use Case for Locally Redundant Storage:

1. Provides highest maximum bandwidth of Azure Storage replication options.
2. With LRS, application data can be easily reconstructed.
3. LRS can be used in cases where applications are restricted to replicating data only within a country due to data governance requirements.

Storage Accounts Supported: GPv2, GPv1 and Blob Storage Account.

Geo Redundant Storage (GRS)

Geo-redundant storage (GRS) replicates your data to a secondary region that is hundreds of miles away from the primary region.

With GRS, data is first replicated 3 times within the primary region and then asynchronously replicated to the secondary region, where it is also replicated three times.

With GRS, data is durable even in the case of a complete regional outage or a disaster in which the primary region is not recoverable.

When you create a storage account, you select the primary region for the account. The secondary region is determined based on the primary region, and cannot be changed.

Storage Accounts Supported: GPv2, GPv1 and Blob Storage Account

Read-access geo-redundant storage (RA-GRS)

Read-access geo-redundant storage (RA-GRS) not only replicates your data to a secondary region but also provides read-only access to the data in the secondary location.

With RA-GRS, data is first replicated 3 times within the primary region and then asynchronously replicated to the secondary region, where it is also replicated three times.

With RA-GRS, data is durable even in the case of a complete regional outage or a disaster in which the primary region is not recoverable.

When you create a storage account, you select the primary region for the account. The secondary region is determined based on the primary region, and cannot be changed.

Storage Accounts Supported: GPv2, GPv1 and Blob Storage Account

Zone-redundant storage (ZRS)

ZRS replicates your data synchronously across three availability zones. ZRS enables customers to read and write data even if a single zone is unavailable or unrecoverable. Inserts and updates to data are made synchronously and are strongly consistent.

ZRS provides durability for storage objects of at least 99.9999999999% (12 9's) over a given year. Consider ZRS for scenarios like transactional applications where downtime is not acceptable.

ZRS provides higher durability than LRS. Data stored in ZRS is durable even if the primary datacenter is unavailable or unrecoverable.

ZRS will not protect your data against a regional disaster where multiple zones are permanently affected. For protection against regional disasters, Microsoft recommends using Geo-redundant storage (GRS): Cross-regional replication for Azure Storage.

Storage Accounts Supported: GPv2

Zone-redundant storage (ZRS) Classic (Deprecated)

Zone-redundant storage (ZRS) Classic replicates data 3 times asynchronously across datacenters within one or two regions.

Note : ZRS Classic replication option is planned for deprecation and require migration by March 31, 2021.

Storage Account endpoints

Every object that you store in Azure Storage has a unique URL address. The storage account name forms the subdomain of that address. The combination of subdomain and domain name, which is specific to each service, forms an **endpoint** for your storage account.

For example, if your storage account is named **mystorageaccount**, then the default endpoints for your storage account are:

Blob service: http://mystorageaccount.blob.core.windows.net
Table service: http://mystorageaccount.table.core.windows.net
Queue service: http://mystorageaccount.queue.core.windows.net
File service: http://mystorageaccount.file.core.windows.net

The URL for accessing an object in a storage account is built by appending the object's location in the storage account to the endpoint. For example, a blob address might have this format:
http://mystorageaccount.blob.core.windows.net/mycontainer/myblob.

You can also configure a custom domain name to use with your storage account..

Storage Account Design Nuggets

1. Storage Account name must be unique within Azure
2. Read-access geo-redundant storage (RA-GRS) is the default replication option when you create a storage account.

Storage Account Limits

Resource	Default Limit
Number of storage accounts per subscription	200
Max storage account capacity	500 TB
Maximum request rate per Standard storage account for VM Disks	20000
Max Throughput for Premium Storage Account for VM Disks.	50 Gbps
Max number of blob containers, blobs, file shares, tables, queues, entities, or messages per storage account	No Limit

Note 1: You can increase Max Storage Account Number & capacity by Contacting Azure Support.

Note 2: MS has announced new Maximums for Blob storage Account. Max capacity for Blob storage accounts is now 5 PB.

Storage Account Pricing

Storage Accounts are free of cost. You are charged for Storage service- Blob Queue, Table or File Storage.

Exercise 14: Create Storage Account (GPv2)

1. In Azure Portal Click create a resource>Storage>Storage Account>Create Storage Account Blade opens> Choose options as per your requirement and click create.

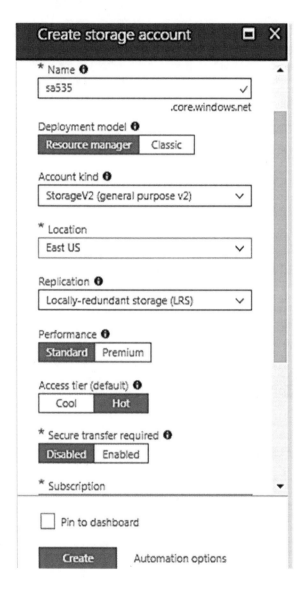

Note 1: Storage Account name has to be unique within Azure.

Note 2: You can choose between Standard or premium (SSD) performance Tier.

Note 3: Note Access Tier option. This is not available with GPv1 Account.

Exercise 15: Demonstrating Storage Account functionalities

1. Figure below shows **dashboard** of the GPv2 Storage Account created in previous step. From here you can create Blob, file, table or queue Storage.

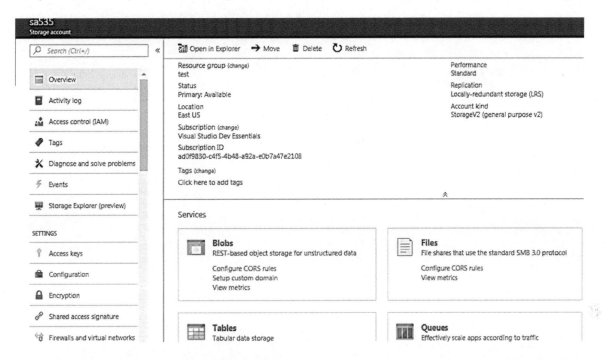

2. **Change configuration of storage account**: Click configuration in left pane.

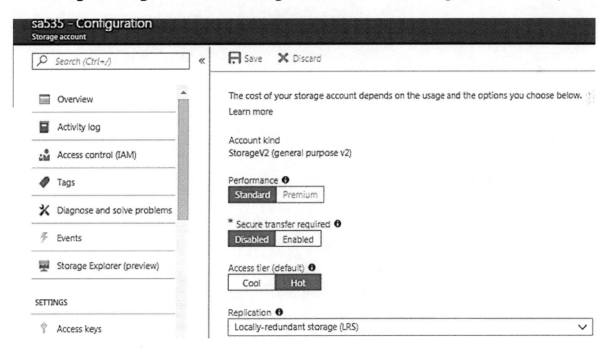

3. **Enabling Encryption at Rest using customer managed keys**: By default Storage Service encryption (SSE) protects your data at Rest using MS managed keys. You can use your own to keys to encryption storage data. Click encryption in left pane.

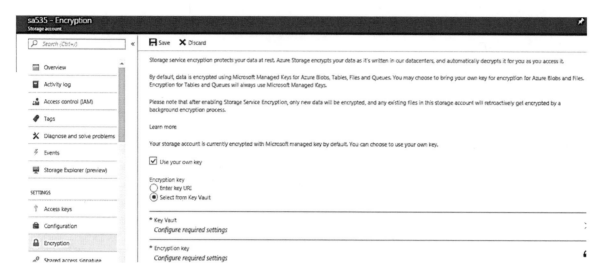

4. **Restricting Access to Storage Account from Virtual Network only**: By default owner can access storage account from internet. This is a security loophole. Click Firewall and Virtual Networks in left pane>Click Add existing Virtual Network>Select your Virtual Network.

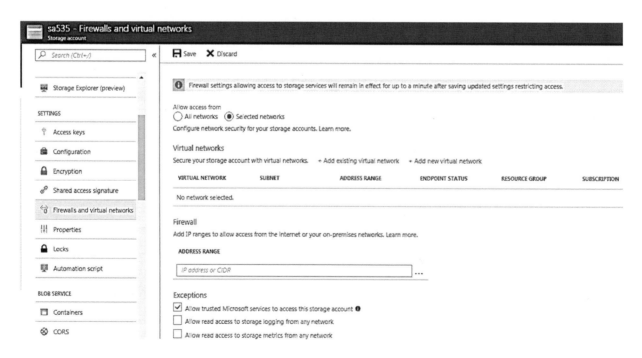

Chapter 4 Azure Storage

This Chapter covers following Topic Lessons

- Azure Storage
- Blob Storage
- File Storage
- Queue Storage
- Table Storage
- Azure Data Box
- StorSimple
- Storage Service Encryption

This Chapter Covers following Lab Exercises to build below topology

- Creating Blob Storage
- Generating shared access signature (SAS)
- Creating and Mounting File Share
- Creating queue Storage

Chapter Topology

In this chapter we will add Blob, File & Queue Storage to the topology.

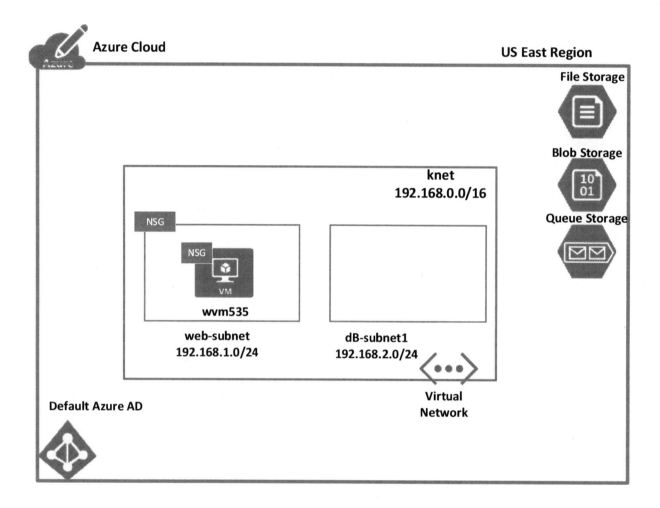

Azure Storage

Azure Storage is the Managed cloud storage solution. Azure Storage is highly available and massively scalable. Azure provides five types of storage - Blob, Table, Queue, Files and Virtual Machine Disk storage (Page Blobs).

Azure Blobs: A massively scalable object store for text and binary data.
Azure Files: Managed file shares for cloud or on-premises deployments.
Azure Queues: A messaging store for reliable messaging between application components.
Azure Tables: A NoSQL store for schemaless storage of structured data.

Figure Below shows five types of Azure Storage Services.

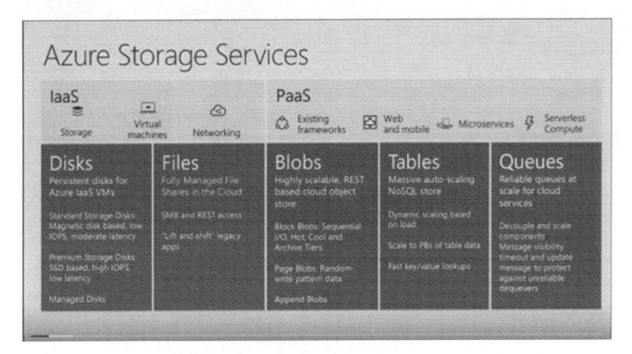

Comparing Different Azure Storage Services types

Azure Storage	Data Type
Blob	Unstructured
Table	Structured
Queue	Messaging
File	Shared Storage

Feature of Azure Storage

Durable and highly available: Redundancy ensures that your data is safe in the event of transient hardware failures. You can also opt to replicate data across datacenters or geographical regions for additional protection from local catastrophe or natural disaster. Data replicated in this way remains highly available in the event of an unexpected outage.

Secure: All data written to Azure Storage is encrypted by the service. Azure Storage provides you with fine-grained control over who has access to your data.

Scalable: Azure Storage is designed to be massively scalable to meet the data storage and performance needs of today's applications.

Managed: Microsoft Azure handles maintenance and any critical problems for you.

Accessible: Data in Azure Storage is accessible from anywhere in the world over HTTP or HTTPS. Microsoft provides SDKs for Azure Storage in a variety of languages -- .NET, Java, Node.js, Python, PHP, Ruby, Go, and others -- as well as a mature REST API. Azure Storage supports scription in Azure PowerShell or Azure CLI. And the Azure portal and Azure Storage Explorer offer easy visual solutions for working with your data.

Blob Storage

Azure Blob storage is massively scalable, highly redundant and secure **object storage** with a **URL/http based access** which allows it to be accessed within Azure or outside the Azure. Though Azure objects are regionally scoped you can access them from anywhere in the world.

Azure Blob Storage is **a Managed Service** that stores large amount of unstructured data in the cloud as objects/blobs. Blob storage can store any type of text or binary data, such as a document, media file, or application installer that can be accessed anywhere in the world via http or https.

Blob storage is also referred to as object storage.

Blobs are basically files like those that you store on your computer. They can be pictures, Excel files, HTML files, virtual hard disks (VHDs), log files & database backups etc. Blobs are stored in containers, which are similar to folders. Containers are created under Storage account.

You can access Blob storage from anywhere in the world using URLs, the REST interface, or one of the Azure SDK storage client libraries. Storage client libraries are available for multiple languages, including Node.js, Java, PHP, Ruby, Python, and .NET.

You can create Blob Storage using 3 ways – General Purpose Storage Account v1, General Purpose Storage Account v2 or Blob storage Account.

Common Use cases for Blob Object Storage

For users with large amounts of unstructured object data to store in the cloud, Blob storage offers a cost-effective and scalable solution. You can use Blob storage to store content such as:

- Serving images or documents directly to a browser.
- Storing files for distributed access.
- Streaming video and audio.
- Storing data for backup and restore, disaster recovery, and archiving.

Blob Storage Service Components

Blob Service contains 3 components.

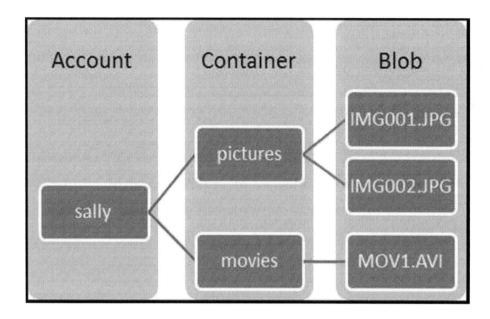

Storage Account:

All access to Azure Storage is done through a storage account. This storage account can be a **General-purpose v1 & v2** or a **Blob storage account** which is specialized for storing objects/blobs.

Containers:

Container is like a folder which store Blob Files. Container provides a grouping of a set of blobs. All blobs must be in a container. An account can contain an unlimited number of containers. A container can store an unlimited number of blobs. Container name must be lowercase.

Blob

A file of any type and size. Azure Storage offers three types of blobs: block blobs, page blobs, and append blobs.
Blob Storage tiering is available with General Purpose v2 Account and Blob Storage Account.

Types of Blob Storage in Azure Cloud

Blob storage offers three types of blobs – Block Blobs, Page Blobs and Append Blobs.

Block blobs are optimized for storing cloud objects, streaming content and and are a good choice for storing documents, media files, backups etc. It is backed by HDD.

Append blobs are similar to block blobs, but are optimized for append operations. An append blob can be updated only by adding a new block to the end. Append blobs are a good choice for scenarios such as logging, where new data needs to be written only to the end of the blob. It is backed by magnetic HDD.

Page blobs are used for storing virtual machine disks (OS and Data Disks) only. Page Blob can use both HDD and SSD. Page Blob was covered in compute chapter.

Comparing 3 types of Blob Storage

Description	Block Blob	Append Blob	Page Blob
Storage Account Supported	General purpose v1 & v2 and Blob Storage Account	General purpose v1 & v2 and Blob Storage Account	General purpose – v1 & v2
Disk Type	**HDD**	**HDD**	**HDD & SSD**
Managed Disk Option	No	No	Yes
Can be used for Virtual Machine Disks	No	No	Yes
Use case	documents, media files, backups	logging	Virtual Machine Disks

In this chapter we will focus only on Block blobs and Append bobs as we already have covered Page Blobs in Azure Compute Chapter.

Azure Blob Storage Tiering: Hot, Cool & Archive Storage tiers

Azure Blob Storage tiering is available with General Purpose v2 Account and Blob Storage Account. General Purpose v1 Account does not offers Blob Storage Tiering. Microsoft Recommends using GPv2 instead of Blob Storage accounts for tiering.

General Purpose v2 Account & Blob storage accounts expose the **Access Tier** attribute, which allows you to specify the storage tier as **Hot** or **Cool**. **The Archive tier** is only available at the blob level and not at the storage account level.

Hot Storage Tier

The Azure **hot storage tier** is optimized for storing data that is frequently accessed at lower access cost but at higher storage cost.

Cool Storage Tier

The Azure **cool storage tier** is optimized for storing data that is infrequently accessed at lower storage cost but at higher access cost.

Archive Storage Tier

Archive storage tier is optimized for storing data that is rarely accessed and has the lowest storage cost and highest data retrieval costs compared to hot and cool storage. The archive tier can only be applied at the blob level.

Blob rehydration (Important Concept)

Data is offline in Archive Storage Tier. To read data in archive storage, you must first change the tier of the blob to hot or cool. This process is known as rehydration and can take up to 15 hours to complete.

If there is a change in the usage pattern of your data, you can also switch between these storage tiers at any time.
Data in hot storage tier has slightly higher availability (99.9%) than cool storage tier (99%). Availability is not applicable for Archive tier as data is offline.

Architecting Microsoft Azure Solutions Study & Lab Guide Part 1: Exam 70-535

Hot Tier use case

1. Data that is in active use or expected to be accessed frequently.
2. Data that is staged for processing and eventual migration to the cool storage tier.

Cold Tier Use case

1. Short-term backup and disaster recovery datasets.
2. Older media content not viewed frequently anymore but is expected to be available immediately when accessed.
3. Large data sets that need to be stored cost effectively while more data is being gathered for future processing.

Archive Tier Use case

1. Long-term backup, archival, and disaster recovery datasets
2. Original (raw) data that must be preserved, even after it has been processed into final usable form.
3. Compliance and archival data that needs to be stored for a long time and is hardly ever accessed. (For example, Security camera footage, old X-Rays/MRIs for healthcare organizations, audio recordings, and transcripts of customer calls for financial services)

Comparison of the storage tiers

Features	Hot Storage Tier	Cool Storage Tier	Archive Tier
Availability	99.9%	99%	NA
Availability (RA-GRS reads)	99.99%	99.9%	NA
Usage charges	Higher storage costs, lower access and transaction costs	Lower storage costs, higher access and transaction costs	lowest storage cost and highest retrieval costs
Minimum Storage Duration	NA	30 days (GPv2 only)	180 days
Latency	Milliseconds	Milliseconds	<15 Hrs

Exercise 16: Creating Blob Storage and uploading a file

1. **Create storage account or use existing storage account.** Go to storage Account sa535 Dashboard created in chapter 3.

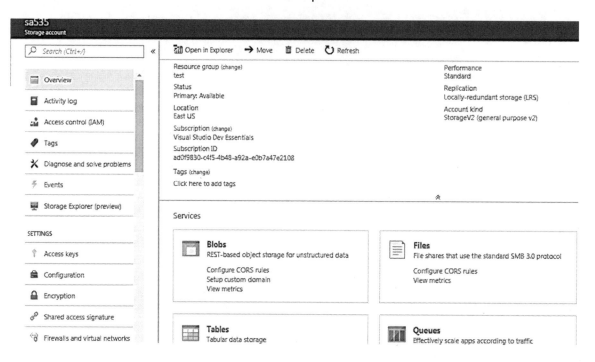

2. **Create container or use existing container**. Click Blobs> Blob Service Pane opens> Click + Container> New Container blade opens> Give a name & choose access level and click ok. For this exercise we have chosen Container (anonymous access for containers and blob).

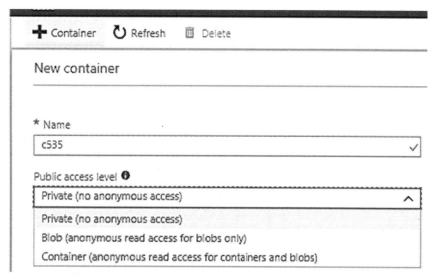

Explanation of Public Access level options (see next section)

Architecting Microsoft Azure Solutions Study & Lab Guide Part 1: Exam 70-535

3. **Upload File to Blob Service**. Select your container in Blob Service pane> Click Upload in Middle pane> Upload blade opens>Select a file> Click upload. For this exercise we have uploaded text file Hello World.

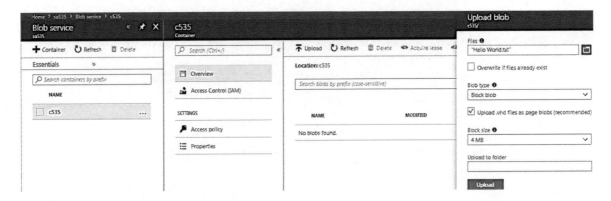

4. **Status of uploaded file**. Click uploaded file in container pane. You can download file. You can see download URL. You can see Uploaded file is in hot tier. You can change the tier to Cool or Archive.

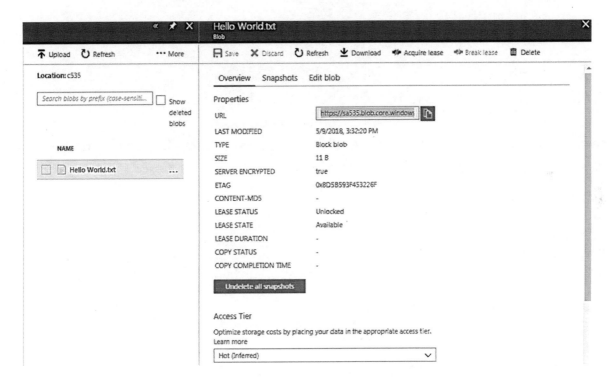

5. **Access the uploaded file anonymously**: Copy the URL of the blob from step
   4. https://sa535.blob.core.windows.net/c535/Hello World.txt
   Open a browser and enter the URL.

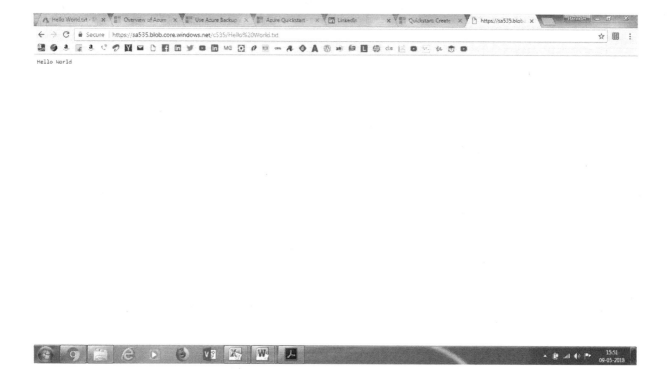

We were able to access the Blob anonymously because we had set the permission to anonymous in step 2.

In case we had chosen Public access level **Private** in step 2 then we would not be able to access the file anonymously.

Options to make blob data available to users

Anonymous access: You can make a container or its blobs publicly available for anonymous access.

Shared access signatures: Shared access signature (SAS), provide delegated access to a resource in your storage account, with permissions that you specify and for an interval that you specify without having to share your account access keys.

Anonymous read access to containers and blobs

By default, a container and any blobs within it may be accessed only by the owner of the storage account (Public Access level: Private). To give anonymous users read permissions to a container and its blobs, you can set the container & Blob permissions to allow full public access.

Container (anonymous read access for containers and blobs): Container and blob data can be read via anonymous request. Clients can enumerate blobs within the container via anonymous request, but cannot enumerate containers within the storage account.

Blob (anonymous read access for blobs only): Blob data within this container can be read via anonymous request, but container data is not available. Clients cannot enumerate blobs within the container via anonymous request.

Http access to Blob data using DNS names

By default the blob data in your storage account is accessible only to storage account owner because of Default **Private (no anonymous access)** Policy. Authenticating requests against Blob storage requires the account access key.

Using DNS names you can http access Blob endpoint if anonymous access is configured.

https://mystorageaccount.blob.core.windows.net/mycontainer/myblob

Here mystorageaccount is storage account name, mycontainer is container name and myblob is uploaded file name.

Controlling access to blob data using Shared access signatures (SAS)

Anybody having access to Storage account key will have unlimited access to storage account.

Shared access signature (SAS), provide delegated access to a resource in your storage account, without having to share your account access keys. SAS is a secure way to share your storage resources without compromising your account keys.

A shared access signature (SAS) is a URI that grants restricted access rights to Azure Storage resources. You can provide a shared access signature to clients who should not be trusted with your storage account key but whom you wish to delegate access to certain storage account resources. By distributing a shared access signature URI to these clients, you grant them access to a resource for a specified period of time.

SAS granular control features

1. The interval over which the SAS is valid, including the start time and the expiry time.
2. The permissions granted by the SAS. For example, a SAS on a blob might grant a user read and write permissions to that blob, but not delete permissions.
3. An optional IP address or range of IP addresses from which Azure Storage will accept the SAS
4. The protocol over which Azure Storage will accept the SAS. You can use this optional parameter to restrict access to clients using HTTPS.

Types of shared access signatures (SAS)

Service SAS delegates access to a resource in just one of the storage services: the Blob, Queue, Table, or File service.

An **Account-level SAS** can delegate access to multiple storage services (i.e. blob, file, queue, table).

Demonstration Exercise 17: Generating shared access signature (SAS)

A shared access signature (SAS) is a URI that grants restricted access rights to Azure Storage resources. By distributing a shared access signature URI to client applications, you grant them access to a resource for a specified period of time and you can also implement additional security parameters like allowed permissions, Allowed IP address from which to connect to storage.

1. From Storage Account Dashboard click Shared Access Signature in left Pane> Select your options and click **generate SAS** Tile. You can now integrate SAS Tokens and SAS URL with your application to access Storage Services.

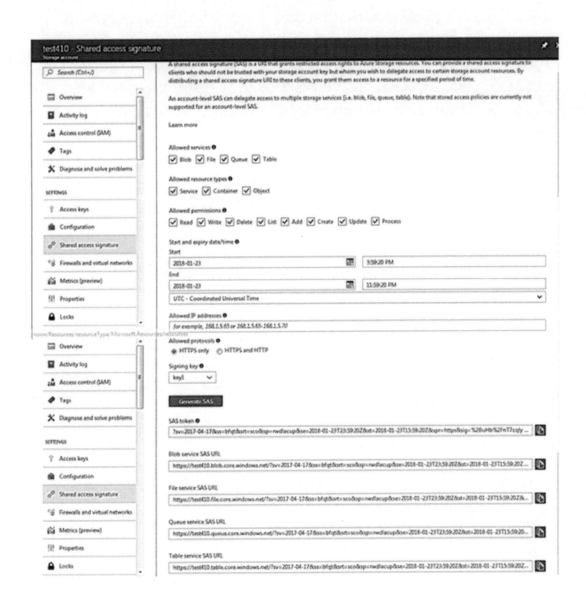

Blob Storage Pricing using GPv2 Storage Account (4 Components)

1. Cost of storing data in Blobs.
2. Operation Prices
3. Geo-Replication Data Transfer charge (Applicable only for GRS & GRS-RA)
4. Cool & Archive Early Deletion

Storage Charges GRS (LRS, ZRS & RA-GRS prices are not shown)

	Hot	Cool	Archive
First 50 terabyte (TB) / month	$0.0368 per GB	$0.02 per GB	$0.004 per GB
Next 450 TB / Month	$0.0354 per GB	$0.02 per GB	$0.004 per GB
Over 500 TB / Month	$0.0339 per GB	$0.02 per GB	$0.004 per GB

Operation Prices GRS

	Hot	Cool	Archive
Write Operations* (per 10,000)	$0.10	$0.20	$0.20
List and Create Container Operations (per 10,000)	$0.10	$0.10	$0.10
Read Operations** (per 10,000)	$0.004	$0.01	$5
Other Operations (per 10,000), except Delete, which is free	$0.004	$0.004	$0.004
Data Retrieval (per GB)	**Free**	**$0.01**	**$0.02**
Data Write (per GB)	Free	Free	Free

Note: Storage Charges are high but Access charges are lower in Hot Tier.

Geo-Replication Data Transfer charge

LRS OR ZRS	GRS OR RA-GRS
NA	$0.02

Cool and Archive early deletion pricing (GPv2)

Any blob that is moved to Cool or Archive tier is subject to an Archive early deletion period of 180 days and Cool early deletion period of 30 days. For example, if a blob is moved to Archive and then deleted or moved to the Hot tier after 45 days, the customer is charged an early deletion fee equivalent to 135 (180 minus 45) days of storing that blob in Archive.

Blob Storage Service Limits

Max size of a single blob container – 500 TB

Max size of a block blob – 4.75 TB

Max size of an append blob – 195 GB

Max size of a page blob – 8 TB

Design Nugget

1. The per-gigabyte cost is lower for the cool storage tier than for the hot storage tier.
2. Access Operation cost is lower in hot storage tier than for Cool Storage Tier.
3. Data Retrieval and Data Write is free in Hot Storage tier.
4. **Changing the storage tier from Cool to Hot**: Changing the storage tier from cool to hot will incur a charge equal to reading all the data existing in the storage account for every transition.
5. **Changing the storage tier from Hot to Cool**: On the other hand, changing the storage tier from hot to cool will be free of cost in Blob storage account. In General Purpose v2 accounts, you will only be charged for write operations (per 10,000).

File Storage

Azure Files Storage offers fully managed file shares in the cloud that are accessible via the industry standard Server Message Block (SMB 3.0) protocol (also known as Common Internet File System or CIFS).

Azure File shares can be mounted concurrently by cloud or on-premises deployments of Windows, Mac OS, and Linux instances.

Figure below shows Multiple Virtual Machines accessing Azure File share.

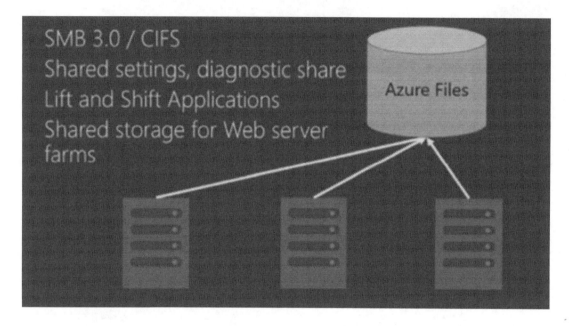

Azure File share Use case

1. Azure Files can be used to completely replace or supplement traditional on-premises file servers or NAS devices.
2. Developers can leverage their existing code and skills to migrate existing applications that rely on file shares to Azure quickly and without costly rewrites.
3. An Azure File share is a convenient place for cloud applications to write their logs, metrics, and crash dumps.
4. When developers or administrators are working on VMs in the cloud, they often need a set of tools or utilities. Copying such utilities and tools to each VM can be a time consuming exercise. By mounting an Azure File share locally on the VMs, a developer and administrator can quickly access their tools and utilities, no copying required.

File Service Architecture and components

Figure below shows the architecture of File share. File share is mounted as a drive on Virtual Machine and is accessed over the network.

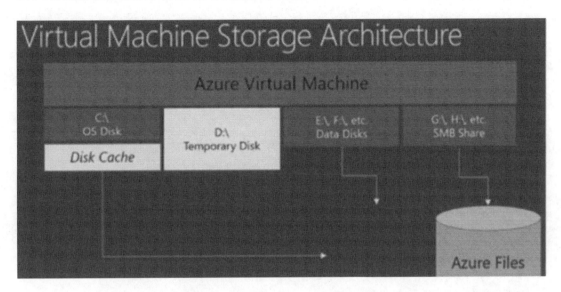

File Service contains 3 components: Storage Account, File Shares and Files.

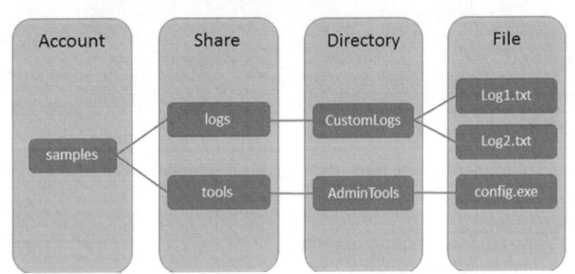

Storage Account: This storage account can be a **General-purpose v1 or v2 storage account.** It supports only Standard Storage for File service.
Share: Share stores the files. Azure File shares can be mounted and accessed concurrently by cloud or on-premises deployments of Windows, Linux, and macOS. A share can store an unlimited number of files.
Directory: Directory is optional. Directory is like a folder for files.
File: A file of any type with max size of 1 TB.

Exercise 18: Creating and using File Share

Creating and using File share is a 2 step process:
1. Create File Share and upload a file.
2. Mount the File share on a Server instance in cloud or on-Prem.

Creating File Share

1. Log on to Azure Portal @ https://portal.azure.com
2. In Storage Account sa535 Dashboard opens>Click Files.

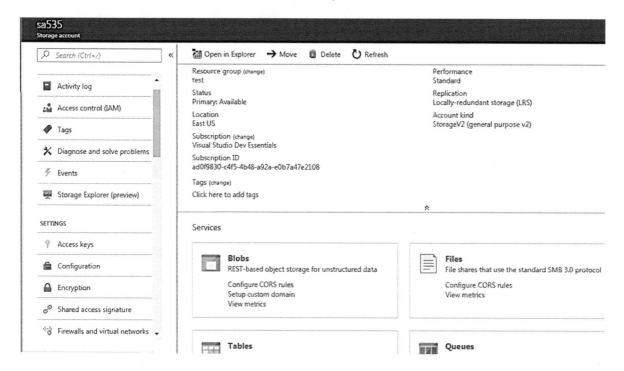

3. File Service Blade opens. Note the File service endpoint http address.

4. Click +File share>New File share Blade opens>Enter name & Size and click ok.

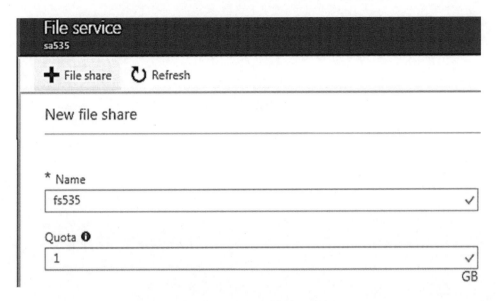

5. Click your Created File share in File service pane> Click upload in Middle pane> Upload File Blade open> Upload a file and click upload.

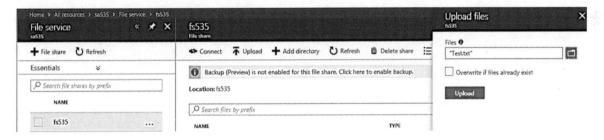

6. Click Connect In Middle pane>In connect pane copy net use Z command shown in the rectangular Box.

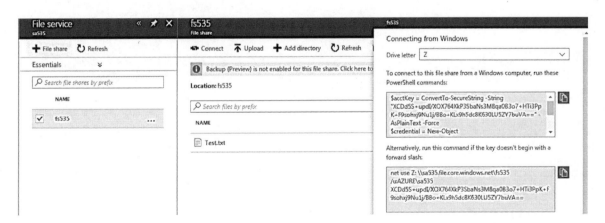

7. In Storage Account Dashboard>Click Access Keys in left pane> Copy the Key1.

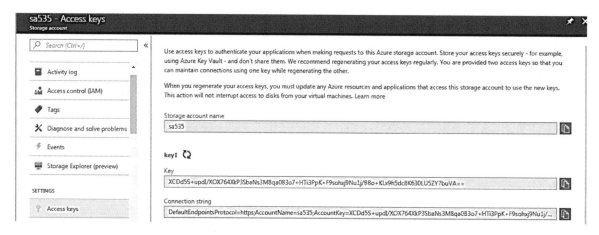

8. Open a Notepad. Paste net use command copied from step 6 in the Notepad.

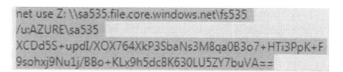

9. Replace the 3rd and 4th line with the Storage Account Access key1 copied from from step 7.

10. Connect to Azure VM wvm535 using RDP> Go to Command Prompt and run the net use command. The command completed successfully.

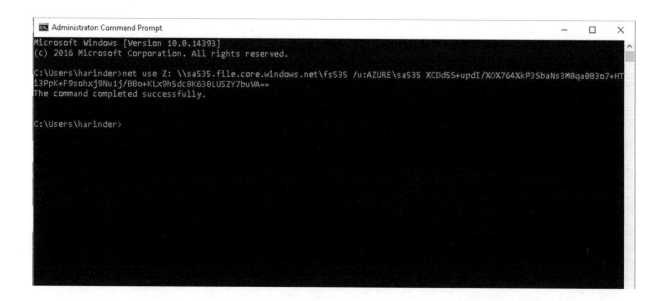

11. Go to File Explorer in wvm535>You can see the file share fs535 mounted.

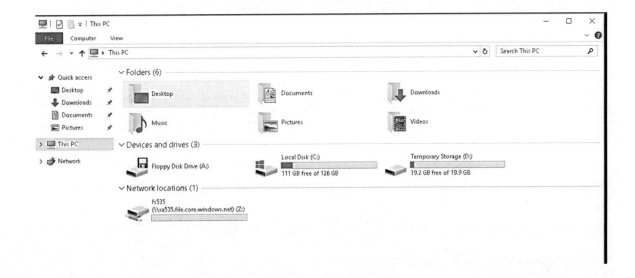

File Share Limits

Max size of a file share	5 TB
Max size of a file in a file share	1 TB
Max number of files in a file share	Only limit is 5 TB file share size
Max IOPS per share	1000
Maximum request rate per storage account	20,000 requests per second for files
Maximum number of share snapshots	200 share snapshots

File Storage Pricing using General Purpose v2 Account

Storage Pricing

LRS	GRS
$0.06/GB/Month	$0.10/GB/Month

Operation & Data Transfer Pricing

Access Prices are transaction for both SMB and REST operations against your Azure File share. These are the costs for operations, such as enumerating a directory or reading a file, against the data you store on an Azure File share.

	LRS	GRS
Put, Create Container Operations (per 10,000)	$0.015	$0.03
List Operations (per 10,000)	$0.015	$0.015
All other operations except Delete, which is free (per 10,000)	$0.0015	$0.0015
Geo-Replication Data Transfer (per GB)	NA	$0.02

Design Nuggets

Azure Files does not support RA-GRS at this time. Support for ZRS is in Preview.

Queue Storage

Azure Queue Storage is a highly reliable, scalable message queuing service that enables asynchronous message-based communication between distributed components of an application.

Azure Queue storage is a Managed service for storing large numbers of messages that can be accessed from anywhere in the world via authenticated calls using HTTP or HTTPS. A single queue message can be up to 64 KB in size. The maximum time that a message can remain in the queue is 7 day. And, queues can contain millions of messages, up to the total capacity limit of a storage account.

Queues Store messages. Messages are generated by one application and consumed by other application. The queue acts as a buffer between the components producing the data and components receiving the data for processing.

Queue storage provides asynchronous decoupling between applications.

Queues are used primarily for messaging between services and applications. Messages are inserted into queues and kept there in order until they are delivered. The maximum time that a message can remain in the queue is 7 days.

Message Producer　　　　　**Queue Storage**　　　　　**Message Consumer**

Queue resolves the issues that arise if the producer is producing faster than the consumer can process it or if the producer and the consumer are intermittently connected to the network.

Queue Use Cases

1. Creating a backlog of work to process asynchronously.
2. Passing messages from an Azure web role to an Azure worker role.

Queue based Load leveling

Queue resolves the issues that arise if the producer is producing faster than the consumer can process it or if the producer and the consumer are intermittently connected to the network.

This figure shows using a queue to level the load on a service. The task and the service run asynchronously. The task posts a message containing the data required by the service to a queue. The queue acts as a buffer, storing the message until it's retrieved by the service.

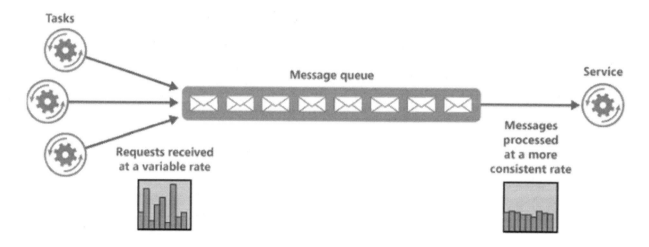

Benefits of Load Leveling

1. It can help to **control costs** because the number of service instances deployed only have to be adequate to meet average load rather than the peak load.

2. It can help to **maximize availability** because delays arising in services won't have an immediate and direct impact on the application, which can continue to post messages to the queue even when the service isn't available or isn't currently processing messages.

3. It can help to **maximize scalability** because both the number of queues and the number of services can be varied to meet demand.

Queue Storage Components

Queue Storage Service contains 2 components.

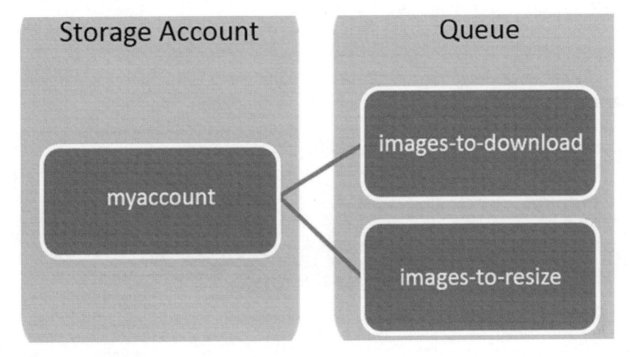

Storage Account

All access to Azure Storage is done through a storage account. This storage account can be a **General-purpose v1 or v2 storage account**. It supports only Standard Storage for File service.

Queue

A queue contains a set of messages. All messages must be in a queue. Queue name must be all lowercase. Queue can hold 500 TB of messages.

Message

A message in any format with Max size of 64 KB. The maximum time that a message can remain in the queue is 7 days.

Accessing Queue Storage using http

https://storage account.queue.core.windows.net/<queue>

Exercise 19: Creating Storage Queue and Accessing Queue from Applications

1. In Storage Account Dashboard >Click Queues>Queue Service Blade Opens> Click +Queue> Enter Queue name in lowercase and click ok.

2. In applications (Application Inserting messages in Queue Storage and Application Processing Queue Messages) add Storage Account connection strings, Storage Account keys and http Queue endpoint. In case you want to protect Storage account keys you can generate and use shared access signatures (SAS).
3. You can also access queue using Azure Storage SDK.

Azure Queue Storage Limits

Max size of single queue	500 TB
Max size of a message in a queue	64 KB
Max number of stored access policies per queue	5
Maximum request rate per storage account	20,000 messages per second assuming 1 KiB message size
Target throughput for single queue	Up to 2000 messages per second

Queue Storage Pricing using General Purpose v2 Account

Queue pricing is based on the storage capacity used, Queue Operations and Geo-Replication Data Transfer.

	LRS	GRS	RA-GRS
Data Storage per GB	$0.045	$0.06	$0.075
Queue Class 1 Operations (in 10,000)	$0.004	$0.008	$0.008
Queue Class 2 Operations (in 10,000)	$0.004	$0.004	$0.004
Geo-replication data transfer (per GB)	NA	$0.02	$0.02

Note 1: Class 1 Queue Operations include CreateQueue, ListQueues, PutMessage, SetQueueMetadata, UpdateMessage, ClearMessages, DeleteMessage, DeleteQueue, GetMessageWrite, GetMessagesWrite.

Note 2: GetMessage, GetMessages, GetQueueMetadata, GetQueueServiceProperties, GetQueueAcl, PeekMessage, PeekMessages, GetMessageRead, GetMessagesRead

Table Storage

Important Note: Microsoft is deprecating table storage and it is recommending Cosmos DB Table API which is also a key-value pair type no SQL Database.

Table Storage is a key-value pair no SQL Database with a schemaless design. They are designed to store large amounts of data for massive scale where some basic structure is required, **but relationships between data don't need to be maintained**.

Tables (Key-Value) stores data in pairs where you have a Key with associated value. For Example take Mobile 8625068410 Pair. Here Mobile is key and the number is value.

Advantage of Table is that Access to data is fast and cost-effective for all kinds of applications. Table storage is typically significantly lower in cost than traditional SQL for similar volumes of data.

Features of Table Storage

Store petabytes of structured data: Azure Table storage store petabytes of semi-structured, non-relational data. You can scale up without having to manually shard your dataset.

Flexible data schema: Table Storage does not lock down the data model to particular schemas. Different rows in the same table can have a different structure—for example, order information in one row, and customer information in another. You can evolve your application and table schema without taking it offline.

Highly Available: With geo-redundant storage, stored data is replicated three times within a region—and an additional three times in another region.

Table Database Use Cases

Key-value databases are optimized for querying against keys. As such, they serve great in-memory caches. Following are some of the use cases:

Session management in Web Applications
Caching for Web Applications.

Table Storage Components

Table Storage Service contains 3 components.

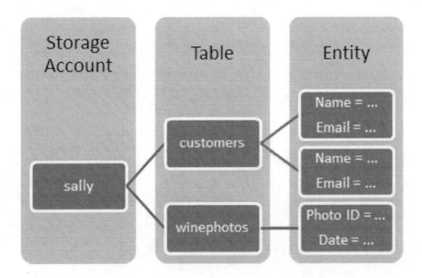

Storage Account: This storage account can be a **GPv2 or GPv1 account.**

Table: A table is a collection of entities. Tables don't enforce a schema on entities, which means a single table can contain entities that have different sets of properties.

Entities: An entity is a set of properties with a Max size of 1MB. Each entity can include up to 252 properties to store data and 3 System Defined Properties.

Properties: A property is a **key-value pair**.

System Defined Properties: Each entity has three system defined properties that specify a partition key, a row key, and a timestamp. You specify value for Partition and Row key. Timestamp value is system generated. An entity's row key is unique within a partition.

Accessing Table Storage using http
https://storage account.table.core.windows.net/<table>

Creating Table Storage

Refer to Table API in Cosmos DB Chapter in Architecting Microsoft Azure Solution Study & Lab Guide Part 2 which is being Published separately.

Azure Table Storage Limits

Max size of single table	500 TB
Max size of a table entity	1 MB
Max number of properties in a table entity	252
Max number of stored access policies per table	5
Maximum request rate per storage account	20,000 transactions per second
Target throughput for single table partition	Up to 2000 entities per second

Table Storage Pricing

Table pricing is based on the storage capacity used, Table Operations and Geo-Replication Data Transfer.

	LRS	GRS	RA-GRS
First 1 TB / month	$0.07 per GB	$0.095 per GB	$0.12 per GB
Next 49 TB (1 to 50 TB) / month	$0.065 per GB	$0.08 per GB	$0.10 per GB
Next 450 TB (50 to 500 TB) / month	$0.06 per GB	$0.07 per GB	$0.09 per GB
Next 500 TB (500 to 1,000 TB) / month	$0.055 per GB	$0.065 per GB	$0.08 per GB
Next 4,000 TB (1,000 to 5,000 TB) / month	$0.045 per GB	$0.06 per GB	$0.075 per GB
Table Operations (in 10,000)	$0.00036	$0.00036	$0.00036
Geo-replication data transfer (per GB)	NA	$0.02	$0.02

Azure Data Box

Azure Data Box is a Secure, Tamper proof and Ruggedised appliance as shown below.

Azure Data Box transfers on-premises data to Azure Cloud.

Azure Data Box is used to transfer large amount of data which otherwise would have taken days, months or years to transfer using Internet or ExpressRoute connection.

Setup & Working

Data Box is ordered to through Azure Portal. Connect the Data Box to your existing Network. Assign an IP directly or through DHCP. Load your data onto the Data Box using standard NAS protocols (SMB/CIFS). Your data is automatically protected using 256-AES encryption. The Data Box is returned to the Azure Data Centre to be uploaded to Azure. After data is uploaded the device is securely erased.

StorSimple

Azure StorSimple is a Hybrid storage solution that stores highly active and less frequently used data locally and moves archival data or inactive data into cloud.

StorSimple offers hybrid management solution wherein you can use StorSimple Device Manager service running in the Azure portal to manage data stored on multiple StorSimple devices and Cloud Storage

Microsoft Offers StorSimple Storage Solution in following Formats:

StorSimple 8000 Series Physical Arrays (8100 & 8600)
StorSimple 8000 Series Cloud Appliance for Azure Cloud
StorSimple on-premises Virtual Appliance - 1200

StorSimple 8000 Series Array

StorSimple 8000 series Physical array is iSCSI SAN Storage Array that has certain amount of Local Storage (SSD & HDD) and can leverage Azure Cloud Storage.

More frequently used data is stored in SSD, less frequently used data is stored in HDD and rarely used is used Data in Azure Storage. The reorganizing of data happens automatically using algorithms built in StorSimple.

Figure below shows the Architecture of the Hybrid Storage Solution using StorSimple 8000 series physical array.

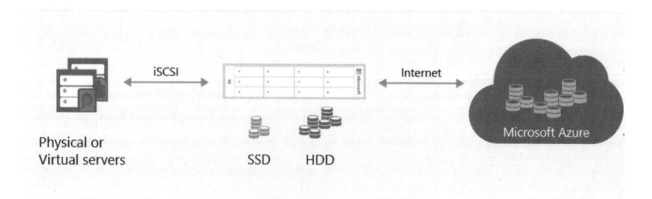

Working of 8000 Series Physical Array

Microsoft Azure StorSimple uses the following software technologies to provide quick access to data and to reduce storage consumption:

Automatic storage tiering
Thin provisioning
Deduplication and compression

Data sent to StorSimple is initially stored in the SSD tier of the hybrid storage array. When it approaches a threshold of fullness, the least recently accessed data will be deduplicated, compressed and then pushed to the HDD tier. When the HDD tier approaches a threshold for fullness, the least recently accessed data will be encrypted, using AES-256 bit encryption, and pushed to the cloud.

Figure below shows working of 8000 Series Physical Storage Appliance.

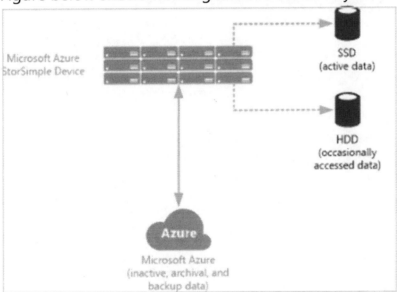

To enable quick access, StorSimple stores very active data (hot data) on SSDs in the StorSimple device. It stores data that is used occasionally (warm data) on HDDs in the device or on servers at the datacenter. It moves inactive data, backup data, and data retained for archival or compliance purposes to the cloud. The reorganizing of data happens automatically using algorithms built in StorSimple.

Pinned Volume: You can specify storage volume as locally pinned in which case the data remains on the local device and is not tiered to the cloud.

Comparing 8100 and 8600 Appliance

StorSimple Physical Array is dual controller array with only one controller active at any point in time. If the active controller fails, the second controller becomes active automatically. It comes with 6 Network interfaces.

	8100	8600
Number of HDDs	8	19
Number of SSDs	4	5
Single HDD capacity	4 TB	4 TB
Single SSD Capacity	400 GB	800 GB
Usable HDD capacity	14 TB	36 TB
Usable SSD capacity	800 GB	2 TB
Total usable capacity (Locally)	15 TB	38 TB
Maximum solution capacity (including cloud)	200 TB	500 TB

StorSimple Cloud Appliance

StorSimple cloud appliance replicates the architecture and capabilities of the 8000 series physical hybrid storage array. The StorSimple Cloud runs on a single node in an Azure virtual machine.

The StorSimple Cloud Appliance is available in two models: the 8010 device & 8020 device. The 8010 device has a maximum capacity of 30 TB and uses Azure Standard Storage (HDD). The 8020 device has a maximum capacity of 64 TB and uses Azure Premium Storage (SSD).

StorSimple on-premises Virtual Appliance – 1200

StorSimple on-premises Virtual Appliance – 1200 is a hybrid storage solution that uses both local storage and cloud storage.

The Virtual Array 1200 is a single-node virtual appliance that can run on Hyper-V or VMware hypervisor. The virtual Array can be configured as iSCSI target or File Server.

The Virtual Array is available in one model. The Virtual Array has a maximum capacity of 6.4 TB on the device (with an underlying storage requirement of 8 TB) and 64 TB including cloud storage.

The virtual array is particularly well-suited for remote office/branch office scenarios.

Figure below shows Architecture of Hybrid storage using Virtual array. It uses heat mapping to determine what data should be tiered in or out

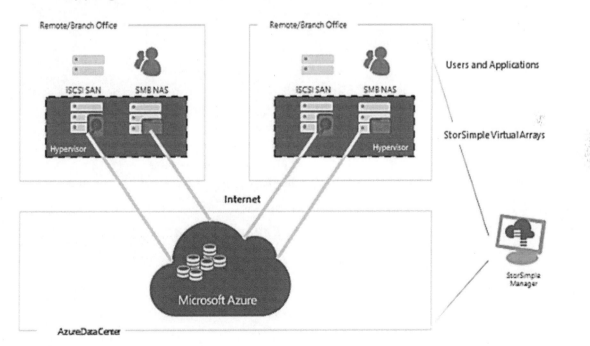

You Configure Virtual array 1200 using Local Web user interface. You can manage the Virtual Array using StorSimple Device Manager Service running in Azure cloud.

StorSimple Device Manager Service

StorSimple Device Manager Service runs in Azure cloud and manages StorSimple device (Physical or Virtual) or StorSimple Cloud Appliance from a single web interface. You can use the StorSimple Device Manager service to create and manage services, view and manage devices, view alerts, manage volumes, shares and view and manage backup policies and the backup catalog.

StorSimple Snapshot Manager – an MMC snap-in that uses volume groups and the Windows Volume Shadow Copy Service to generate application-consistent backups. In addition, you can use StorSimple Snapshot Manager to create backup schedules and clone or restore volumes.

Figure below shows StorSimple Device Manager Service running in Azure cloud managing StorSimple Physical array running on –premises and StorSimple Cloud Appliances. Not shown in the figure is StorSimple Virtual Array 1200.

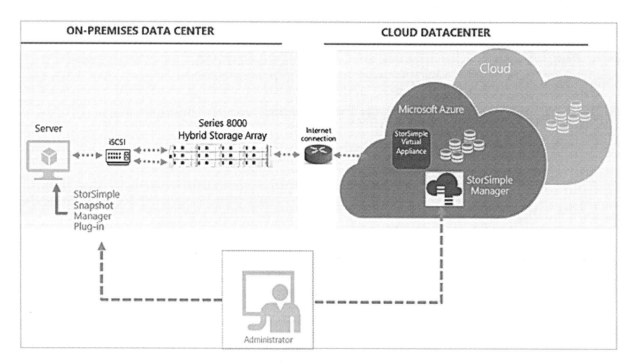

StorSimple Data Manager

The StorSimple Data Manager allows you to seamlessly access StorSimple data in the cloud. This service provides APIs to extract data from StorSimple and present it to other Azure services in formats that can be readily consumed. The formats supported initially are Azure blobs, Azure Files and Azure Media Services assets.

This enables you to use data stored on StorSimple 8000 series devices with Azure Media Services, Azure HDInsight, Azure Machine Learning and Azure Search.

Figure below shows working of StorSimple Data Manager.

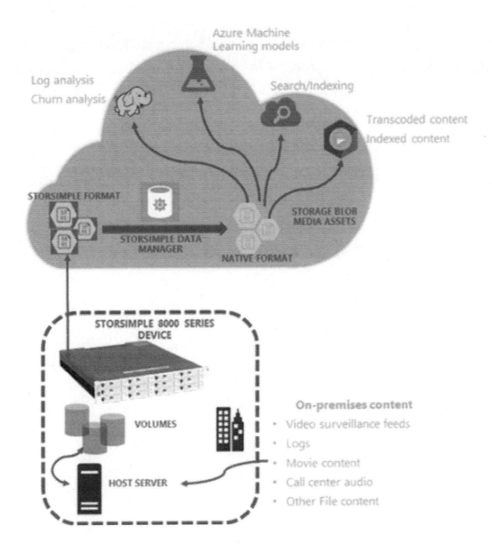

StorSimple Pricing

Model	Daily Rate	Monthly Rate
Physical appliance—8100	$43.84	$1,359.04
Physical appliance—8600	$63.01	$1,953.31
Cloud array 8010 or 8020	$4.11	$127.41
Virtual appliance—1200	$4.11	$127.41

StorSimple Data Manager Pricing

StorSimple Data Manager Pricing is based on the number of data transformation jobs run and how much data is transformed.

Data Transformation (per Job)	$1.50
Data Transformation (per GB)	$0.005

Storage Service Encryption (SSE)

Storage Service encryption (SSE) protects data at Rest.

Storage Storage Service encryption (SSE) automatically encrypts Azure Storage data (Blobs, Files, Queues and Tables) at Rest using Azure Managed keys. SSE automatically decrypts it for you as you access it.

You may choose to bring your own key for encryption for Azure Blobs and Files. Encryption for Tables and Queues will always use Microsoft Managed Keys.

SSE is enabled automatically and you don'y have to do anyhting.

Figure below shows dashboard of Azure Storage Account with Encryption selected from left pane. You have the option of selecting your own key.

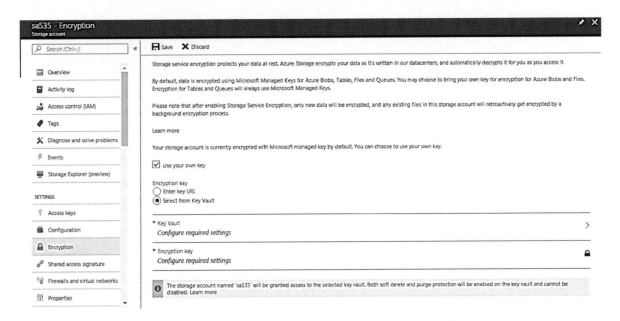

Design Nugget: After enabling Storage Service Encryption, only new data will be encrypted, and any existing files in this storage account will retroactively get encrypted by a background encryption process.

Chapter 5 Virtual Machine Scale Set (VMSS)

This Chapter covers following Topic Lessons

- Virtual Machine Scale Set
- Virtual Machine Scale Set Architecture
- Autoscaling with VMSS
- VIRTUAL MACHINE SCALE SET (VMSS) MAXIMUMS
- Monitoring Autoscaling

This Chapter Covers following Lab Exercises

- Deploying Virtual Machine Scale Set

Chapter Topology

In this chapter Virtual Machine Scale Set (VMSS) will be deployed in System Generated Virtual Network. Azure Basic Load Balance with public IP is also deployed automatically by the System. All VMs specified in Create VMSS dialog box are deployed in a single system specified subnet.

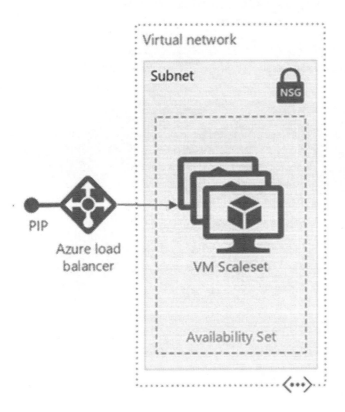

Virtual Machine Scale Set (VMSS)

Virtual Machine Scale Set creates scalable & high available Virtual Machine infrastructure by deploying and managing identical VMs as a set. An Azure Load Balancer and Virtual Network with a single subnet are also deployed along with set of identical VMs.

By enabling Autoscaling on VMSS, Virtual Machines instances in the set can be added or removed automatically.

VMs in the scale set are managed as a unit. All VMs in the scale set are identical and are either Windows VM or Linux VMs. All VMs are of same size and series.

VMSS supports Azure Windows and Linux images and Custom images.

Main Advantages of VMSS against Load Balanced VMs deployed with Load Balancers

1. Scale-out or Scale-in also known as Autoscaling is automatic based on predefined metrics. Whereas you need to manually deploy Virtual machines yourself and add to the pool or can be deployed using Azure Automation scripts.
2. VMs in the scale set are managed as a unit. Whereas you need to manage each VM individually.
3. Virtual Network & Azure Load Balancer are automatically created during VMSS deployment.

VM-specific features not available in Scale Set

1. You can snapshot an individual VM but not a VM in a scale set.
2. You can capture an image from an individual VM but not from a VM in a scale set.
3. You can migrate an individual VM from native disks to managed disks, but you cannot do this for VMs in a scale set.

Virtual Machine Scale Set (VMSS) Architecture

Virtual Machine Scale Set (VMSS) deploys set of Identical VMs in a single subnet of a Virtual Network. Figure below shows Architecture of Virtual Machine Scale Set (VMSS) deployed in single subnet with Single Placement group.

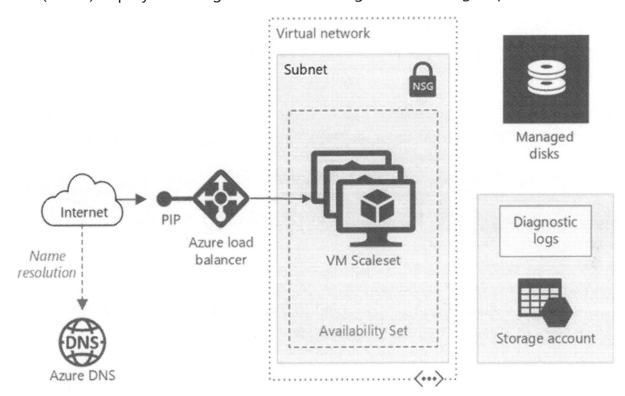

VM Scaleset deploys set of identical VMs in the Single Subnet of Virtual Network.

Virtual Network with Single Subnet is automatically created during VM Scaleset deployment.

Azure Load Balancer is automatically created during VMSS deployment.

Placement group is availability set with five fault domains and five update domains and support up to 100 VMs. Placement group is automatically created by VMSS. Additional Placement groups will be automatically created by VMSS if you are deploying more than 100 instances.

Storage: VMSS can use managed disks or unmanaged disks for Virtual Machine storage. Managed disks are required to create more than 100 Virtual Machines. Unmanaged disks are limited to 100 VMs and single Placement Group.

VM Diagnostic Logs are guest OS performance counters and are streamed to Azure storage Account. VMSS uses this data for making Autoscaling decisions.

Autoscaling with VMSS

With Autoscaling, Virtual Machines can be added (scale-out) or removed (scale-in) automatically from Virtual Machine Scale Set (VMSS) based on rules configured for metrics (CPU utilization, Memory utilization etc.).

During Autoscaling the application continues to run without interruption as new resources are provisioned. When the provisioning process is complete, the solution is deployed on these additional resources. If demand drops, the additional resources can be shut down cleanly and de-allocated automatically.

How to Enable Autoscaling in VMSS

You can enable Autoscaling during VMSS creation or after the creation from VMSS dashboard or Azure Monitor Dashboard. If enabled during VMSS creation then only CPU metrics can be used for Autoscaling. Autoscaling can be based on schedule or on metric condition.

Autoscaling Metrics

Autoscaling is enabled by configuring rules on Metrics or on Schedule. VMSS supports following types of metrics for configuring Autoscaling rules:

Host level Metrics: Host level metrics such as % CPU Utilization, Disk Read/write, Network in/out traffic at Network interface etc are emitted by Virtual Machines by default.

Guest OS level Metrics: You need to enable Guest OS diagnostics to use OS level metrics. OS level metrics are Operating system performance counters. Performance metrics are collected from inside of each VM instance and are streamed to an Azure storage account. VMSS can configure Autoscaling rules based on Guest OS level metrics,.

Application Insights: Application insights provide performance data for application running on VM.

Azure Resources: Azure resources such as Azure Storage queue length can be used as a metric for configuring Autoscaling rules. For Example you can configure Autoscaling rule which scale-out by 2 instances when queue length is greater than 5.

Autoscaling Working

When threshold for a metric is reached scale-out or scale-in happens. For Example a rule configured for CPU utilization states that if CPU utilization crosses 80% then scale-out by 2 instances and if CPU utilization drops below 30% then scale-in by one instance.

All thresholds are calculated at an instance level (Average of all instances in VMSS). For example scale- out by 2 instance when average CPU > 80%, means scale-out happens when the average CPU across all instances is greater than 80%.

VIRTUAL MACHINE SCALE SET (VMSS) MAXIMUMS

1. Maximum Number of VMs in a scale set when using Azure Platform images is 1000.
2. Maximum Number of VMs in a scale set when using Custom VM images is 300.
3. To have more than 100 VMs in the scale set you need to use Managed Disks for VM storage.
4. A scale set configured with unmanaged disks for VM storage is limited to 100 VMs.

DESIGN NUGGETS

Design Nugget: If Multiple Rules are configured then *scale-out* happens if any rule is met and *scale-in* happens when all rules are met.

Design Nuggets: You can only attach data disks to a scale set that has been created with Azure Managed Disks.

Design Nuggets: If you are not using managed disks, we recommend no more than 20 VMs per storage account with overprovisioning enabled and no more than 40 VMs with overprovisioning disabled.

Exercise 20: Deploying VMSS

1. In Azure Portal click +New> In search box type scale set and click enter>In the result click Virtual Machine Scale set>Click create>Create Virtual Machine Scale set blade opens> enter information as per your req and click create.

Note: You can enable Autoscaling during VMSS deployment but you get only CPU metrics to configure Autoscaling rules. We will enable from VMSS portal. Figure below Metrics available for configuring Autoscaling rules during VMSS creation. We are not enabling Autoscaling here.

AUTOSCALE

Autoscale ❶	Disabled **Enabled**
* Minimum number of VMs ❶	1
* Maximum number of VMs ❶	10

Scale out

* CPU threshold (%) ❶	75
* Number of VMs to increase by ❶	1

Scale in

* CPU threshold (%) ❶	25
* Number of VMs to decrease by ❶	1

2. After clicking create in step 1 VMSS deployment begins. It will take around 4-5 minutes for deployment to succeed. Figure below shows VMSS dashboard.

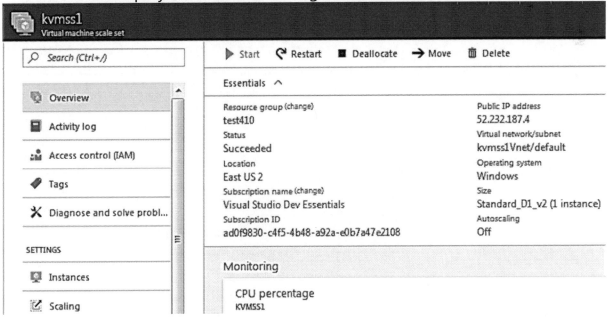

In the above figure a VNET (kvmss1Vnet) was automatically created and Virtual Machine is created in default subnet. An Azure load balancer was also created with VMSS. To see the created Azure load Balancer go to all resources and click the Azure Load Balancer created.

Enabling Autoscaling

1. Click Scaling in VMSS dashboard>Scaling blade opens in right pane.

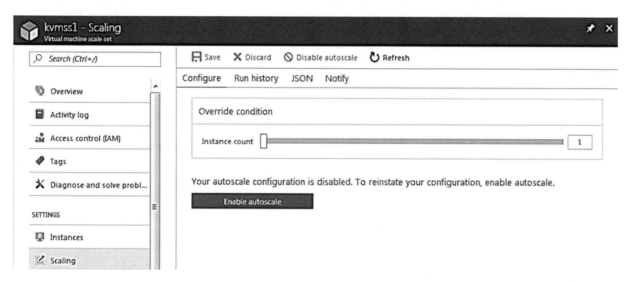

2. Click Enable Autoscale>Scale Condition Blade opens> Here we can create Autoscaling based on metric or on schedule. For our example we will use metric. Here Maximum specifies number of instances which can scale out.

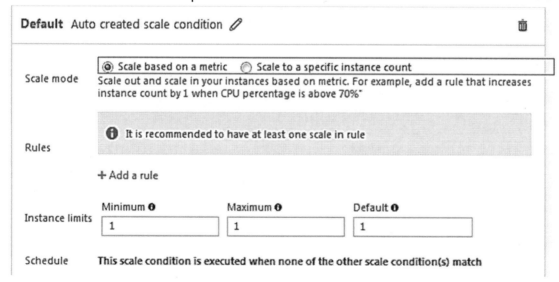

3. We will add 5 as Maximum Scale-out limit.

4. **Add scale-out rule**: Click + Add a rule>Scale rule opens in right pane. Note the metrics sources we can use here. See dropdown box for other metric also.

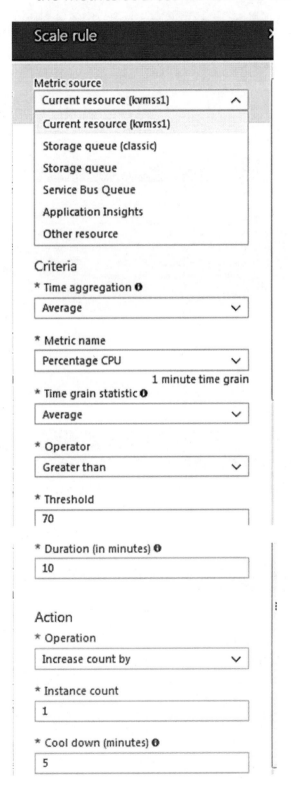

5. **Add scale-in rule**: Similarly add scale-in rule by selecting decrease count in operation dropdown box.

Figure below shows the dashboard of Load Balancer which was automatically created.

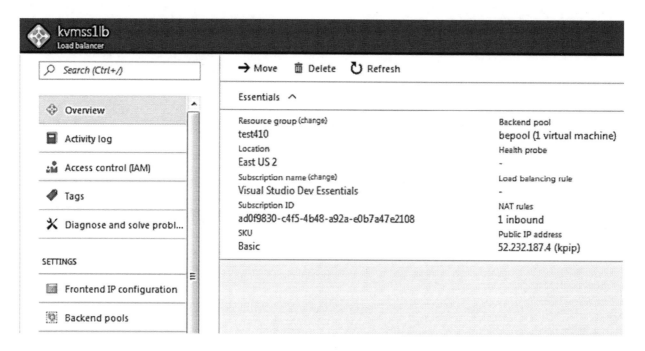

Figure below shows the dashboard of Virtual Network which was automatically created.

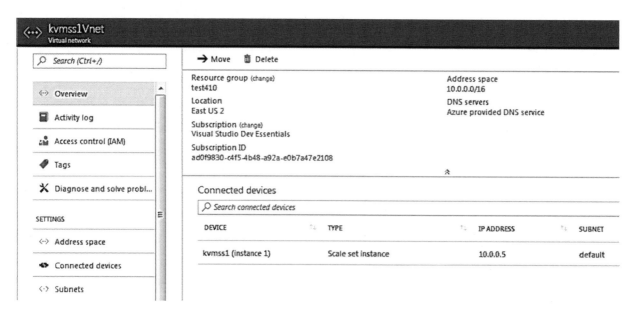

Monitoring Autoscaling

All Autoscale successful and failures actions are logged to the Activity Log. You can then configure an activity log alert so that you can be notified via email, SMS & webhook whenever there is an Autoscale success or failure.

Chapter 6 Azure Backup

This Chapter covers following

- Azure Backup
- Recovery services Vault
- Backup scenarios with Azure Backup
- Architecture of Azure Backup using Azure Backup Agent
- Architecture of Azure Backup using System Center Data Protection Manager
- Architecture of Azure Backup using Azure Backup Server
- Azure IaaS VM Backup
- Azure Backup Limits
- Azure Backup Pricing
- Monitoring Azure Backup

This Chapter Covers following Lab Exercises to build below topology

- Create Recovery Services Vault
- Backup Files & Folder on Windows Server VM using Backup Agent option
- Azure VM-level backup
-

Chapter Topology

In this Chapter we will add Recovery Services Vault to the topology and Deploy Azure Backup agent on wvm535.

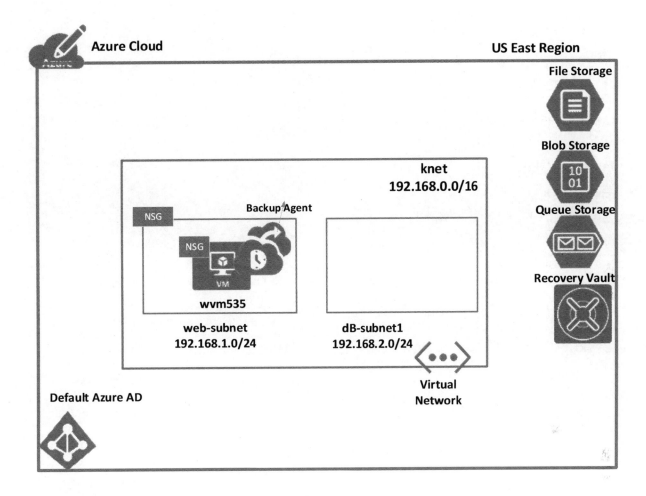

Azure Backup

Azure Backup is Backup as a service (BaaS) which you can use to backup and restore your data in Azure cloud.
You can backup both on Premises workloads and Azure workloads.
Azure Backups are stored in Recovery Services Vault.
Advantage of Azure backup is that we don't have to set up Backup infrastructure.

Feature of Azure Backup

1. No backup infrastructure to setup. It uses pay-as-you-use model.
2. Azure Backup manages backup storage scalability and high availability. Azure Recovery Services Vault offers unlimited Storage. For high availability, Azure Backup offers two types of replication: locally redundant storage and geo-redundant storage.
3. Azure Backup supports incremental backup. Incremental backup transfers changes made since the last full backup.
4. Data is encrypted for secure transmission between on-premises and Azure Cloud. The backup data is stored in the Recovery Services vault in encrypted form.
5. Backups are compressed to reduce the required storage space in Vault.
6. Azure Backup provides application-consistent backups, which ensured additional fixes are not needed to restore the data. Restoring application consistent data reduces the restoration time, allowing you to quickly return to a running state. This option is only available when we use either System Center DPM or Azure Backup server.

Recovery services Vault

A Recovery Services Vault is a storage entity in Azure that houses backup data.

You can use Recovery Services vaults to hold backup data for on-premises workload and for various Azure services such as IaaS VMs (Linux or Windows) and Azure SQL databases. **Azure Backup offers two types of replication:** locally redundant storage (LRS) and geo-redundant storage (GRS)**.**

Backup scenarios with Azure Backup

Azure Backup provides 4 options to Backup on-premises and Cloud workloads – Azure Backup Agent, System Center DPM Server, Azure Backup Server and Azure IaaS VM Backup.

Table below shows comparison of Azure Backup options.

Backup Option	Features	Deployment	Target Storage
Azure Backup Agent	Backs up Files and Folders on Windows Server and VMs. No Linux support. No backup server required.	On-premises and Cloud	RSV
System Center DPM	Backs up Files, folders, Volumes, VMs & Application aware backup (SQL, Exchange). Other features include Restore granuality and Linux support. Cannot back up Oracle workload.	On-premises and Cloud	RSV, Local Disk on DPM server and Tape (on-site only)
Azure Backup Server	Backs up Files, folders, Volumes, VMs & Application aware backup (SQL, Exchange). Restore granuality and Linux support. Cannot back up Oracle workload. Requires live Azure subscription. No support for tape backup. Does not require a System Center license	On-premises and Cloud	RSV, Local Disk on Azure Backup Server
Azure IaaS VM Backup	Backup Integrated in VM dashboard. Backs up VMs and Disks. No specific agent installation required. Fabric-level backup with no backup infrastructure needed	Cloud only	RSV

RSV: Recovery Services Vault

Architecture of Azure Backup using Azure Backup Agent

Azure Backup agent backs up Windows server or Windows VM to Recovery Services Vault in Azure. Azure Backup Agent option can be used to backup both on-premises and cloud workloads.

Backup to Azure requires following components.

1. Recovery services Vault
2. Azure backup agent

Azure Backup Agent can backup following workloads

Files & Folders: Azure Backup agent backs up files and folders on Window server or Windows VM to Recovery Services Vault.

Windows System State

Backup Location:

Backs up data to Recovery Services Vault in Azure. There is no option to backup Data locally.

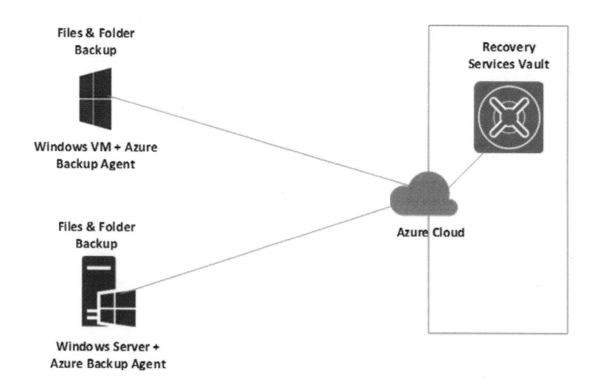

Installing & Configuring Azure Backup Agent option

1. Create Recovery Services vault.
2. Download Backup Agent and Vault Credentials to the on Premises server by configuring the Backup goal in Recovery services vault dashboard.
3. Install Azure Backup Agent on the on Premises Server and register the server with Recovery Services vault using Vault credentials.
4. Schedule the backup by opening Azure backup agent in the on premises server and configuring the backup policy.

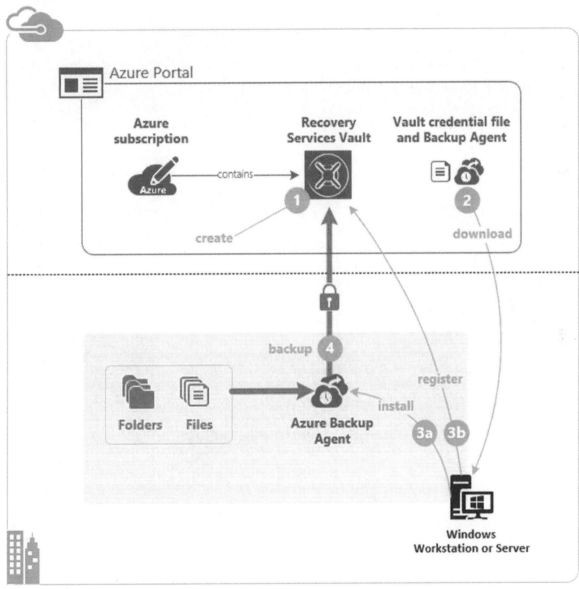

Architecture of Azure Backup using System Center Data Protection Manager

This option not only backs up workload to Azure Recovery Service Vault but backup is also available locally on disk as well as on tape. This option can be used to backup both on-premises and cloud workloads.

Backup to Azure requires following components

1. Recovery services Vault
2. Azure backup agent
3. System Center Data Protection Manager (DPM)

In this case backup agent will be installed on DPM server.

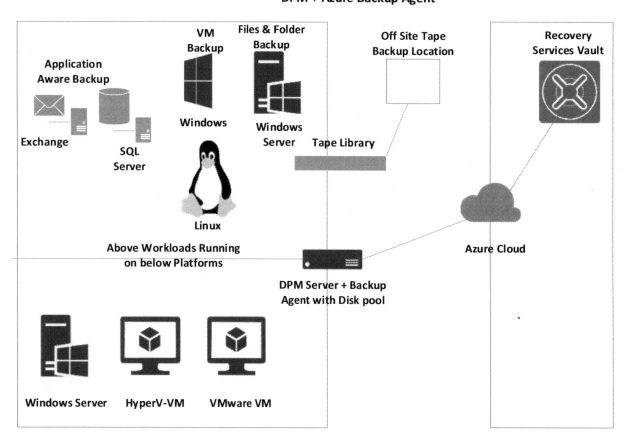

DPM can backup following workloads

Application-aware backup: Application-aware back up of Microsoft workloads, including SQL Server, Exchange, and SharePoint.

File backup: Back up files, folders and volumes for computers running Windows server and Windows client operating systems.

System backup: Back up system state or run full, bare-metal backups of physical computers running Windows server or Windows client operating systems.

Hyper-V backup: Back up Hyper-V virtual machines (VM) running Windows or Linux. You can back up an entire VM, or run application-aware backups of Microsoft workloads on Hyper-V VMs running Windows.

VMware VMs backup

DPM Backup Workload Locations

Disk: For short-term storage DPM backs up data to disk pools.

Azure Recovery Services Vault: For both short-term and long-term storage off-premises, DPM data stored in disk pools can be backed up to the Azure Recovery Services Vault using the Azure Backup service.

Tape: For long-term storage you can back up data to tape, which can then be stored offsite. This option is only available for on-premises workload.

Advantages of DPM backup

1. Backup is also available locally.
2. Linux VM backup.
3. Application Aware Backup.
4. Tape Backup option.

Architecture of Azure Backup using Azure Backup Server

This option is same as DPM option except for following 2 differences.

1. Tape option is not there with Azure backup server.
2. You don't have to pay license for Azure Backup server.

Backup to Azure requires following components

1. Recovery services Vault
2. Azure backup agent
3. Azure Backup Server

In this case backup agent will be installed on Azure Backup Server.

Rest everything is same as discussed in Data protection Server in previous section.

Azure Backup Server + Azure Backup Agent

Azure IaaS VM Backup

Azure IaaS VM Backup provides Native backups for Windows/Linux. This option can be used to backup Azure VMs only. The benefit of this option is that Backup option is built in VM dashboard.

Backup to Azure requires following components.

1. Recovery services Vault
2. Azure backup agent extension is automatically enabled when backup is enabled in the VM.

Azure IaaS VM Backup can backup following workloads

Full Azure Windows/Linux VM backup.
VM Disk Backups (Using Powershell)

Backup Location:

Backs up data to Recovery Services Vault in Azure.

Exercise 21: Create Recovery Services Vault

1. In Azure Portal click create a resource> Storage> Backup and Site Recovery (OMS)> Create Recovery Services Vault Blade opens> Enter as per your requirement and click create.

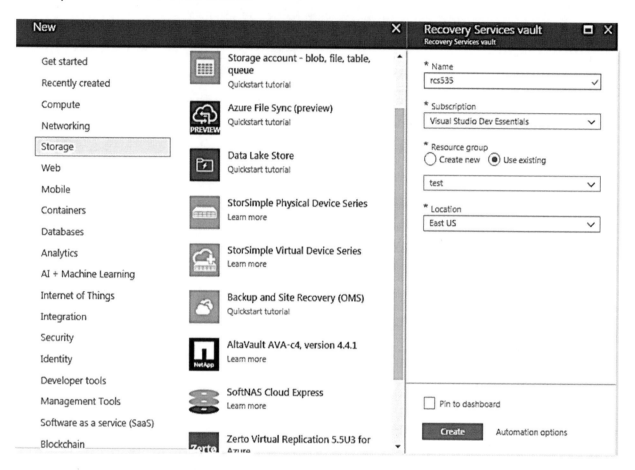

2. **Choosing Storage Replication of Recovery Services Vault**: In RCS Vault Dashboard click Backup Infrastructure in left pane (Not shown)>Backup Configuration >Backup Configuration Blade opens>Select Replication option as per your requirement. Default is Geo-redundant.

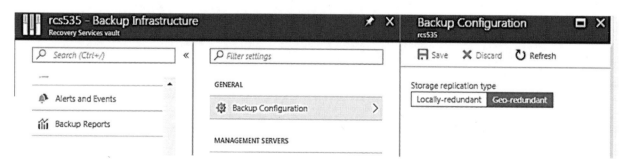

Architecting Microsoft Azure Solutions Study & Lab Guide Part 1: Exam 70-535

Exercise 22: Backup Files & Folder on Windows Server VM using Backup Agent option

In this exercise we will backup Files & Folders & System State of Azure VM wvm535 using Azure Backup Agent option. For this exercise we will RDP into wvm535. Here we will select workload location as on-premises.

1. RDP into wvm535.
2. Create an empty folder name test on the wvm535 desktop.
3. In wvm35 Open internet explorer and log on to Azure portal> Go to Recovery Services Vault Dashboard>Click Backup in left pane>Select on-premises and select Files and Folder & System State>Click Prepare Infrastructure>Prepare Infrastructure Blade opens

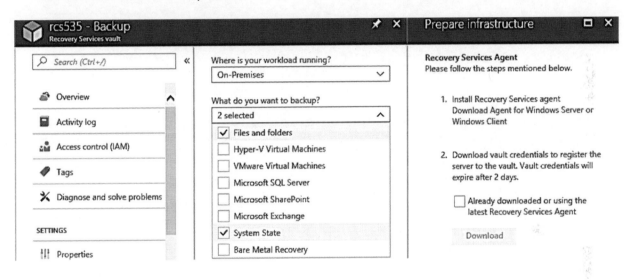

Note: Options available to backup windows server (Vmware VMs, Exchange etc).

4. Download both Recovery Services agent & Vault Credentials. Vault credential is used to register windows server to Recovery Services Vault.

5. Install Recovery services agent on Azure VM wvm535 and register server with RCS using vault credentials downloaded in step 4 and also enter paraphrase for encrypting backup.

6. **Create a Backup Schedule & Select Backup items**. Open the Microsoft Azure Backup agent in wvm535>Click Action> Click schedule backup> Schedule Backup Wizard opens> In Select Items to backup select test folder created in step 2 and for rest select all default values> Click close.

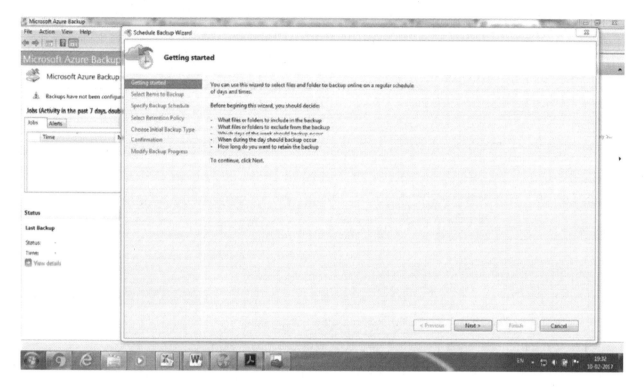

7. **To back up files and folders for the first time**. Open the Microsoft Azure Backup agent in wvm535>Click Action>Click backup now> On confirmation page click back up>Click close>Monitor the progress in agent console. Once the job is completed go to Recovery Services Vault in Azure to see the status of the backup job.

8. **Monitor the Backup Job**: Go to Recovery Service vault Dashboard>Click Backup Items>Click Backup Agents> You can see the backup listed.

Architecting Microsoft Azure Solutions Study & Lab Guide Part 1: Exam 70-535

Exercise 23: Azure VM-level backup

1. In Azure Portal go to VM wvm535 dashboard>click Backup in left pane>Enable Backup blade opens> Select RSV created in Exercise 10 or create new>click enable backup. This will backup system state of the wvm535.

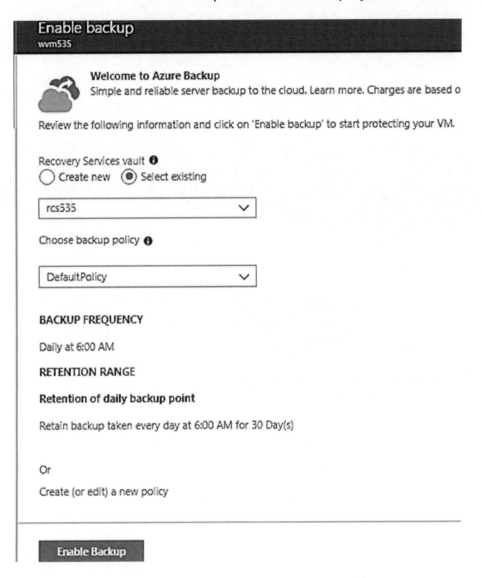

Note: You can create a new RSV or use existing Recovery Services Vault.
Note: You can also create a new policy or edit existing daily policy.

Design Nugget: Azure Backup provides **VM-level backup** for Azure VMs using the VM extension. To protect files and folders on the guest Windows OS, install the **Azure Backup agent** on the guest Windows OS as shown in Previous Exercise.

Azure Backup Limits

Limit Identifier	Default Limit
Number of servers that can be registered against each vault	50 for Windows Server/ SCDPM 200 for IaaS VMs
Maximum Storage Capacity of Vault	Unlimited
Max Size of a data source which can be stored in Azure vault storage	54400 GB
Number of backup vaults that can be created in each Azure subscription	25 Recovery Services vaults per region
Number of times backup can be scheduled per day	3 per day for Windows Server/Client 2 per day for SCDPM Once a day for IaaS VMs

Azure Backup Pricing

Azure Backup pricing consist of 2 factors.

1. Size of the backed-up data of an instance.
2. Azure Storage consumed.

SIZE OF EACH INSTANCE	AZURE BACKUP PRICE PER MONTH
Instance < or = 50 GB	$5 + storage consumed
Instance is > 50 but < or = 500 GB	$10 + storage consumed
Instance > 500 GB	$10 for each 500 GB increment + storage consumed

Backup Storage Pricing

Azure Backup uses Block Blob storage for backing up your instances. You have the option to choose between locally redundant storage (LRS) or geo-redundant storage (GRS) for Recovery Services Vault.

For Pricing of Blob Storage Refer to Storage Chapter.

Monitoring Azure Backup

You can configure OMS workspaces to receive key backup data across multiple Recovery Services vaults by adding Management Solution to Log Analytics Workspace.

The OMS monitoring solution **allows you to monitor key backup parameters such as** backup and restore jobs, backup alerts, and cloud storage usage **across Recovery Services vaults and subscriptions.**

You can then utilize OMS log analytics capabilities to raise further alerts for events that you deem important for the business to be notified of. You could even open tickets through webhooks or ITSM integration using the OMS log analytics capabilities.

Figure below shows Backup Management Solution which is to be added to Log Analytics Workspace.

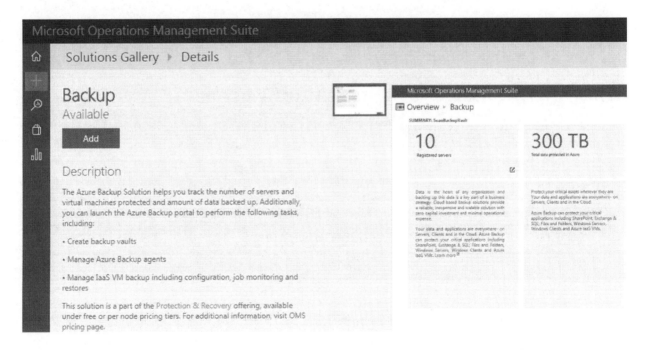

Chapter 7 Azure Site Recovery

This Chapter covers following

- Replication scenarios with Azure Site Recovery
- Disaster Recovery Site option with Azure Site Recovery
- Architecture for Disaster Recovery to Azure
- Architecture for Disaster Recovery to Secondary Data Center
- Replication Architecture of Hyper-V VMs Managed by VMM to Azure
- Replication Architecture of VMware VMs or Physical Servers to Azure
- Replication Architecture of Hyper-V VMs to Azure
- Replication Architecture of Hyper-V VMs Managed by VMM to Secondary Data Center
- Replication Architecture of Azure VMs in Azure Cloud to Azure Cloud
- Azure Site Recovery Pricing

This Chapter Covers following Lab Exercises to build below topology

- Enabling Disaster Recovery for Azure VM using Azure Site Recovery

Chapter Topology

In This chapter we will add Azure Site Recovery to the topology to replicate wvm535 from US East region to US East 2 region.

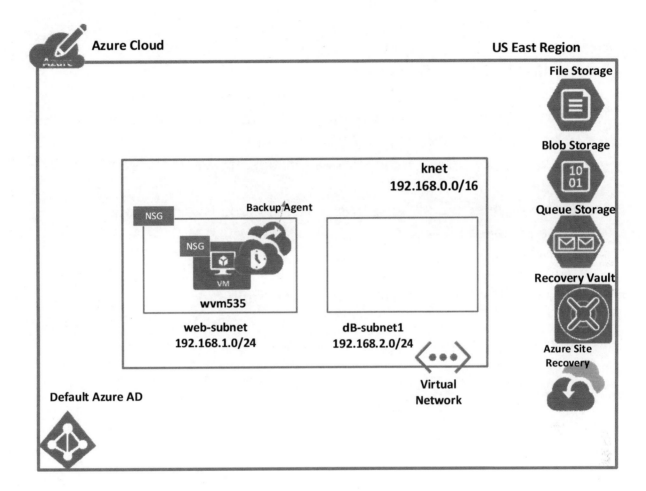

Azure Site Recovery

Azure Site Recovery provides Disaster Recovery as a Service (DRaaS).

Azure Site Recovery is an Azure Managed service that orchestrates and replicates Azure VMs and on-premises physical servers and virtual machines to the Azure cloud or to a secondary datacenter.

When outages occur in your primary location, you fail over to the secondary location to keep apps and workloads available. You fail back to your primary location when it returns to normal operations.

You can replicate Azure VMs in one Azure region to another Azure region.

You can replicate on-premises VMware VMs, Hyper-V VMs, Windows and Linux physical servers to Azure cloud or to a secondary datacenter.

Azure Recovery Services contribute to your BCDR strategy. The Azure Backup service keeps your data safe and recoverable. Site Recovery replicates, fails over, and recovers workloads when failure occurs.

Replication scenarios with Azure Site Recovery

Replicating on-premises VMs and Physical servers to Azure Cloud: You can replicate on-premises VMware VMs, Hyper-V VMs, Hyper-V VMs managed by SC VMM, Windows and Linux physical servers to Azure cloud.
Replicating to Secondary Data Center: You can replicate on-premises VMware VMs, Hyper-V VMs managed by VMM, Windows and Linux physical servers to Secondary Data Center. Note in this case we cannot replicate Hyper-V VMs to secondary Data Center.
Replicating Azure VMs in one region to another region in Azure Cloud: You can replicate Azure VMs from one Azure region to another Azure region.

Disaster Recovery Site option with Azure Site Recovery

1. Azure Cloud
2. Secondary Data Center (Non applicable for Azure VMs)

Architecture for Disaster Recovery to Azure

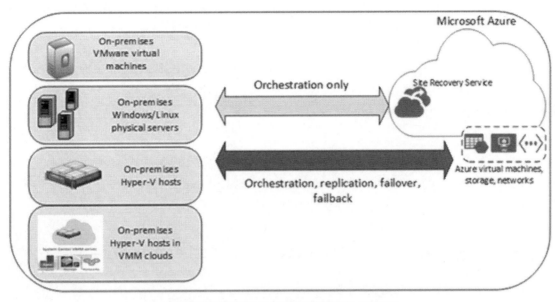

ON-PREMISES DATACENTER TO AZURE

Architecture for Disaster Recovery to Secondary Data Center

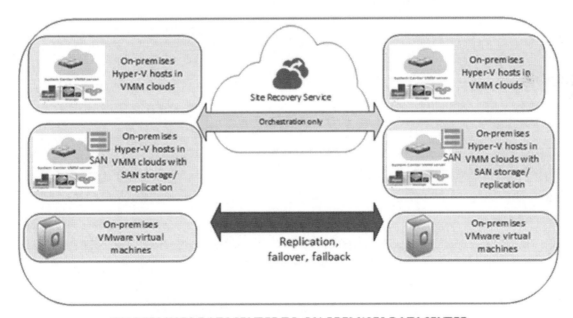

ON-PREMISES DATACENTER TO ON-PREMISES DATACENTER

Replication Architecture of Hyper-V VMs Managed by VMM to Azure

You can Replicate VMs located on-premises Hyper-V hosts managed by System Center Virtual Machine Manager (VMM) to Azure Storage. You can replicate Hyper-V VMs running any guest operating system <u>supported by Hyper-V and Azure</u>.

Figure below shows the Replication Architecture of Hyper-V VMs Managed by System Center VMM.

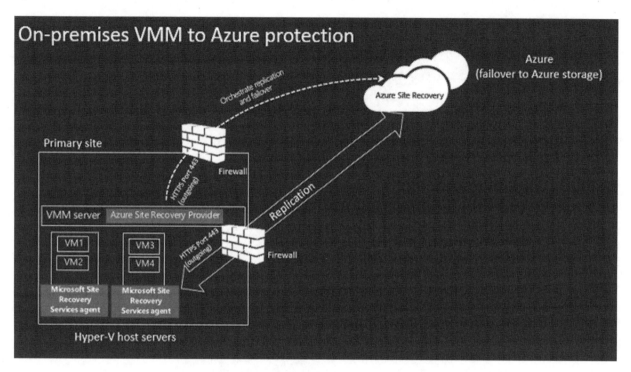

Requirements on Azure Side

1. **Storage Account**: You need an Azure storage account to store replicated data. Azure VMs are created from Replicated data when failover occurs.
2. **Virtual Network**: You need an Azure virtual network that Azure VMs will connect to when they're created at failover.
3. **Recovery Services Vault**: Create Recovery Services Vault

Requirements on-premises side

1. **SC VMM**: You need one or more on-premises VMM servers running System Center VMM 2012 R2 with Azure Site Recovery Provider Installed.
2. **Hyper-V host**: You need one or more Windows Server 2016 or Windows Server 2012 R2 Hyper-V host server. During Site Recovery deployment you'll install the Microsoft Azure Recovery Services agent on the host.
3. **Azure Site Recovery Provider (Installed on VMM)**: The Provider coordinates and orchestrates replication with the Site Recovery service over the internet.
4. **Azure Recovery Service Agent (Installed on Hyper-V host)**: The agent handles data replication data over HTTPS 443. Communications from both the Provider and the agent are secure and encrypted. Replicated data in Azure storage is also encrypted.

Step by Step Deployment in Brief

1. Set Recovery Services Vault in Azure.
2. Set up Resource Group, Storage Account & Virtual Network for DR Site.
3. In Recovery Services Vault dashboard click Site Recovery in left pane>Prepare Infrastructure> Configure settings including Protection goals, source and target preparation and setting up a replication policy.

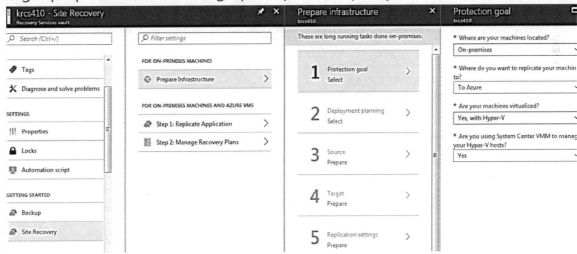

4. As part of specifying source settings, Register VMM server and download and install the Azure Site Recovery Provider on the VMM server and the Azure Recovery Services agent on each Hyper-V host. The source will be the VMM server. In SC VMM Create a VMM cloud on-premises.

5. As part of specify target settings select your Azure Subscription. Site Recovery will check for compatible storage account and Network.

6. In replication settings, **create a replication policy** for the VMM cloud. The policy is applied to all VMs located on hosts in the VMM cloud.

7. **Create Network Mapping** by clicking Site Recovery Infrastructure in Recovery services vault>Click Networking Mapping for Hyper VMs managed by VMM.

8. **Enable replication** for Hyper-V VMs managed by VMM as shown in figure below. Here you will specify the target Storage Account created in step 2. Selects the VMs for which you want replication. Initial replication occurs in accordance with the replication policy settings. Data changes are tracked, and replication of delta changes to Azure begins after the initial replication finishes.

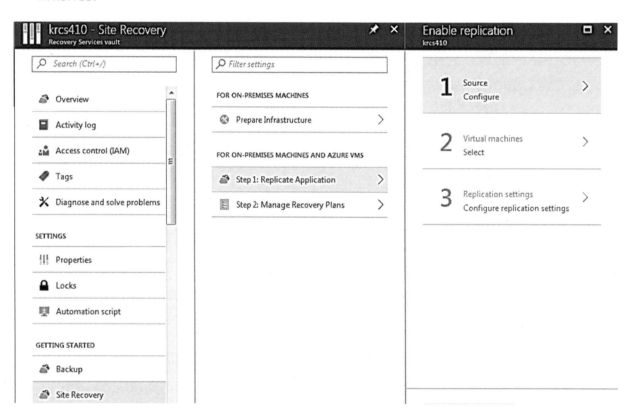

9. Run a test failover to make sure everything's working as expected.

Replication Architecture of VMware VMs or Physical Servers to Azure

Replicate VMs located on-premises VMware hosts managed by vCenter to Azure Storage. vCenter is not compulsory but it is recommended.

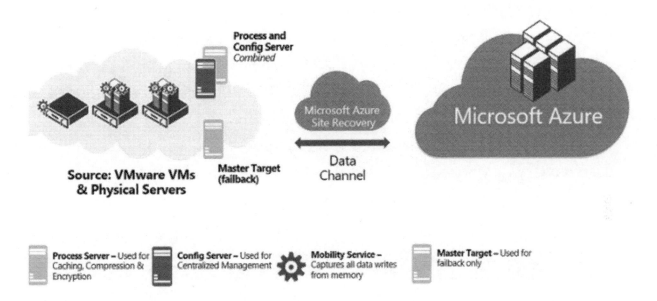

VMware to Azure: Architecture

Requirements on Azure Side

1. Storage Account: You need an Azure storage account to store replicated data. Azure VMs are created from Replicated data when failover occurs.
2. Virtual Network: You need an Azure virtual network that Azure VMs will connect to when they're created at failover.
3. Recovery Services Vault.

Requirements on-premises side

1. **Configuration Server**: Coordinates communications between on-premises and Azure and manages data replication.
2. **Process server**: It receives replication data from VMware Virtual Machines or Physical Servers and optimizes it with caching, compression, and encryption and sends it to Azure Storage. Installed by default on the configuration server.

3. **Master target server**: It handles replication data during failback from Azure. For large deployments, you can add an additional, separate master target server for failback. Installed by default on the configuration server.
4. **Mobilty Service**: Mobility Service captures all data writes on VMware virtual machine and Physical Server and sends it to Process Server. Mobility Service is installed on each VMware VM and Physical Server that you replicate.
5. **VMware Virtual Machines with Mobility service Installed.**
6. **VMware ESXi Hosts and vCenter Server**: Requires vSphere 6.5, 6.0, or 5.5 and vCenter Server 6.5, 6.0, or 5.5.

Replication Process

VMware Virtual Machines replicate in accordance with the replication policy configured. Initial copy of the VM data is replicated to Azure Storage.

After initial replication finishes, replication of delta changes to Azure begins. Changes for a machine are held in a .hrl file.

1. Machines send replication data to the process server.
2. The process server receives data from source machines, optimizes and encrypts it, and sends it to Azure Storage.
3. The configuration server orchestrates replication management with Azure.

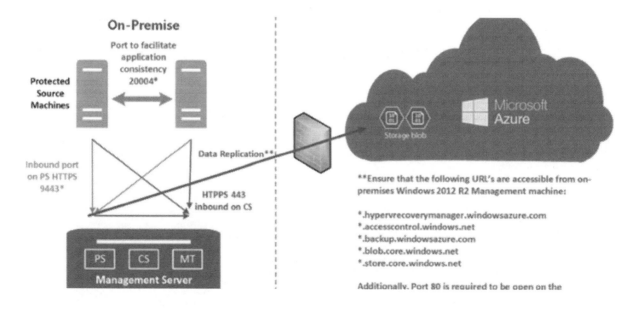

Failover process

After replication is set up and you can run a disaster recovery drill (test failover) to check that everything's working as expected.

1. You can fail over a single machine or create recovery plans to fail over multiple VMs.
2. When you run a failover, Azure VMs are created from replicated data in Azure storage.

Replication Architecture of Hyper-V VMs to Azure

You can Replicate VMs located on-premises Hyper-V hosts to Azure Storage. You can replicate Hyper-V VMs running any guest operating system <u>supported by Hyper-V and Azure</u>.

Figure below shows the Replication Architecture of Hyper-V VMs to Azure Cloud.

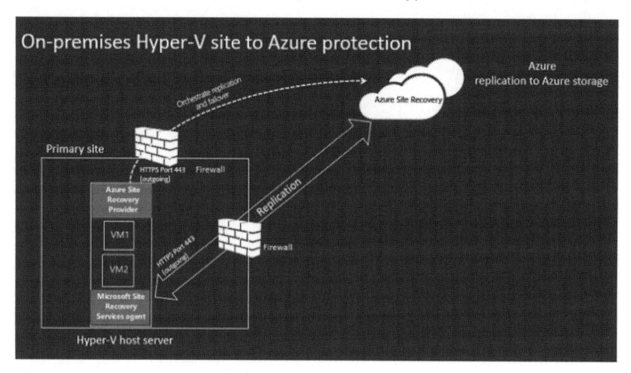

Requirements on Azure Side

1. Storage Account: You need an Azure storage account to store replicated data. Azure VMs are created from Replicated data when failover occurs.
2. Virtual Network: You need an Azure virtual network that Azure VMs will connect to when they're created at failover.
3. Recovery Services Vault.

Requirements on-premises side

1. **Hyper-V host**: You need one or more Windows Server 2016 or Windows Server 2012 R2 Hyper-V host server. Azure Recovery Services agent and Azure Site Recovery Provider will be installed on Hyper-V host.

2. **Azure Site Recovery Provider (Installed on Hyper-V host)**: The Provider coordinates and orchestrates replication with the Site Recovery service over the internet.

3. **Azure Recovery Service Agent (Installed on Hyper-V host)**: The agent handles data replication data over HTTPS 443. Communications from both the Provider and the agent are secure and encrypted. Replicated data in Azure storage is also encrypted.

Replication Architecture of Hyper-V VMs Managed by VMM to Secondary Data Center

You can Replicate VMs located on-premises Hyper-V hosts managed by VMM to secondary data center.

Figure below shows the Replication Architecture of Hyper-V VMs managed by VMM to Secondary Data Center.

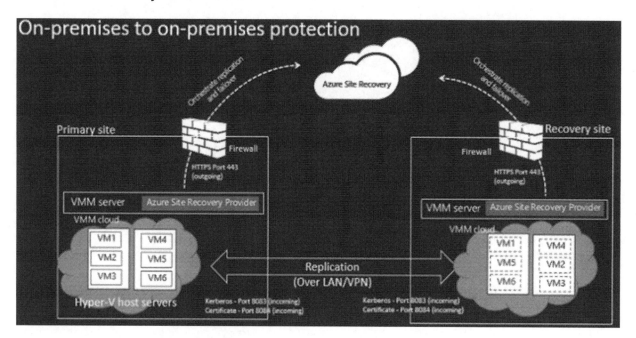

Requirements on Azure Side

1. Recovery Services Vault.

Requirements on-premises side

1. **VMM Server**: You need VMM server in both primary and secondary location.
2. **Hyper-V host**: You need one or more Hyper-V host server (Windows Server 2016 or 2012 R2) in both primary and secondary Datacenter. Azure Site Recovery Provider will be installed on Hyper-V host.
3. **Azure Site Recovery Provider (Installed on Hyper-V host)**: The Provider coordinates and orchestrates replication with the Site Recovery service over the internet.

Replication Architecture of Azure VMs in Azure Cloud to Azure Cloud

You can replicate Azure VMs from one Azure region to another Azure region using Azure Site Recovery. Biggest advantage of this option is that ASR is integrated in the VM dashboard.

Figure below shows Azure to Azure replication architecture.

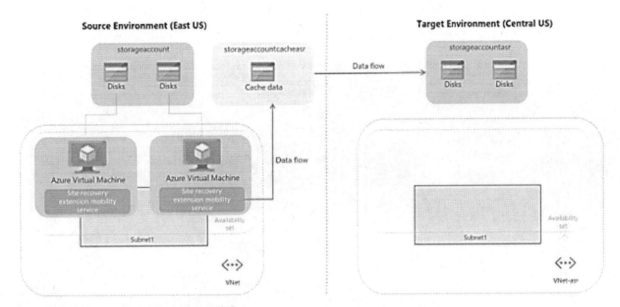

Requirements on Source Side

1. **Cache storage accounts:** Before source VM changes are replicated to a target storage account, they are tracked and sent to the cache storage account in source location.
2. **Site Recovery extension Mobility service**: Mobility Service captures all data writes on VM disks and transfers it to Cache Storage Account.

Requirements on Target Side

Target resource group: The resource group to which Source VMs are replicated.
Target virtual network: The virtual network in which replicated VMs are located after failover. A network mapping is created between source and target virtual networks, and vice versa.
Target storage accounts: Storage accounts in the target location to which the data is replicated.
Target availability sets: Availability sets in which the replicated VMs are located after failover.

Failover process

When you initiate a failover, the VMs are created in the target resource group, target virtual network, target subnet, and in the target availability set. During a failover, you can use any recovery point.

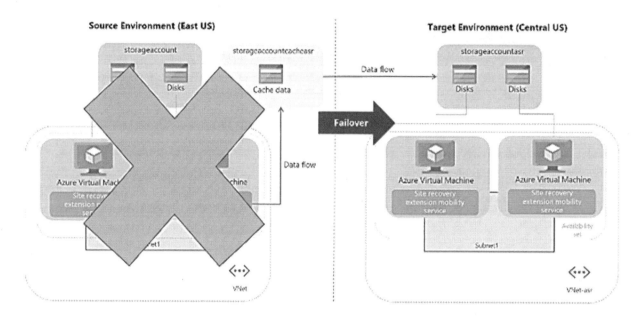

Exercise 24: Enabling Disaster Recovery for Azure VM using ASR

In this exrcise we will enable DR for wvm535 in US East Loaction to East US 2.

2. In Azure Portal go to VM wvm535 dashboard>click Disaster Recovery in left pane> Configure Disaster Recovery blade opens>click enable replication.

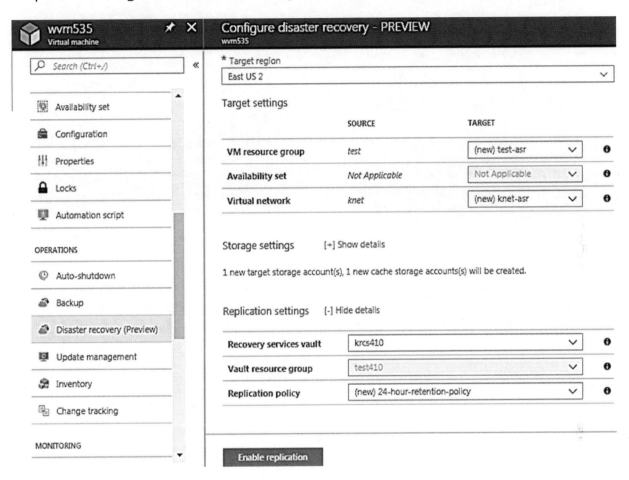

Note 1: Target Resource Group is automatically created. You have option to select existing Resource Group.

Note 2: Target Virtual Network and Storage account are automatically created in East US 2. You have option to select existing Virtual Network in East US 2.

Note 3: System selects existing Recovery Services vault or creates a new vault.

Design Nuggets

1. A Hyper-V site that mixes hosts running Windows Server 2016 and 2012 R2 Hyper-V hosts isn't currently supported.
2. ASR does not support replicating VMs to Azure cloud which are in FC SAN.
3. ASR is great for Azure VM to Azure VM replication with Premium storage. Premium Storage offers LRS as replication option which replicates Data within a Datacenter only. With ASR you can Replicate VMs in one region to another region.

Azure Site Recovery Pricing

Azure Site Recovery is billed based on number of instances protected.

	PRICE FOR FIRST 31 DAYS	PRICE AFTER 31 DAYS
Azure Site Recovery to customer owned sites	Free	$16/month/instance
Azure Site Recovery to Azure	Free	$25/month/instance

If you are replicating VMs to Azure, then you also will be charged for consumed storage and storage transactions.

If a failover occurred and protected VMs in Azure become active, then you also will be charged for consumed Compute resources.

Chapter 8 Containers

This Chapter covers following

- Containers
- Virtual Machines V/S Containers
- What is required to run Containers
- Benefits of Container Technology
- Drawbacks of Container Technology
- Container Deployment Options in Azure
- Deploying Containers on Azure Ubuntu Linux VM
- Azure Container Instances
- Azure Web App for Containers
- Azure Container Service (ACS)
- Azure Kubernetes Service (AKS)

This Chapter Covers following Lab Exercises to build below topology

- Deploying Containers on Azure Ubuntu Linux VM
- Deploying Container Instances
- Deploying Web App for Containers
- Deploying Azure Kubernetes Services

Chapter Topology

In this chapter we will add Ubuntu Linux VM to the topology and install Docker Engine on the VM and then deploy Hello World container on the VM.
In this chapter we will also add Azure Container instance to the topology.
Note: We are not showing above in the topology diagram.

In this chapter Azure Kubernetes Service (AKS) Cluster will be deployed in System Generated Virtual Network using basic networking option. Azure DNS Zone and Azure Basic Load Balance with public IP are also deployed automatically by the System.

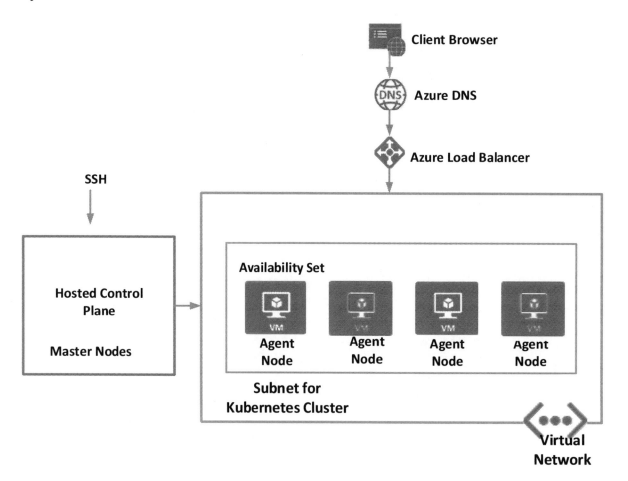

Containers

Containers provide alternate method of running applications.

Before going into containers let's discuss currently how applications are deployed. Application runs on top of Operating system. Operating System can be running on Bare Metal host or in a Virtual Machine known as Server Virtualization.

Containers provide operating system virtualization on Windows and Linux. Multiple Independent containers can run within a single Linux or Windows instance avoiding the overhead of starting and maintaining virtual machines.

Containers allow you to package application with their entire runtime environment—all of the files necessary to run. Container image contains all application's dependencies, it is portable and consistent as it moves from development, to testing, and finally to production.

Figure below shows the Architecture of Containers.

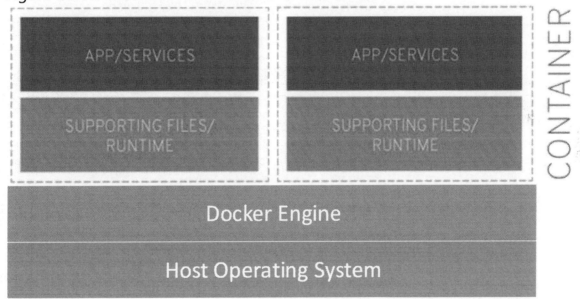

Docker uses the resource isolation features of the Linux kernel such as cgroups and kernel namespaces, and a union-capable file system such as OverlayFS. The Linux kernel's namespaces isolates an application's view of the operating environment, including process trees, network, user IDs and mounted file systems, while the kernel's cgroups provide resource limiting, including the CPU, memory, block I/O, and network.

Virtual Machines V/S Containers

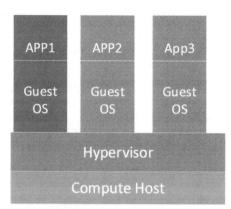

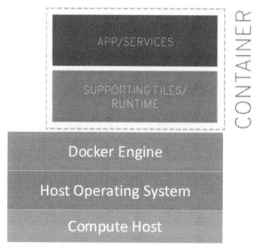

Virtual Machines: A hypervisor installed on compute host creates and runs Virtual Machines. Each virtual machine runs a unique guest operating system. VMs with different operating systems can run on the same physical server—a Windows VM can sit alongside a Linux VM.

Containers: Containers provide operating system virtualization. Multiple Independent containers can run within a single Linux or Windows instance. Containers allow you to package application with their entire runtime environment—all of the files necessary to run.

Feature	Container	VM
Defination	OS virtualization.	Server Virtualization.
Operating System	Containers shares Host OS	Each VM has its own OS
Size	Megabytes	Gigabytes
Time to start	Seconds	Minutes
Kernel	Shared with host	Each VM has its own Kernel
Density of Application workloads	Containers can run 2-3 times more applications.	
Benefits	Containers share a common OS which reduces mgmt. overhead. Containers are light weight and are more portable than VMs and can be deployed across public- private cloud and Traditional Data Centres.	Consolidates Multiple applications on a single system reducing server footprint.
Drawbacks	Higher Fault Domain and are less secure than VMs.	VMs are not portable across Public-Private Clouds.

What is required to run Containers

You require 2 components to run Docker Containers – Docker Engine and Docker image.

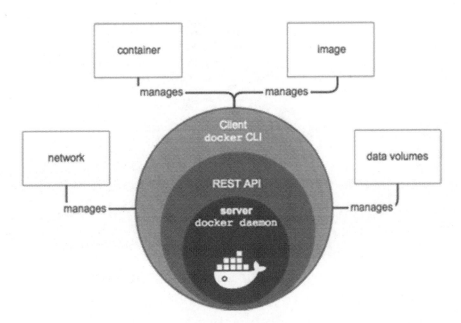

A **Docker Engine** need to be installed on a Linux or a Windows host or VM. The engine creates a server-side docker daemon process that hosts images, containers, networks and storage volumes.
The engine also provides a client-side command-line interface (CLI) that enables users to interact with the daemon through the Docker Engine API.
Docker Engine provides 3 Network Models including Bridge Network and Overlay Networks.

Docker Image is used to create containers. It can be downloaded from Azure Container registry or Docker Hub or from any accessible container registry.

Containers are built from images that are stored in one or more repositories. These repositories can belong to public or private container registries. An example of a public registry is Docker Hub. An example of a private registry is the Docker Trusted Registry, which can be installed on-premises or in a virtual private cloud. There are also cloud-based private container registry services including Azure Container Registry.

Benefits of Container Technology

1. Containers are more portable than VMs and can be deployed across Public Clouds, Private Cloud and Traditional Data Centers without any conversion.

2. Container Streamline software development lifecycle across development, test and production systems as you don't need to have similar hardware and software environment across development and production systems. The container application has the necessary configurations (and files) so that you can move it from development, to test, to production without any side effects.

3. Testing and bug tracking also become less complicated since there is no difference between running your application locally, on a test server, or in production.

4. Containers are light weight and can start in seconds. If there is spike in traffic you can Provision additional containers in few seconds.

5. Containers share a common OS which reduces management overhead as you need to Patch or bug fix a single Operating System.

6. Containers are a very cost effective solution. They help decrease operating cost (less servers, less staff) and development cost (develop for one consistent runtime environment).

7. Running containers is less resource intensive then running VMs so you can add more computing workload onto the same server.

8. Containers are a great option for DevOps and continuous deployment.

Drawbacks of Container Technology

1. Containers have higher fault domain as containers share host OS.

2. Containers are less secure than VMs. Containers share the kernel and other components of the host OS and have root access. If there is vulnerability in the kernel it can jeopardize the security of the containers.

3. Less flexibility in operating systems. You need to start a new server to be able to run containers with different operating systems.

4. Implementing container networking and Storage is still a challenge as compared to virtual machines.

Container Deployment Options in Azure

Container can be deployed in Azure in following ways:

1. Azure Linux or Windows VM with Docker engine installed.
2. Azure Container Instances
3. Azure Web App for Containers
4. Container Orchestration Platform. Orchestration platform provide a cluster of container ready virtual machines. Azure offers following Container Orchestration platforms:
   Azure Container Service (ACS) (DC/OS, Docker Swarm & Kubernetes)
   Azure Kubernetes Service (AKS)
   Azure Service Fabric Cluster

Exercise 25: Deploying Container on Azure Ubuntu Linux VM

1. In Azure Portal click create a resource> Compute>Ubuntu Server 16.04 LTS>Create VM blade opens> Enter Information and click create.

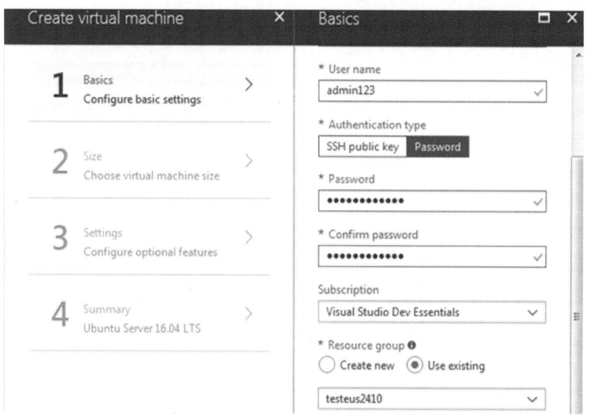

2. From VM dashboard note the IP address. From your desktop open putty client and connect to Ubuntu server using IP address and enter username and password from step 1.

3. To Install Docker engine enter command **sudo apt install docker.io**

```
admin123@kcu410: ~
admin123@kcu410:~$ sudo apt install docker.io
```

4. To check Docker version enter command **docker version**

```
admin123@kcu410:~$ docker version
Client:
 Version:      1.13.1
 API version:  1.26
 Go version:   go1.6.2
 Git commit:   092cba3
 Built:        Thu Nov  2 20:40:23 2017
 OS/Arch:      linux/amd64
```

5. Pull NGINX hello-world server image from Docker Hub. Enter command **sudo docker pull hello-world.**

6. Check the downloaded image: **sudo docker images**

7. Run the hello-world image to create container. Enter command **sudo docker run hello-world**

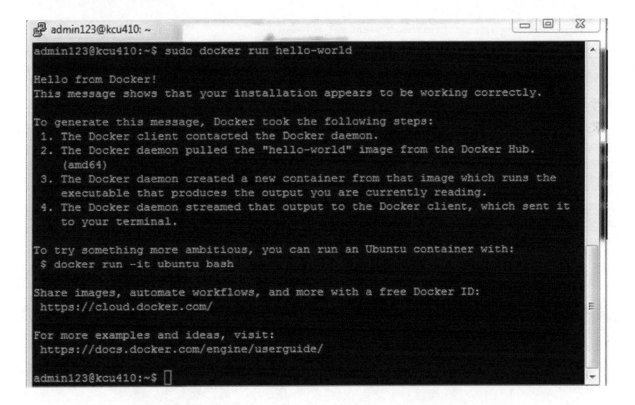

Azure Container Instances (ACI)

Azure Container Instances offers simple way to run a container in Azure, without having to provision any virtual machines and without having to adopt a higher-level service.

The benefit of using Azure Container Instances is that you don't need to provision or manager underlying Virtual Machines.

Features of Azure Container Instances (ACI)

Fast startup times: Azure Container Instances can start containers in Azure in seconds, without the need to provision and manage VMs.

Public IP connectivity and DNS name: Azure Container Instances enables exposing your containers directly to the internet with an IP address and a fully qualified domain name (FQDN).

Hypervisor-level security: With Azure Container Instances application is as isolated in a container as it would be in a VM.

Custom sizes: With Azure Container Instances you can specify CPU cores and memory for your container instance.

Persistent storage: By default, Azure Container Instances are stateless. To persist state with Azure Container Instances, you have the option to mount container instances on Azure Files shares.

Linux and Windows containers: Azure Container Instances can schedule both Windows and Linux containers with the same API. Simply specify the OS type when you create your container groups.

Container Groups: A container group is a collection of containers that get scheduled on the same host machine. The containers in a container group share a lifecycle, local network, and storage volumes. It's similar in concept to a pod in Kubernetes and DC/OS.

Exercise 26: Deploying Azure Container Instance (ACI)

1. In Azure Portal click create a resource> Containers>Container Instances> Container Instances blade opens>Enter Information and click Ok.

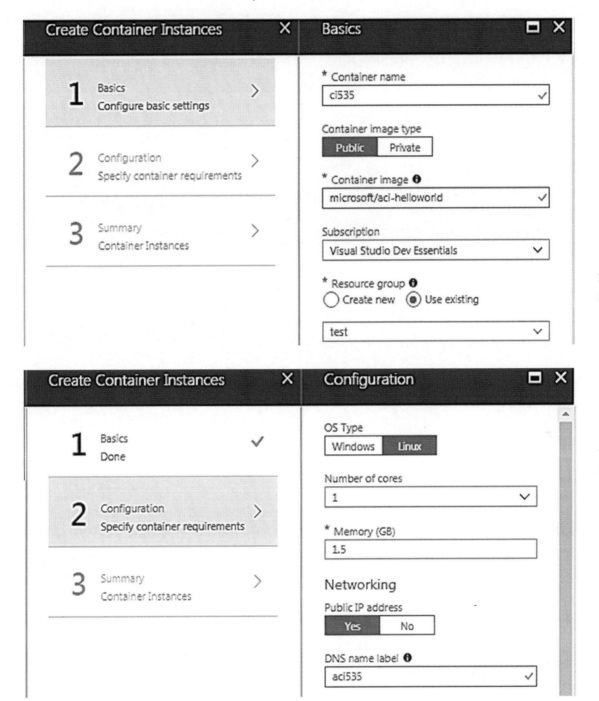

Note: here we have chosen Hello World image from Public Container Registry.

2. Figure below shows the Dashboard of aci535 container instance.

3. From Dashboard copy the FQDN of the aci535 container instance and open it in a browser. FQDN is aci535.eastus.azurecontainer.io.

Container Groups in ACI

A container group is a collection of containers that get scheduled on the same host machine. The containers in a container group share a lifecycle, local network, and storage volumes. It's similar in concept to a pod in Kubernetes.

The following diagram shows an example of a container group that includes multiple containers:

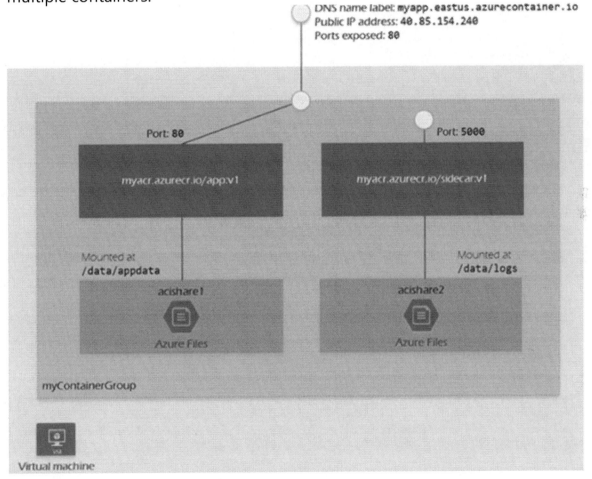

From the above Container Group Example we can infer following:
- Is scheduled on a single host machine.
- Is assigned a DNS name label.
- Exposes a single public IP address, with one exposed port.
- Consists of two containers. One container listens on port 80, while the other listens on port 5000.
- Includes two Azure file shares as volume mounts, and each container mounts one of the shares locally.

Azure Container Instance use case scenarios

Azure Container Instances is a great solution for any scenario that can operate in isolated containers, including simple applications, task automation, and build jobs. Use Container Orchestration Platform such as AKS or ACS for scenarios where you need full container orchestration, including service discovery across multiple containers, automatic scaling, and coordinated application upgrades.

Elastic bursting with AKS: When you run out of capacity in your AKS cluster, scale out additional pods in ACI without any additional servers to manage.

Event-driven applications with Azure Logic Apps: Combine ACI with the ACI Logic Apps connector, Azure queues and Azure Functions to build robust infrastructure which can elastically scale out containers on demand.

Cost Savings: Use Azure Container Instances for data processing where source data is ingested, processed and placed in a durable store such as Azure Blob storage. By processing the data with ACI rather than statically-provisioned virtual machines, you can achieve significant cost savings through per-second billing.

Azure Web App for Containers

Web App for containers is a fully managed compute platform (PaaS) that is optimized for running container applications.

Web Apps for container is a managed Linux VM with **pre-installed Docker Engine.** Figure below shows difference between IaaS and PaaS Platform.

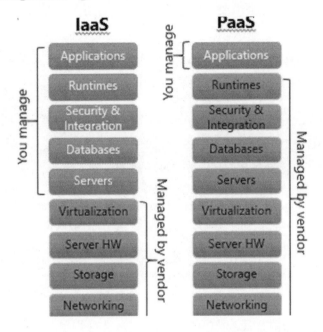

Features and Benefits of Web App for Containers

1. Web App for containers comes with Pre-Installed Docker Engine.
2. It is a managed platform (PaaS) which means Azure automatically takes care of OS and Docker engine patching and updates.
3. Deploy containers in seconds by pulling images from Docker Hub and Azure Container Register.
4. Supports Continuous Integration and Deployment (CI/CD) for custom container image from Docker Hub and Azure Container Registry. CI/CD will automatically deploy your container image hosted in Docker Hub or Azure Container Registry if you push changes to your image.
5. Built in Auto Scaling and Load Balancing for automatically scaling up and scaling out container applications.
6. Web apps have a deployment slot where you can deploy containers for testing. You can validate changes in a staging deployment slot before swapping it with the production slot without any downtime.

Exercise 27: Deploying Web App for Containers

In Azure Portal click create a resource> Containers >Web App for containers > create web App for containers blade opens>Enter as per your requirement and click create. Here I have chosen Public Docker Hub Registry for images.

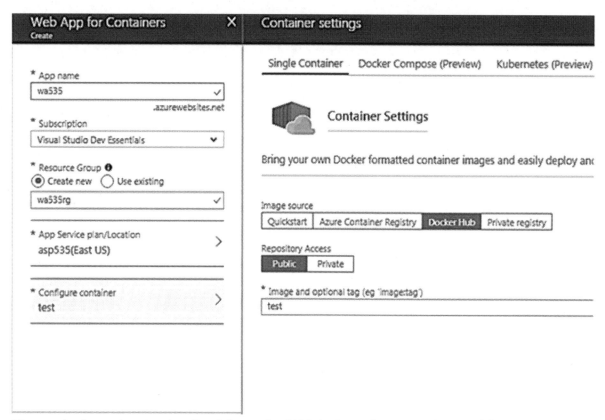

Figure below shows the Dashboard of Web App for container with Container settings selected in left pane. From here you can deploy your containers.

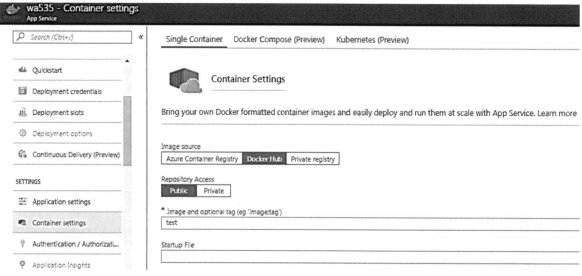

Container Orchestration Platform - Azure Container Service

Azure Container Service (ACS) is a container orchestration platform to create, configure and manage a cluster of virtual machines that are preconfigured (Docker Engine Pre-Installed) to run containerized applications.

ACS provides option to choose from Kubernetes, DC/OS or Docker Swarm for orchestration. ACS consists of 2 components: Master Node and Agent Node Cluster.

Master Node cluster is highly available and runs the management component which can be DC/OS, Swarm or Kubernetes Orchestration Platform. Agent cluster is a cluster of container ready virtual machines which runs container workloads.

You are only charged for the compute instances you choose, as well as the other underlying infrastructure resources consumed such as storage and networking. There is no charge for the Management Cluster.

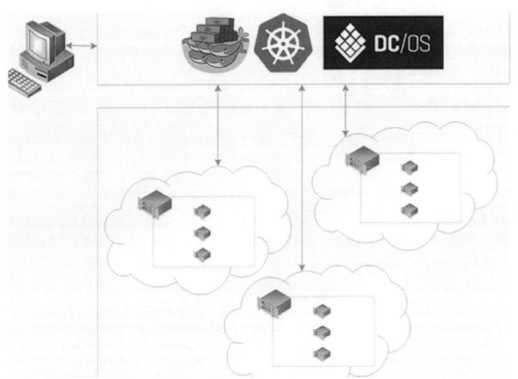

Important note 1: ACS is not a managed Service. Azure just provides template for the deployment.
Important Note 2: MS will be deprecating Azure Container Service (ACS) and will focus on Azure Kubernetes Service (AKS).

Architecting Microsoft Azure Solutions Study & Lab Guide Part 1: Exam 70-535

Architecture of DC/OS

DC/OS includes a set of Master nodes and Agent nodes. DC/OS includes the Marathon orchestration platform. Marathon provides a web UI from which you can deploy your container workloads on agent nodes.

Master nodes are Fault-tolerant replicated master and slaves using Apache ZooKeeper Key-Value Datastore. Master nodes run the Marathon Orchestration Platform.
Agent Nodes is a Cluster of Container ready Virtual Machines deployed in Virtual Machine Scale Set (VMSS). Agent Node runs the container workloads.

Figure below shows the Architecture of Mesosphere DC/OS deployed in Azure Virtual Network. Master nodes are deployed in Availability Set in a separate Subnet. Agent nodes are deployed in VM Scale Set (VMSS) in a separate subnet. Load balancer is automatically deployed with VM Scale Set (VMSS).

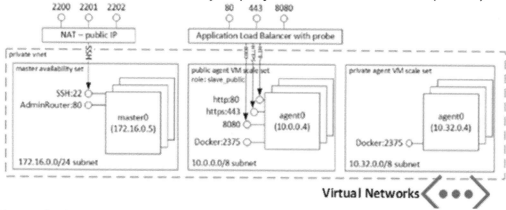

Figure below shows Marathon Web UI which used for Managing and deploying workload on Agent Nodes.

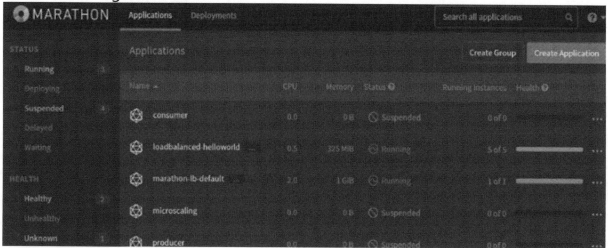

Architecture of Docker Swarm

Docker Swarm consists of Cluster of Master Nodes and Agent Nodes. Master Nodes are fault-tolerant replicated master and slaves using Apache Zookeeper Key-Value Datastore.

Master Node run Docker Swarm Orchestration Platform which schedules workloads on Agent Nodes. It also scales, manages and monitors Agent Nodes.

Agent Nodes is a Cluster of Container ready Virtual Machines deployed in Virtual Machine Scale Set (VMSS). Agent Node runs the container workloads.

Figure below shows the Architecture of Docker Swarm deployed in Azure Virtual Network. Master nodes are deployed in Availability Set in a separate Subnet. Agent nodes are deployed in VM Scale Set (VMSS) in a separate subnet. Load balancer is automatically deployed with VM Scale Set (VMSS).

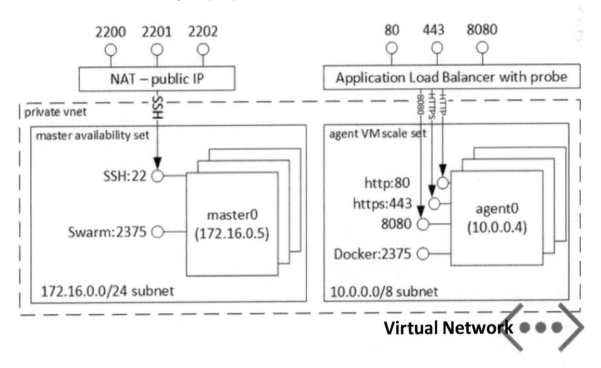

Note 1: Virtual Network (VNET) is automatically created when you deploy ACS with DC/OS or Swarm or Kubernetes.
Note 2: Docker Swarm or DC/OS or Kubernetes in ACS are not a managed service.

Architecture of Kubernetes

Kubernetes consists of Cluster of Master Nodes and Agent Nodes.

Master Node run Kubernetes Orchestration Platform which schedules workloads on Agent Nodes. It also scales, manages and monitors Agent Nodes. Master Node use Load balancer and etcd key-value datastore for high Availability.

Agent Nodes is a Cluster of Container ready Virtual Machines deployed in Availability Set. A Load Balancer is also deployed with Agent cluster. Agent Node runs the container workloads.

Figure below shows the Architecture of Kubernetes deployed in Azure VNET.

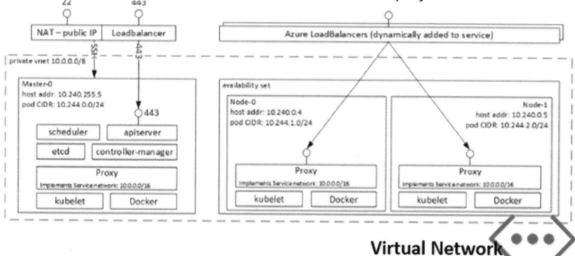

Components

Apiserver: It is the front-end for the Kubernetes control plane and exposes the Kubernetes API.

etcd: Key-value Datastore used for storing cluster data. All communication between components often happens via etcd.

Scheduler: The scheduler assigns a node to the pod.

Controller-manager: It runs multiple controllers. All controllers are compiled into a single binary and run in a single process. Controllers include Node, replication, endpoint, Route, service and volume controllers.

Kubelet: An agent that runs on each node in the cluster. It makes sure that containers are running in a pod.

Proxy: Maintains network rules on the host and performs connection forwarding.

Docker Engine: Responsible for running containers.

Azure Kubernetes Service (AKS)

Azure Kubernetes Service (AKS) is a managed service. Azure Kubernetes Service (AKS) is a container orchestration platform to deploy containers on a cluster of virtual machines (Agent Nodes) that are preconfigured (Docker Engine Pre-Installed) to run containerized applications.

AKS uses Google's open source Kubernetes Orchestration Platform.

Kubernetes consists of Cluster of Master Nodes and Agent Nodes deployed in Virtual Network.

By using AKS, you can take advantage of the enterprise-grade features of Azure, while still maintaining application portability through Kubernetes and the Docker image format.

Features of AKS

Kubernetes automates deployment, scaling, and management of containerized applications. It has a rich set of features including:

- Self-healing hosted/managed control plane (masters nodes).
- Automated Kubernetes version upgrades and patching.
- Easy cluster scaling of agent nodes with a single click.
- Cost savings - pay only for running agent pool nodes.
- Service discovery and load balancing.
- Secret and configuration management.
- Storage orchestration.

Pre-Installed Components on Agent Nodes

- **Kubelet**: An agent that runs on each node in the cluster. It makes sure that containers are running in a pod.
- **Proxy**: Maintains network rules on the host and performing connection forwarding.
- **Docker Engine**: Responsible for running containers.

AKS Architecture

Kubernetes consists of Cluster of Master Nodes and Agent Nodes deployed in Virtual Network.

Master nodes are Azure Managed and are highly available. Configuration and number of master nodes is known to Microsoft only.
Master Node runs the managed Kubernetes Orchestration Platform which manages, monitors and schedules workloads on Agent Nodes.

Agent Nodes is a Cluster of Container ready Virtual Machines deployed in Virtual Network in an Availability Set.
Virtual Network: A Pre-configured VNET or a custom VNET is deployed with AKS Cluster depending upon networking option chosen.
Load Balancer is also deployed with Kubernetes Cluster.
DNS Zone

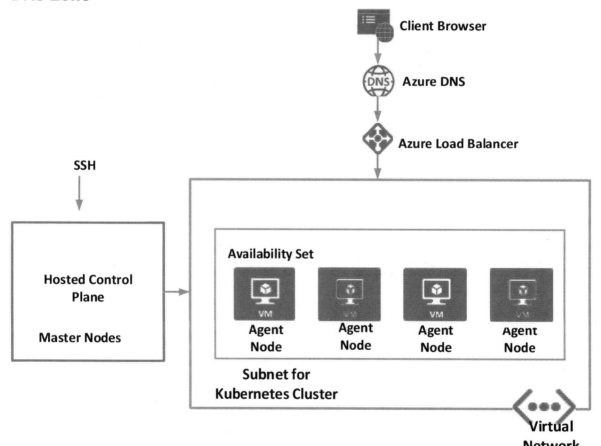

PODs in Kubernetes: A POD is a collection of containers that get scheduled on the same host or Virtual Machine.

Exercise 28: Create AKS Cluster with Basic Networking

1. In Azure Portal click create a resource> Containers>Kubernetes Service> Create Kubernetes Cluster blade opens>Enter Information and click next.

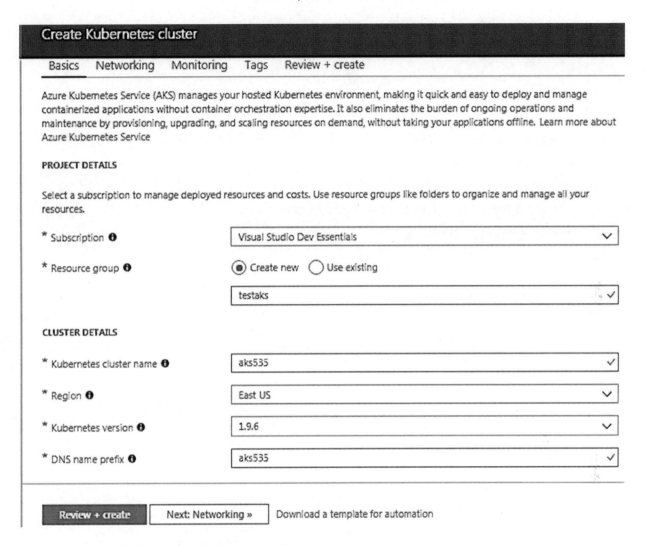

Note: I have changed the node count from 3 to 1. Node count is not shown in above figure. You need to scroll down.

2. For Networking select Basic and select yes for Application Routing. Rest select default values and click create to create AKS Cluster.

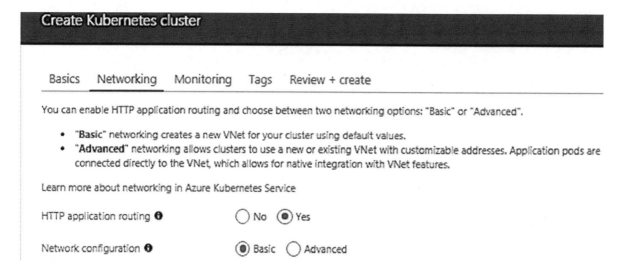

3. Figure below shows dashboard of AKS Cluster.

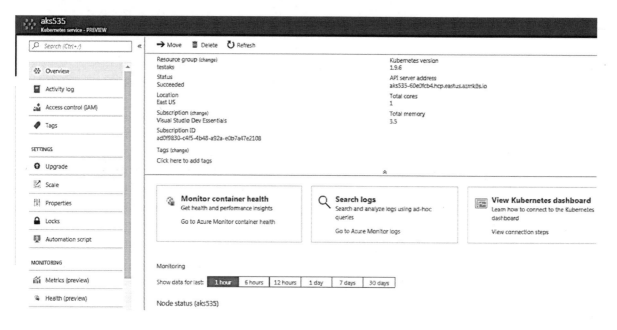

Exercise 29: Connect to Kubernetes Cluster using kubectl

Use kubectl, the Kubernetes command-line client to manage Kubernetes cluster.
The kubectl client is pre-installed in the Azure Cloud Shell.

Open Azure Cloud Shell using the button 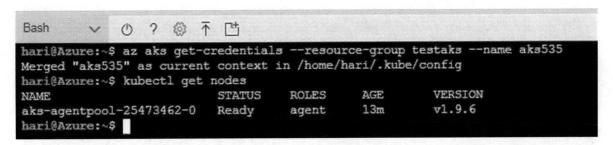 on the top right-hand corner of
the Azure portal> Use the az aks get-credentials command to configure kubectl
to connect to your Kubernetes cluster.
az aks get-credentials --resource-group testaks --name aks535.
I also ran the command **kubectl get nodes** to see information about the agent
pool.

```
hari@Azure:~$ az aks get-credentials --resource-group testaks --name aks535
Merged "aks535" as current context in /home/hari/.kube/config
hari@Azure:~$ kubectl get nodes
NAME                      STATUS    ROLES    AGE    VERSION
aks-agentpool-25473462-0  Ready     agent    13m    v1.9.6
hari@Azure:~$ █
```

You can deploy your application from the command line as shown above or
configure your setup to use Kubernetes GUI Dashboard for Deploying
applications. Figure below shows Kubernetes Dashboard.

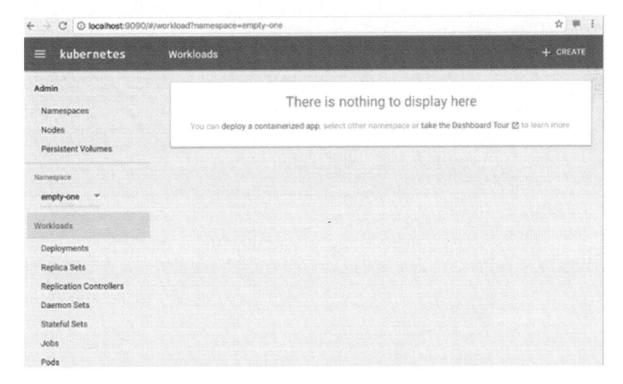

Following are also deployed along with Kubernetes Cluster

VNET

Load Balancer

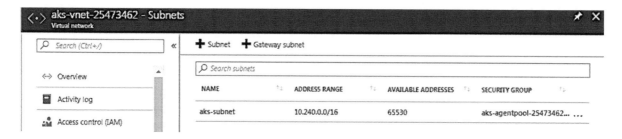

DNS Zone

Availability Set

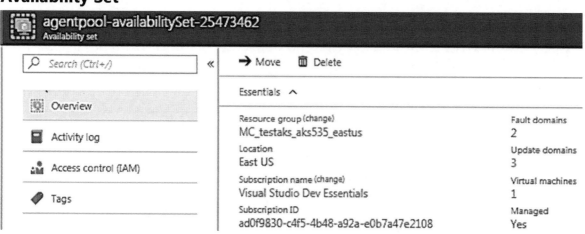

AKS Networking Options

Basic networking creates a new VNET for your cluster using Azure provided default values. You do not have control over network configuration such as subnets or the IP address ranges assigned to the cluster.

Advanced networking allows clusters to use a new or existing VNET with customizable addresses. Application pods are connected directly to the VNET which allows for native integration with VNET features.
Nodes in an AKS cluster configured for advanced networking use the Azure Container Networking Interface (CNI) Kubernetes plugin.

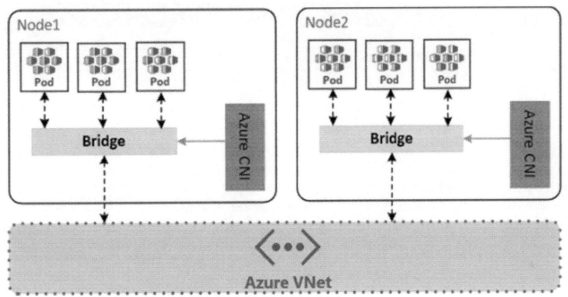

Features of Advanced Networking

1. Pod in the cluster is assigned an IP address in the VNET and can directly communicate with other pods in the cluster and other VMs in the VNET.
2. A pod can connect to other services in a peered VNET and to on-premises networks over ExpressRoute and site-to-site (S2S) VPN connections. Pods are also reachable from on-premises.
3. Expose a Kubernetes service externally or internally through the Azure Load Balancer. Also a feature of Basic networking.
4. Pods in a subnet that have service endpoints enabled can securely connect to Azure services, for example Azure Storage and SQL DB.
5. Use user-defined routes (UDR) to route traffic from pods to a Network Virtual Appliance.

Chapter 9 Load Balancers

This Chapter covers following Topic Lessons

- Load Balancer
- Azure Load Balancer
- Traffic Manager
- Application Gateway

This Chapter Covers following Case Studies

- Load Balancing e-commerce server
- Highly Available Multisite Website

This Chapter Covers following Lab Exercises

- Create Internet facing Azure Load Balancer
- Create Traffic Manager
- Create Application Gateway

Chapter Topology

In this chapter we will add Azure Load Balancer, Traffic Manager and Application Gateway to the topology. Virtual Machine **wvm35** will be added as an endpoint to the Azure Load Balancer, TM and Application Gateway. We will then access default website on wvm35 using public IPs of the Load Balancers.

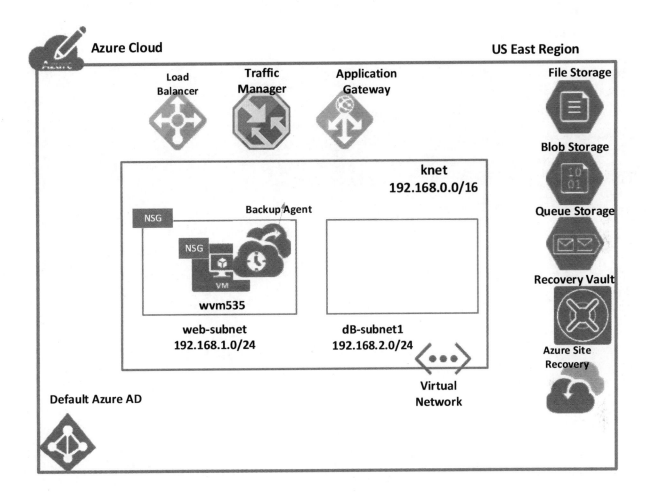

Load Balancers

Load balancing distributes traffic across multiple computing resources.

Microsoft Azure offers three types of load Balancers: Azure Load Balancer, Application Gateway & Traffic Manager.

Azure Load Balancer is a Layer 4 (TCP, UDP) load balancer that distributes incoming traffic among healthy instances defined in a load-balanced set.

Application Gateway works at the application layer (Layer 7). Application Gateway deals with web traffic only (HTTP/HTTPS/WebSocket). It acts as a reverse-proxy service, terminating the client connection and forwarding requests to back-end endpoints.

Traffic Manager works at the DNS level. It uses DNS responses to direct end-user traffic to globally distributed endpoints. Clients then connect to those endpoints directly.

Comparing Different Types of Azure Load Balancers

Feature	Load Balancer	Application Gateway	Traffic Manager
Working	Transport level (Layer 4)	Application level (Layer 7)	DNS level
Application protocols supported	Any	HTTP, HTTPS, and WebSockets	Any (An HTTP endpoint is required for endpoint monitoring)
Endpoints	Azure VMs and Cloud Services role instances	Any Azure internal IP address, public internet IP address, Azure VM, or Azure Cloud Service	Azure VMs, Cloud Services, Azure Web Apps, and external endpoints
VNET support	Can be used for both Internet facing and internal (VNET) applications	Can be used for both Internet facing and internal (VNET) applications	Only supports Internet-facing applications
Endpoint Monitoring	Supported via probes	Supported via probes	Supported via HTTP/HTTPS GET

Azure Load Balancer

Azure Load Balancer is a managed Layer 4 (TCP, UDP) load balancer that distributes incoming traffic among healthy instances of services defined in a load-balanced set.

Azure Load Balancer Types: Basic & Standard. Standard Load Balancer is currently in preview.

Azure Load Balancer can be configured as Internet facing Load Balancer or Internal Load Balancer.

Internet Facing Load Balancer distributes incoming Internet traffic to virtual machines. Figure below show shows internet traffic being distributed between Virtual Machines. LB has public IP and DNS name.

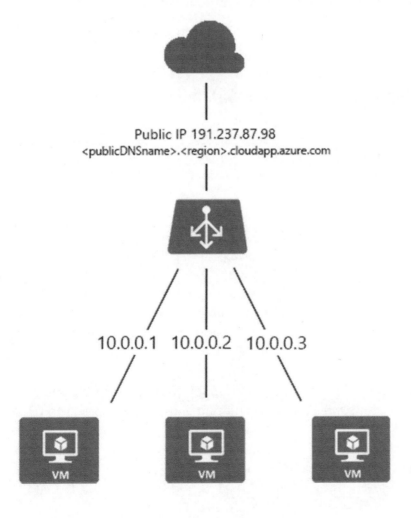

Internal load Balancer

In Multi-Tier applications, Internal Load Balancer distributes traffic coming from Internet tier to virtual Machines which are in back-end tiers and are not Internet-facing.

Internal Load Balancers can distribute traffic coming from application tier which is not internet facing to Database tier which is also not internet facing.

An internal load balancer is configured in a virtual network.

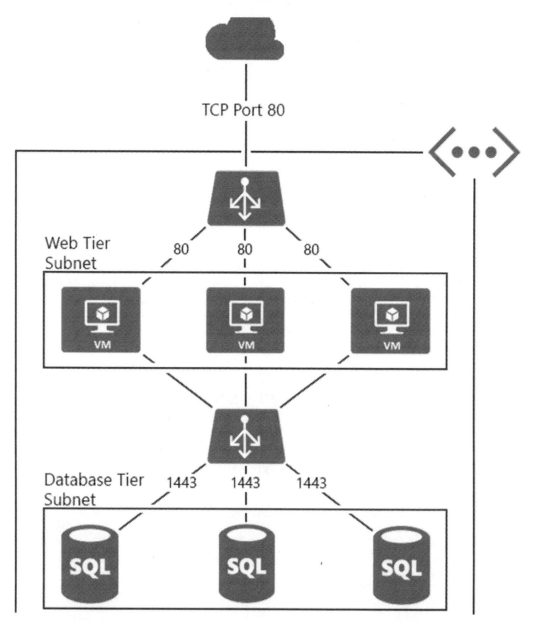

Azure Load Balancer Types

Azure Load Balancer comes in 2 types: Basic & Standard. Standard Load Balancer is currently in preview. Basic Load Balancer is free of charge whereas Standard Load Balancer is charged.

Standard includes all the functionality of Basic Load Balancer and provides additional functionalities.

Azure Load Balancer Standard and Public IP Standard together enable you to provide additional capabilities such as multi-zone architectures, Low latency, high throughput, and scalability for millions of flows for all TCP and UDP applications.

Additional Features in Standard Load Balancer (Preview)

Enterprise scale: With Standard Load Balance you can design Virtual Data Center which can support up to 1000 Virtual Machine instances.

Cross-zone load balancing: With Standard Load Balancer you can load balance Virtual Machines in backend pool spread across Availability Zones. Note that Availability Zones are also in Preview.

Resilient virtual IPs (VIP): A single front-end IP address assigned to Standard Load Balancer is automatically zone-redundant. Zone-redundancy in Azure does not require multiple IP addresses and DNS records.

Improved Monitoring: Standard Load Balancer is integrated with Azure Monitor (Preview) which provides new metrics for improved monitoring. Monitor your data from front-end to VM, endpoint health probes, for TCP connection attempts, and to outbound connections. New Metrics include VIP Availability, DIP Availability, SYN Packets, SNAT connections, Byte counters and Packets counters.

New SNAT: Load Balancer Standard provides outbound connections for VMs using new port-masquerading Source Network Address Translation (SNAT) model that provides greater resiliency and scale. When outbound connections are used with a zone-redundant front-end, the connections are also zone-redundant and SNAT port allocations survive zone failure.

Traffic Distribution Mode for Azure Load Balancer

Traffic Distribution mode determines how Load Balancer will distribute client traffic to load balanced set.

Traffic Distribution mode is selected in Load Balancing Rules.

Hash-based distribution mode

It uses 5 tuple hash of source IP, source port, destination IP, destination port, protocol type to map client traffic to available load balanced servers.

It provides stickiness only within a transport session. Packets in the same session will be directed to the same datacenter IP (DIP) instance behind the load balanced endpoint.

When the client starts a new session from the same source IP, the source port changes and causes the traffic to go to a different DIP endpoint.

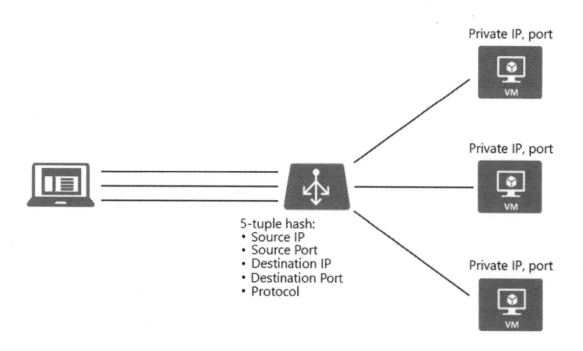

Source IP affinity distribution mode

Source IP Affinity also known as session affinity or client IP affinity use a 2-tuple (Source IP, Destination IP) or 3-tuple (Source IP, Destination IP, Protocol) to map traffic to the available servers.

By using Source IP affinity, connection initiated from the same client IP goes to the same datacenter IP (DIP) instance.

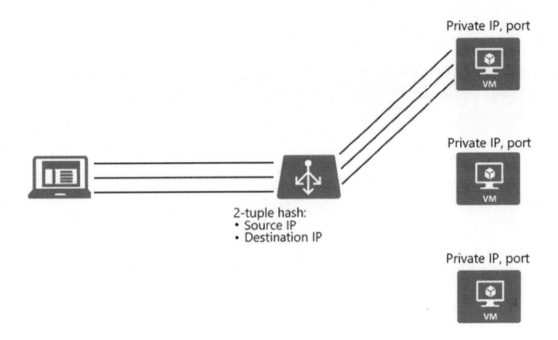

Source IP Affinity distribution method provides session affinity based on Client IP address.

Source IP Affinity distribution method can result in uneven traffic distribution if clients are coming behind a proxy.

Steps to creating Internet facing Azure Basic Load Balancer

1. Create Load Balancer with Public option.
2. In the Load Balancer Dashboard create backend address pool and add end points (VMs) to it.
3. Create a probe for monitoring end points (VMs).
4. Create Load Balancing rules (add backend address pool & probe created in step 2 and step 3 respectively and choose session persistence method)
5. Create inbound NAT rules (optional). If VMs in the backend pool have Public IPs assigned then inbound NAT rules are not required.

Steps to creating Internal Azure Basic Load Balancer

1. Create Load Balancer with internal option.
2. Create backend address pool and add end points to it.
3. Create a probe for monitoring end points
4. Create Load Balancing rules (add backend address pool, probe created in step 2 and step 3 respectively and choose session persistence method).

Exercise 30: Create Internet facing Azure Load Balancer and access default website on Azure VM wvm35 through Load Balancer Public IP

For this Exercise we will use single Virtual Machine wvn535 and connect to default website using Public IP of the Load Balancer.

Step 1 Create Load Balancer: In Azure Portal Click +Create a Resource>Networking>Load Balancer>Create Load Balancer Blade opens. Specify following and click create. For Public IP address create new IP address.

Dashboard of Load Balancer

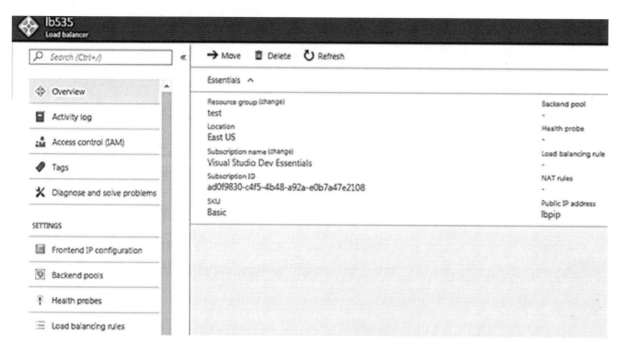

Step 2 Create Backend Address Pool and Add Endpoints: Click Backend pools in left pane of Load Balancer Dashboard> Add Backend pool Blade opens> Give a name and then add Virtual Machines from dropdown box> Select target Network IP configuration of Virtual Machine from Dropdown box and click Ok.

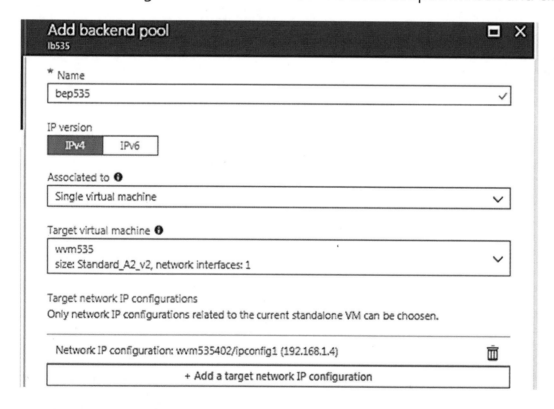

Step 3 Create a Load Balancer Health Probe: Health probes are used to check availability of virtual machines instances in the back-end address pool. When a probe fails to respond, Load Balancer stops sending new connections to the unhealthy instance. Probe behavior depends on:

1. The number of successful probes that allow an instance to be labeled as up.
2. The number of failed probes that cause an instance to be labeled as down.
3. The timeout and frequency value set in SuccessFailCount determine whether an instance is confirmed to be running or not running.

Go to Load Balancer Dashboard>Click Health Probes in left Pane>+Add>Add health Probe blade opens>specify following and click ok.

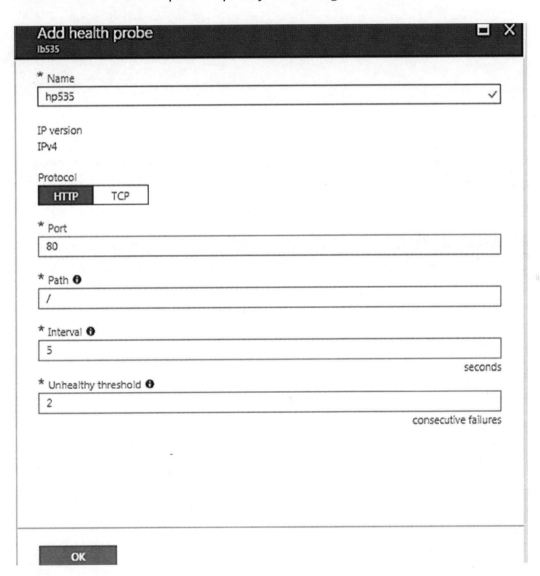

Step 4a Create a Load Balancer Rule: Load Balancer rule to define how traffic is distributed to the VMs. You define the front-end IP configuration for the incoming traffic and the back-end IP pool to receive the traffic, along with the required source and destination port, Health probe, session persistence and TCP idle timeout.

Go to Load Balancer Dashboard and Click Load Balancing Rules in left Pane> +Add> Add load Balancing Rule blade opens>specify following.

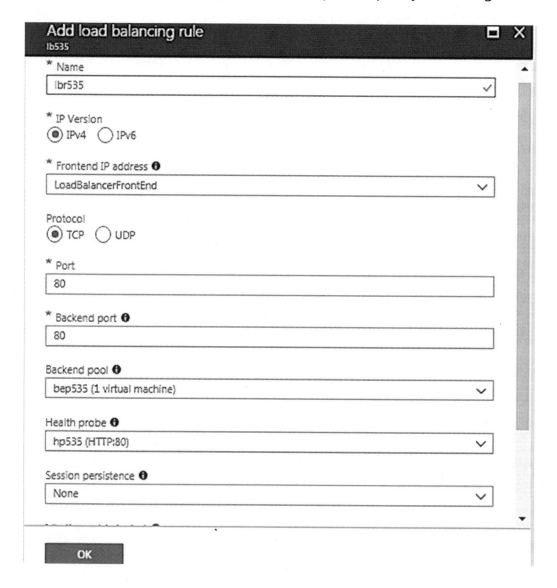

Note: There is idle Timeout setting is also there which is not shown in above figure. You just need to scroll down.

Step 4b Check the default website of wvm535 using Public IP of Load Balancer: Go to Load Balancer Dashboard and click Frontend IP configuration in left pane> In right pane note down the IP Address.

Open a browser and http://168.62.168.92. Default Website of wvm535 opens as shown below.

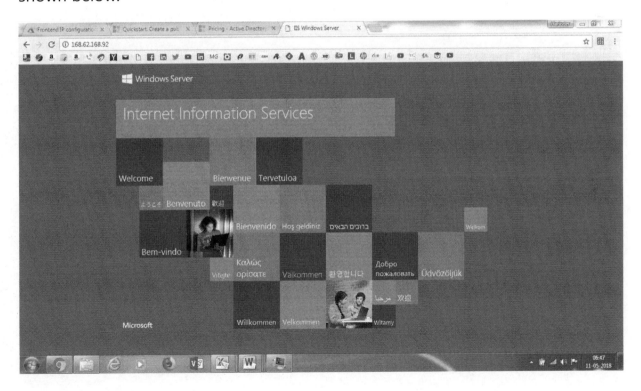

Idle timeout settings for Azure Basic Load Balancer

In its default configuration, Azure Load Balancer has an idle timeout setting of 4 minutes. If a period of inactivity is longer than the timeout value, there's no guarantee that the TCP or HTTP session is maintained between the client and your cloud service.

A common practice is to use a TCP keep-alive so that the connection active for a longer period. With keep-alive enabled, packets are sent during periods of inactivity on the connection. These keep-alive packets ensure that the idle timeout value is never reached and the connection is maintained for a long period.

TCP Idle timeout is configured in Load Balancing Rules.

Outbound connections of Load Balanced VMs

Load-balanced VM with no Instance Level Public IP address: Azure translates the private source IP address of the outbound flow to the public IP address of the public Load Balancer frontend.

Azure uses Source Network Address Translation (SNAT) to perform this function. Ephemeral ports of the Load Balancer's public IP address are used to distinguish individual flows originated by the VM. SNAT dynamically allocates ephemeral ports when outbound flows are created.

Load-balanced VM with Instance Level Public IP address (ILPIP): When an ILPIP is used, Source Network Address Translation (SNAT) is not used. The VM uses the ILPIP for all outbound flows.

Azure Basic Load Balancer Pricing

Azure Basic Load Balancer is free of charge.

Azure Standard Load Balancer Pricing (Preview)

The pricing for standard Load Balancer will be based on the number of rules configured (load balancer rules and NAT rules) and data processed for inbound originated flows.

Load Balancer rules: (free during preview period)
First five rules—$0.025/hour
Additional rules—$0.01/rule/hour

NAT Rules: (free during preview period)
NAT rules are free.

Data processed: (free during preview period)
$0.005 per GB

Traffic Manager

Traffic Manager works at the DNS level. It uses Public DNS responses to direct end-user traffic to globally distributed endpoints. Clients then connect to those endpoints directly. Traffic Manager does not see the traffic passing between the client and the service.

An endpoint is any Internet-facing service hosted inside or outside of Azure with public DNS name. Endpoints can be in different Data centers or in different regions.

Endpoints supported by Traffic Manager include Azure VMs, Web Apps, Cloud Services and Non Azure Endpoints. Traffic Manager also supports Azure Load Balancers and Application Gateway as Endpoints.

Traffic Manager Working.

Traffic Manager uses the Domain Name System (DNS) to direct client requests to the most appropriate endpoint based on a traffic-routing method and the health of the endpoints. Figure below shows the working of Traffic Manager.

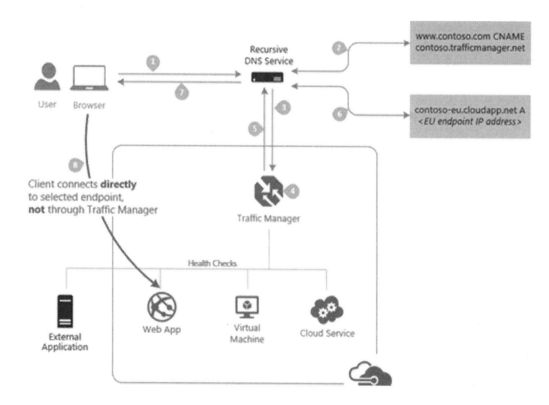

Traffic Manager Working (Continued from Previous Page)

Azure Traffic Manager distributes traffic across application endpoints. An endpoint is any Internet-facing service hosted inside or outside of Azure.

Traffic Manager does two things:

1. Distribution of traffic according to one of several traffic-routing methods.
2. Continuous monitoring of endpoint health and automatic failover when endpoints fail

When a client attempts to connect to a service, Traffic Manager first resolve's the DNS name of the service to an IP address. The client then connects to that IP address directly to access the service.

The most important point to understand is that Traffic Manager works at the DNS level. Traffic Manager uses DNS to direct clients to specific service endpoints based on the rules of the traffic-routing method. Clients connect to the selected endpoint **directly**. Traffic Manager does not see the traffic passing between the client and the service.

Exercise 31: Create & Implementing Traffic Manager in 2 Steps

Note: For this Exercise we are using wvm535 as endpoint. DNS name of wvm35 is wvm535.eastus.cloudapp.azure.com.

Step 1 Creating TM Profile: In Azure Porta Click + Create a resource> Networking> Traffic Manager Profile > create Traffic Manager profile blade opens>specify following and click create. Choose Routing Method as per your requirement.

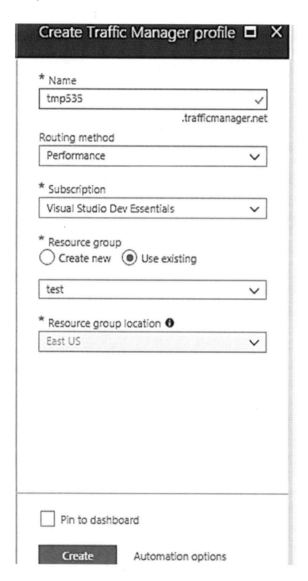

Traffic Manager Dashboard

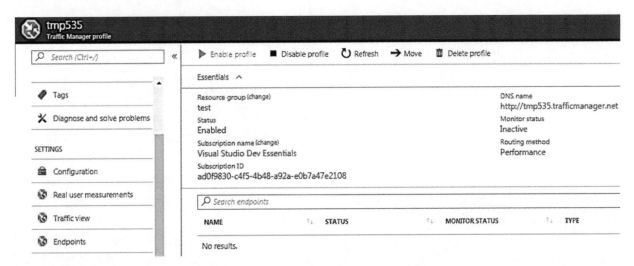

Adding Endpoints (wvm35) in Traffic Manager Profile: In Traffic Manager dashboard click endpoints in left pane>In Right pane click +Add>Add endpoint blade opens>specify following.

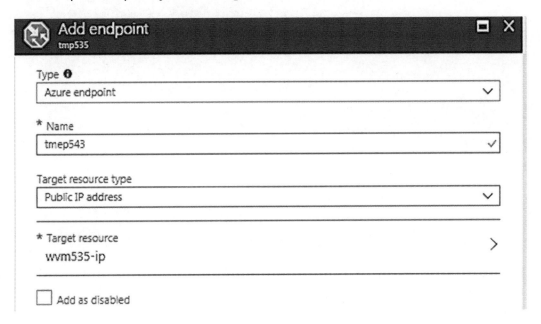

The above step is to be repeated for each endpoint to be added.

Step 2b Check the default website of wvm535 using DNS name of Traffic Manager: Go to TM Profile Dashboard and note down DNS name of Traffic Manager Profile which in this case is http://tmp535.trafficmanager.net

Open a browser and http://tmp535.trafficmanager.net. Default Website of wvm535 opens as shown below.

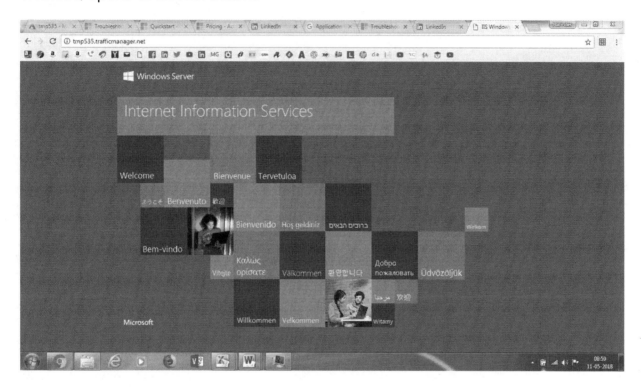

Traffic Manager routing methods

Azure Traffic Manager supports **four** traffic-routing methods to determine how to route network traffic to the various service endpoints.

Priority
Weighted
Performance
Geographic

Priority: With Priority you use a primary service endpoint for all traffic, and provide backups in case the primary endpoints are unavailable.

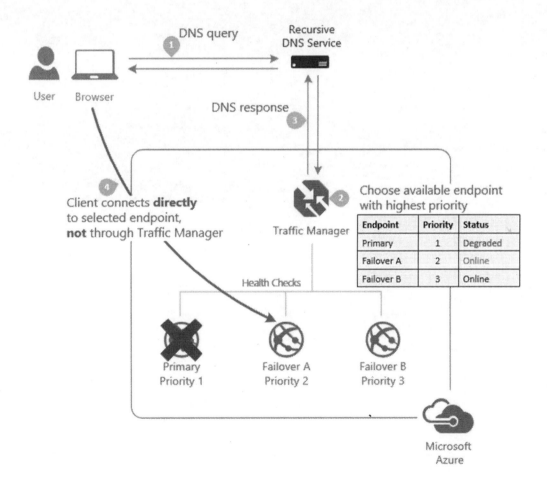

Weighted: Weighted traffic routing method distributes traffic across a set of endpoints, either evenly or according to weights defined.

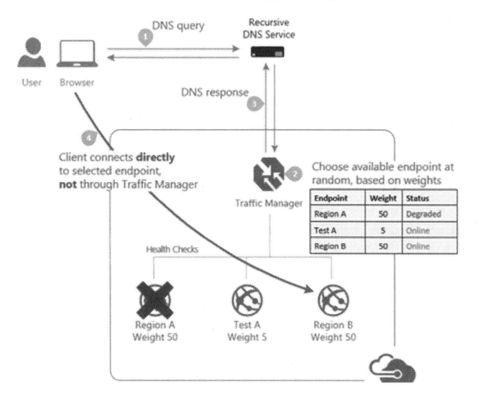

Performance: With Performance routing method users connect to the endpoint which offers lowest network latency.

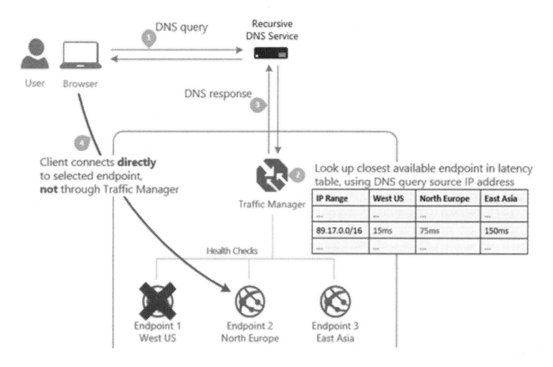

Geographic: With Geographic routing method users are directed to specific endpoints (Azure, External or Nested) based on which geographic location their DNS query originates from.

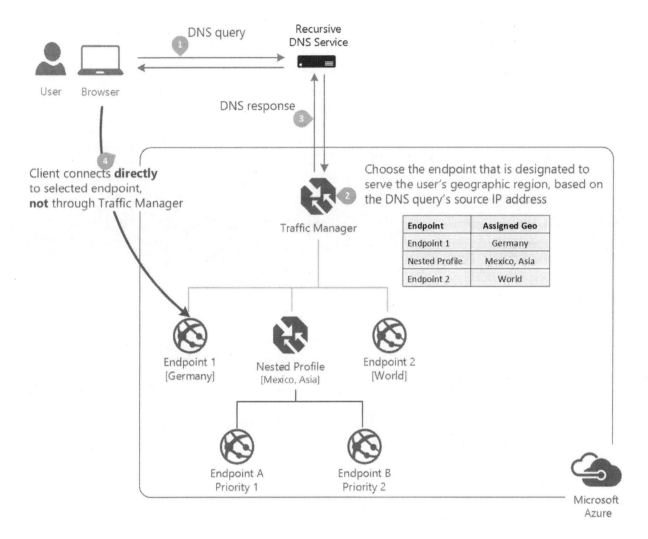

Traffic Manager Pricing

Traffic Manager Pricing consists of 2 components.

1. Number of DNS queries received
2. Health check charge for each monitored endpoint.

Pricing Details	Pricing
First 1 billion DNS queries / month	$0.54 per million queries
Over 1 billion DNS queries / month	$0.38 per million queries
Health Checks (Azure)	$0.36 per Azure endpoint / month
Health Checks (External)	$0.54 per External endpoint / month

Application Gateway

Azure Application Gateway is an Azure managed layer-7 load balancer.

Application Gateway deals with **web traffic only (HTTP/HTTPS/WebSocket).**

Application Gateway is highly available and scalable service, which is fully managed by Azure.

Application Gateway can be configured as Internet facing or as internal load balancer and is deployed in dedicated subnet in your virtual network. The subnet used for application gateway cannot contain any other types of resources. Only resources that are allowed in the subnet are other application gateways.

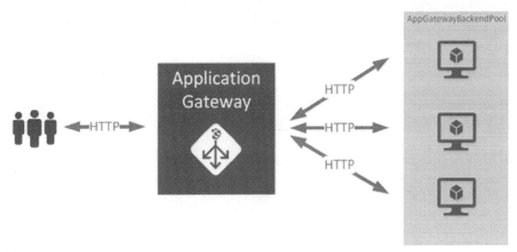

Use cases

1. **Application Gateway is used in cases where application layer session persistence is required.**
2. To improve performance of web applications by freeing web server farms from SSL termination overhead.
3. Applications that support websocket traffic.
4. Protecting web applications from common web-based attacks like SQL injection, cross-site scripting attacks, and session hijacks.

Important Application Gateway Features

1. **HTTP/HTTPS load balancing** - Load balancing is done at Layer 7 and is used for HTTP or HTTPS traffic only.

2. **Cookie-based session affinity** - This feature keeps a user session on the same back-end. By using gateway managed cookies, the Application Gateway is able to direct subsequent traffic from a user session to the same back-end for processing.

3. **Secure Sockets Layer (SSL) offload** - By terminating the SSL connection at the Application Gateway and forwarding the request to server unencrypted, the web server is unburdened by the decryption. Application Gateway re-encrypts the response before sending it back to the client. This feature is useful in scenarios where the back-end is located in the same secured virtual network as the Application Gateway in Azure.

4. **URL-based content routing** - This feature provides the capability to use different back-end servers for different traffic. Traffic for a folder on the web server or for a CDN could be routed to a different back-end, reducing unneeded load on backends that don't serve specific content.

5. **Multi-site routing** - Application gateway consolidate up to 20 websites on a single application gateway.

6. **Websocket support** - Application Gateway provides native support for Websocket.

7. **Web Application Firewall** - The web application firewall (WAF) in Azure Application Gateway protects web applications from common web-based attacks like SQL injection, cross-site scripting attacks, and session hijacks.

8. **Integration with Azure Services**: Application Gateway can be integrated with Azure Traffic Manager to support multi-region redirection & failover. Application Gateway is also integrated with Azure Load Balancer to support scale-out and high-availability for Internet-facing and internal-only web front ends.

Application Layer Persistence using Cookie-based session affinity (Very Important concept)

Cookie-based session affinity keeps a user session on the same back-end server by using Application Gateway managed cookies.

With cookie based session affinity even if client IP address is changed it is still directed to the same backend server. This feature is important in cases such as e-commerce web sites where user must be directed to same backend server even if user IP address is changed.

Cookies are small pieces of information that are sent in response from the web server to the client. **Cookies are used for storing client state.**
Cookies are stored on client's computer. They have a lifespan and are destroyed by the client browser at the end of that lifespan.

Design Nuggets

1. Application Gateway is configured inside a virtual network in its own dedicated subnet. The subnet created or used for application gateway cannot contain any other types of resources. Only resources that are allowed in the subnet are other application gateways.
2. **Application Gateway does not support static public IP**. The VIP can change if the gateway is stopped and started by the customer. The DNS associated with Application Gateway does not change over the lifecycle of the gateway. Use a CNAME alias and point it to the DNS address of the Application Gateway.
3. Application Gateway can talk to instances outside of the virtual network that it is in as long as there is IP connectivity. If you plan to use internal IPs as backend pool members, then it requires VNET Peering or VPN Gateway.
4. A default backend pool is automatically created with the application gateway.
5. An application gateway automatically configures a default health probe when you create Backend pool and add instances to the pool.

Difference between Azure Load Balancer and Application Gateway

Feature	Azure Load Balancer	Application Gateway
Protocols	TCP/UDP	HTTP/HTTPS
Load balancing mode 1	5-tuple(source IP, source port, destination IP, destination port, protocol type)	Round Robin Routing based on URL
Load balancing mode 2 (Source IP/Sticky sessions)	2-tuple (source IP and destination IP), 3-tuple (source IP, destination IP, and port). IP based session persistence.	Cookie-based Session Persistence. Routing based on URL
Health probes	Default: probe interval - 15 secs. Taken out of rotation: 2 Continuous failures. Supports user-defined probes	Idle probe interval 30 secs. Taken out after 3 consecutive live traffic failures or a single probe failure in idle mode. Supports user-defined probes
SSL offloading	Not supported	Supported

Application Gateway Editions

Application Gateway comes in two SKUs. A Standard SKU and a Web Application Firewall (WAF) SKU.

Web application firewall (WAF) is a feature of Application Gateway that provides centralized protection of your web applications from common exploits and vulnerabilities.

Application Gateway Standard SKU is currently offered in three sizes : Small, Medium & Large.

Application Gateway WAF SKU is currently offered in two sizes : Medium & Large.

Exercise 32: Create Application Gateway and access default website of Azure VM wvm35 through Application Gateway Public IP.

Note: Application Gateway Load Balancer is created in a dedicated subnet in the Virtual Network. For this Exercise we will use Virtual Network knet and db-subnet which we created in Exercise 1 & Exercise 2 respectively.

Step 1: In Azure portal click +Create a resource> Networking> Application Gateway> Create Application Gateway Blade open>Enter the information as per your requirement and click ok.

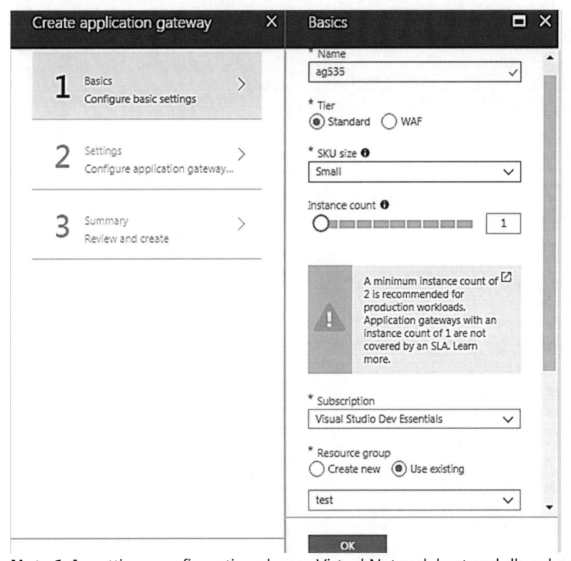

Note 1: In settings configuration choose Virtual Network knet and db-subnet which were created in Exercise 1 & 2 respectively.
Note 2: Choose Listener configuration as http and select Public IP create new.

Dashboard of Application Gateway

Step 2 Create backend address pool and add endpoints: Go to Application Gateway Dashboard> click backend pool in left pane>+Add> Add backend pool blade opens> Select wvn535 from drop down box and click ok.

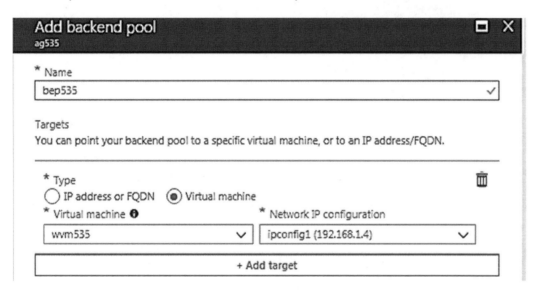

Backend pools can be composed of NICs, virtual machine scale sets, public IPs, internal IPs, and fully qualified domain names (FQDN). Members of backend pools can be across clusters, data centers, or outside of Azure as long as they have IP connectivity.

Note: Application gateway automatically configures a default health probe.

Endpoint health monitoring with Probes

Azure Application Gateway automatically monitors the health of the back-end instances through basic or custom health probes. Health probes, ensures that only healthy hosts respond to traffic.

Application Gateway automatically removes any resource considered unhealthy from the pool. Application Gateway continues to monitor the unhealthy instances and adds them back to the healthy back-end pool once they become available and respond to health probes.

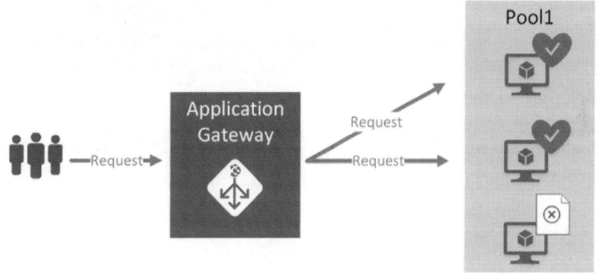

Default Health Probe: An application gateway automatically configures a default health probe when you create Backend pool and add instances to the pool. Default Health probe monitors endpoint by making an HTTP/HTTPS request to the IP addresses configured for the back-end pool.

Probe Property	Value	Description
Interval	30	Probe interval in seconds
Time-out	30	Probe time-out in seconds
Unhealthy threshold	3	Probe retry count. The back-end server is marked down after the consecutive probe failure count reaches the unhealthy threshold.

Design Nugget: You cannot change Default Health probe values.

URL-based content routing

This feature provides the capability to use different back-end servers for different traffic. URL Traffic for a folder on the web server or URL traffic for Images could be routed to a different back-end, reducing unneeded load on backend that don't serve specific content.

Path Based Routing allows you to route traffic to back-end server pools based on URL Paths of the request.

In the Figure below, Application Gateway is serving traffic for contoso.com from three back-end server pools: VideoServerPool, ImageServerPool, and AppGatewayBackendPool (Not shown below). AppGatewayBackendPool is automatically created with application gateway.

Requests for http://contoso.com/video/* are routed to VideoServerPool, and http://contoso.com/images/* are routed to ImageServerPool. AppGatewayBackendPool is selected if none of the path patterns match.

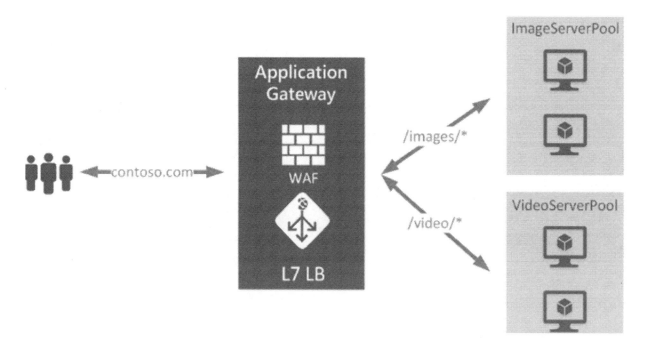

Configuring Path based Routing for above Example

1. Create Application Gateway.
2. Create backend Pools (ImageServerPool & VideoServerPool) and add instances. Note a default backend pool is created with application gateway.
3. Create Basic listener with name mybackendlistener.
4. **Create Path Based Routing Rules**. In Application Gateway Dashboard click Rules in left pane>Path based>Add path-based rule blade opens>Enter following and click ok.

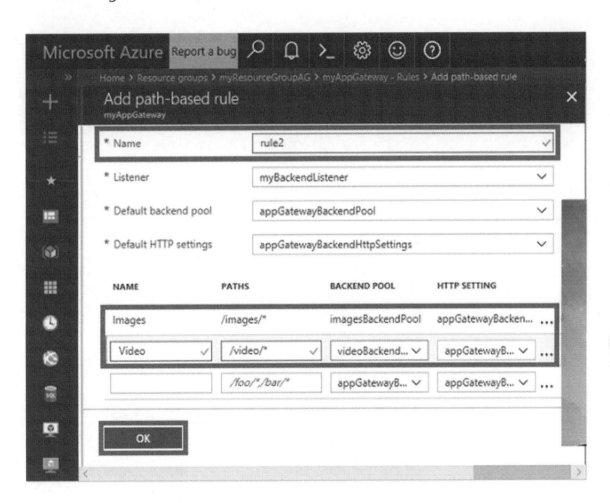

Multiple site hosting

Multiple site hosting feature allows you to configure up to 20 websites to one application gateway. Each website can be directed to its own backend pool.

In the following example, application gateway is serving traffic for contoso.com and fabrikam.com from two back-end server pools called ContosoServerPool and FabrikamServerPool.

Requests for http://contoso.com are routed to ContosoServerPool, and http://fabrikam.com are routed to FabrikamServerPool.

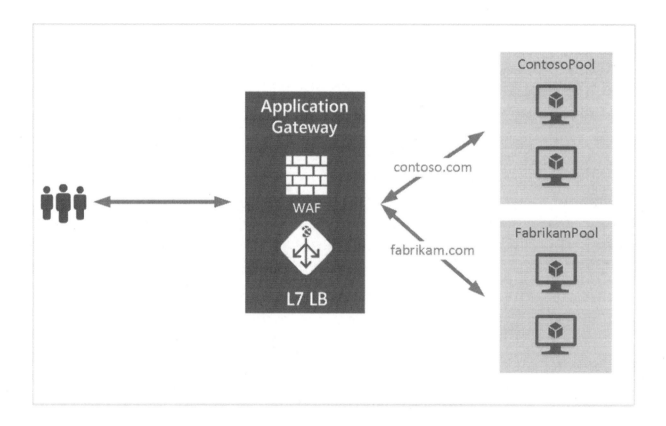

Application Gateway relies on HTTP 1.1 host headers to host more than one website on the same public IP address and port. This is the preferred mechanism for enabling multiple site hosting on the same infrastructure. The sites hosted on application gateway can also support SSL offload with Server Name Indication (SNI) TLS extension.

Configuring Multiple Site hosting for above Example

1. Create Application Gateway.
2. Create backend Pools (ContosoPool & FabrikamPool) and add instances.
3. Create first Multi-site listener with name *contosoListener.*
4. Create second Multi-site listener with name *fabrikamListener.*
5. **Create first Basic Rules**. In Application Gateway Dashboard click Rules in left pane>Basic>Add basic rule blade opens>Enter following and click ok.

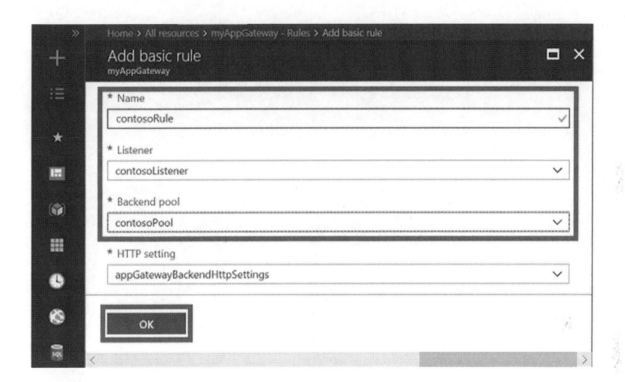

6. **Create second Basic Rules**. In Application Gateway Dashboard click Rules in left pane>Basic>Add basic rule blade opens>Enter Following:
   Name: fabrikamrule
   Select Listener: fabrikamlistener
   Select Backend pool: fabrikampool

Web Application Firewall (WAF)

Web application firewall (WAF) is a feature of Application Gateway that provides centralized protection to web applications from common exploits and vulnerabilities. With Application Gateway WAF SKU, WAF (web application firewall) is directly integrated into the ADC offering.

Web application firewall is based on rules from the Open Web Application Security Project (OWASP) core rule sets.

The OWASP Core Rule Set (CRS) is a set of generic attack detection rules. The CRS protects web applications from a wide range of attacks, including SQL Injection, Cross Site Scripting, Locale File Inclusion, etc.

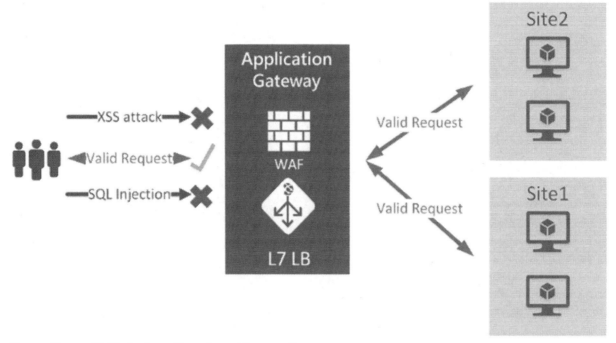

Benefits of Web Application Firewall

A WAF solution reacts to a security threat faster by patching a known vulnerability at a central location versus securing each of individual web applications.

Protect multiple web applications at the same time behind an application gateway. Application gateway supports hosting up to 20 websites behind a single gateway that could all be protected against web attacks with WAF.

Architecting Microsoft Azure Solutions Study & Lab Guide Part 1: Exam 70-535

Application Gateway Pricing

Application Gateway Pricing consists of 2 components.

1. Amount of time that the gateway is provisioned and available
2. Amount of data processed by the Application Gateways.

Application Gateway Type	APPLICATION GATEWAY	WAF APPLICATION GATEWAY
Small	$0.03 per gateway-hour	NA
Medium	$0.07 per gateway-hour	$0.126 per gateway-hour
Large	$0.40 per gateway-hour	$0.448 per gateway-hour

DATA PROCESSING	Small	Medium	Large
First 10 TB/month	$0.008 per GB	Free	Free
Next 30 TB	$0.008 per GB	$0.007 per GB	Free
Over 40 TB/month	$0.008 per GB	$0.007 per GB	$0.0035 per GB

Data Transfer Pricing

Inbound data transfers (data going into Azure data centers) is free.

Outbound Data Transfer (data going out of Azure data centers from application gateways) is charged.

Case Study 6: Load Balancing e-commerce server

You are connected to e-commerce website through a wired broadband connection. This internet connection goes down during your purchase cycle. You now re-connect to e-commerce website by connecting your computer to internet using mobile phone as hot spot.

Which Load Balancer you will use to load balance e-com application – layer 4 Azure Load Balancer or Layer 7 Azure Application Gateway so that client session reconnect to same e-com application server.

Note: Both layer 4 and layer 7 load balancer support session Persistence.

Solution

We will use Azure Application Gateway to load balance e-com application.

If e-commerce website is load balanced with Application gateway you will be re-directed to the same backend server because of cookies stored in client computers irrespective of which internet connection you use.

If e-commerce website is load balanced with azure layer 4 load balancer configured with client IP affinity, you will not know which e-com server you will be re-directed as in this case client IP has changed. If client IP was not changed then client will be re-directed to same e-com application.

Case Study 7: Highly Available Multisite Website

An IT giant located in Pala Alto, California does business with customers and partners located across the world.

There existing website on a single server is located in Palo Alto and is heavily accessed. End users (Customers and Partners) are complaining about slow performance of the website.

They want to give best experience to customers and partners visiting there website. They have short listed 3 locations for their website. Palo Alto serving North America and South America region, Germany serving EMEA region and Singapore serving APAC region including Australia and New Zealand.

There requirement is that each region should have highly available website and should be accessed by the users of that region only. Load Balancing solution in each region must support cookie based session affinity, SSL termination & URL based content routing.

Suggest a solution which satisfies above requirement.

Solution

We will use combination of Traffic Manager and Application Gateway to satisfy the customer requirement.

Each region will have multiple servers hosting the website to provide highly available website.

Application gateway in each region will provide round robin distribution of incoming traffic to the servers hosting the website. Application Gateway will also provide SSL termination, cookie based session affinity and URL based content routing.

Traffic Manager will provide DNS based Load Balancing and will route the user request to the Application Gateway in the respective region using Geographic routing method.

Figure below shows the Architecture of the solution.

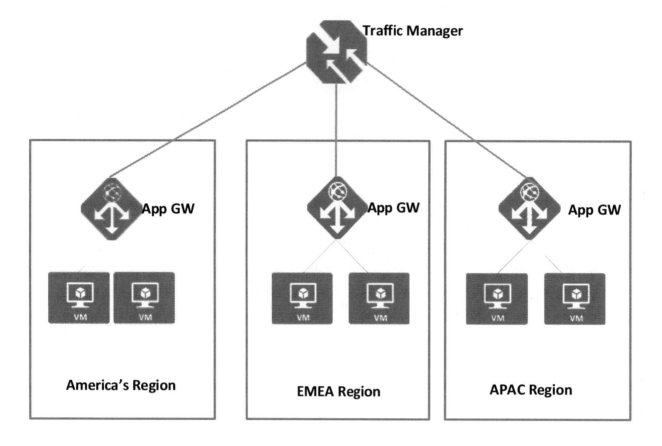

Chapter 10 Virtual Network External Connectivity

This Chapter covers following Topic Lessons

- Virtual Network (VNET) External Connectivity
- VNET External Connectivity over internet
- VPN Type
- VPN Gateway Editions
- Site to Site VPN (S2S)
- Point to Site VPN (P2S)
- VPN Gateway Redundancy
- Border Gateway Protocol (BGP) with Azure VPN Gateways
- VPN Gateway Pricing
- VNET External Connectivity over Private WAN connection using ExpressRoute Gateway
- ExpressRoute Routing Domains
- ExpressRoute Gateway SKU
- ExpressRoute Bandwidth options
- ExpressRoute Connection Tiers
- Connecting Virtual Networks (VNET) to ExpressRoute circuit
- Site-to-Site and ExpressRoute co-existing connections
- ExpressRoute Gateway Pricing
- Comparing ExpressRoute and VPN
- Forced Tunneling

This Chapter Covers following Lab Exercises

- Demonstration Exercise: Connecting VNET to on-premises Data Center using Site to Site (S2S) VPN

Chapter Topology

This is demonstration exercise. We will show configuration on Azure side only. Configuration of on-premises VPN device and connectivity to on-premises will not be shown.

In this chapter we will add GatewaySubnet to the topology. We will deploy Virtual Network Gateway and Local Network Gateway.

To make some space we will not show db-subnet in the topology.

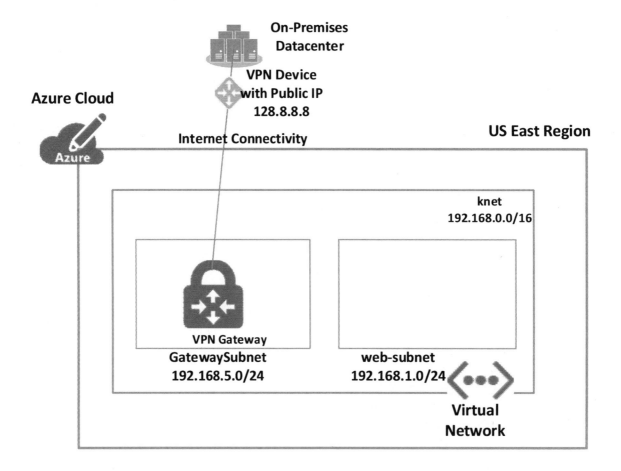

Virtual Network (VNET) External or Hybrid Connectivity

You can connect Virtual Network to on-premises Datacenter through virtual network gateway located in GatewaySubnet using either Internet VPN (P2S or S2S VPN) or ExpressRoute Private WAN connectivity.

For Internet VPN you deploy virtual network gateway of type VPN. For Private WAN connectivity you deploy virtual network gateway of type ExpressRoute.

Figure below shows Virtual Network Connected to on-premises Datacenter.

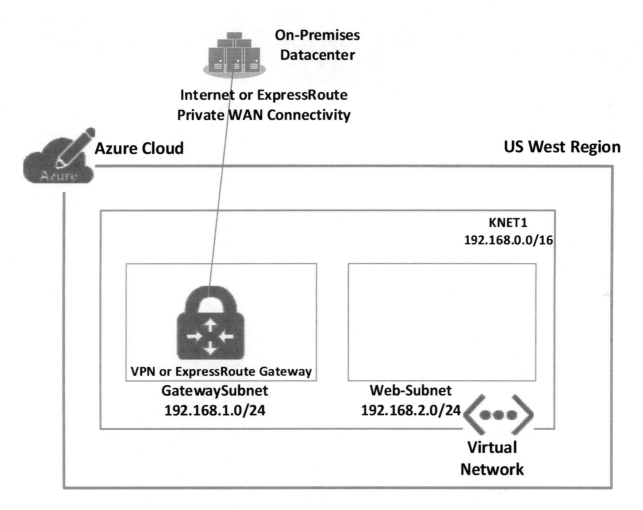

Every Azure VPN gateway consists of two instances in an active-standby or active-active configuration.

VNET External Connectivity over internet

You can connect Virtual Network (VNET) to your on-premises networks over public internet using Azure VPN Gateway. A VPN gateway is a type of virtual network gateway that sends encrypted traffic across a public connection. The connectivity uses the industry-standard protocols Internet Protocol Security (IPsec) and Internet Key Exchange (IKE).

VPN gateway connects VNET to on-premises network using Site to Site VPN (S2S) or Point to Site VPN (P2S). S2S VPN uses **VPN device** on-premises. P2S VPN uses **VPN client software** on client computers in on premises infrastructure.

VPN Gateway is created in GatewaySubnet. A GatewaySubnet is created in Azure Virtual Network (VNET).

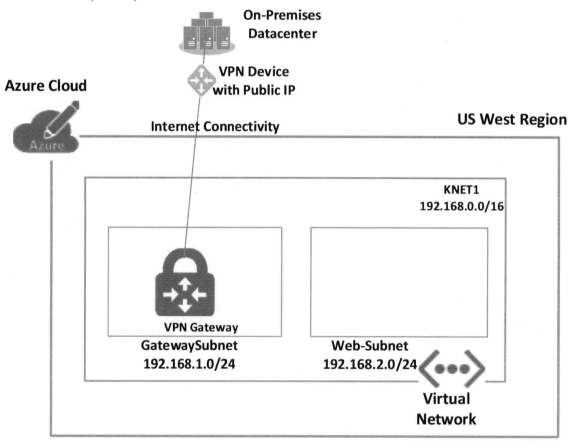

Every Azure VPN gateway consists of two instances in an active-standby configuration.

VPN Type

VPN gateway supports following 2 type of VPN. VPN Types are selected when you are creating Virtual Network gateway of type VPN.

PolicyBased: PolicyBased VPNs were previously called static routing gateways. Policy-based VPNs encrypt and direct packets through IPsec tunnels based on the IPsec policies configured with the combinations of address prefixes between your on-premises network and the Azure VNet.

1. PolicyBased VPNs can **only** be used on the Basic gateway SKU.
2. You can have only 1 tunnel when using a PolicyBased VPN.
3. You can only use PolicyBased VPNs for S2S connections.
4. PolicyBased VPN does not support Point to Site VPN (P2S).

RouteBased: RouteBased VPNs were previously called dynamic routing gateways. RouteBased VPNs use "routes" in the IP forwarding or routing table to direct packets into their corresponding tunnel interfaces. The tunnel interfaces then encrypt or decrypt the packets in and out of the tunnels.

Table below shows comparison between Route-Based and Policy Based VPN.

Features	Route-Based	Policy-Based
Point-to-Site (P2S)	Supported	Not Supported
Site-to-Site (S2S)	Supported	Supported
S2S VNet-to-VNet	Supported	Not Supported
S2S Multi-Site	Supported	Not Supported
S2S and ExpressRoute coexist	Supported	Not Supported
Max IPSec Tunnels	128	1
Authentication	Pre-shared key for S2S connectivity, Certificates for P2S connectivity	Pre-shared key
Gateway SKU	Basic, VpnGw1, VpnGw1, VpnGw1	Basic

VPN Gateway Editions

VPN gateway comes in following 4 Editions or SKUs.

Features	Basic Gateway	VpnGw1	VpnGw2	VpnGw3
Gateway throughput	100 Mbps	650 Mbps	1 Gbps	1.25 Gbps
Gateway max IPsec tunnels for Route Based VPN	10	30	30	30
Gateway max IPsec tunnels for Policy Based VPN	1	NA	NA	NA
Max P2S connections	128	128	128	128
Active-Active S2S VPN	No	Yes	Yes	Yes
BGP support	No	Yes	Yes	Yes
Route-Based VPN	Yes	Yes	Yes	Yes
Policy-Based VPN	Yes	No	No	No

VPN Gateway SKUs Use cases

Workloads	SKUs
Production & critical workloads	VpnGw1, VpnGw2, VpnGw3
Dev-test or proof of concept	Basic

Site to Site VPN (S2S)

A Site-to-Site (S2S) VPN gateway connects Virtual Network (VNET) to on premises infrastructure over IPsec/IKE VPN tunnel. This type of connection requires a VPN device located on-premises that has public IP address assigned to it and is not located behind a NAT.

Site to Site VPN can also be used to connect VNET to VNET.

Figure below shows VNET to on-premises connectivity. A VPN Device is required on-premises with Public IP (Not shown in below Figure).

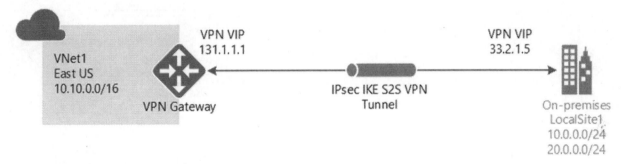

Figure below Shows VNET to on-premises Connectivity (Multisite).

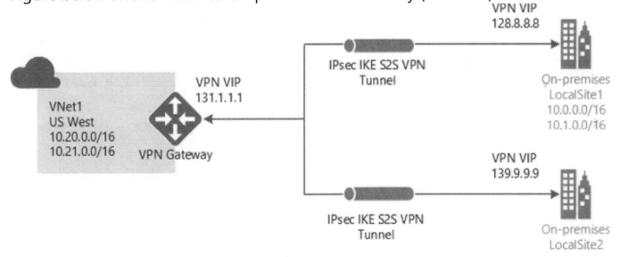

Figure below shows VNET to VNET connectivity.

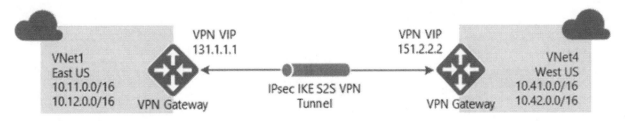

Design Nuggets for S2S VPN

3. VPN Gateway is created in GatewaySubnet (Not shown above).
4. By default VPN gateway consists of two instances in an active-standby configuration.
5. On-Premises require a VPN device with Public IP (Not shown above).
6. On premises addresses should not overlap with VNET addresses.
7. **S2S VPN only supports pre shared key as Authentication.**
8. Public IP is dynamically assigned. Static IP is not supported for VPN Gateway.
9. Do not assign Network Security Group (NSG) to GatewaySubnet.

Step by Step Creating Site to Site (S2S) VPN

1. **Create or use existing Virtual Network**.
2. **Create GatewaySubnet in Virtual Network**.
3. **Create Virtual Network Gateway in GatewaySubnet**: Specify Virtual Network of step 1, Choose Gateway type as VPN, Choose VPN Type (Route Based or Policy based), Gateway SKU (choose Basic, VpnGw1, VpnGw2 or VpnGw3), create or choose Dynamic Public IP.
4. **Create a Local Network gateway**. The local network gateway refers to your on-premises location. Specify the public IP of the VPN device and address ranges for the network that this local network represents. You can add multiple address space ranges.
5. Configure on Premises VPN Device.
6. **Create a Site-to-Site VPN connection.** Specify the Virtual Network Gateway created in step 3, Specify the Local Network Gateway created in step 4 and specify the Pre shared key.

Point to Site VPN (P2S)

A Point-to-Site (P2S) VPN gateway creates a secure connection between virtual network and on-premises using VPN client software installed on individual client computers. P2S is a VPN connection over SSTP (Secure Socket Tunneling Protocol). P2S connections do not require a VPN device or a public-facing IP address to work.

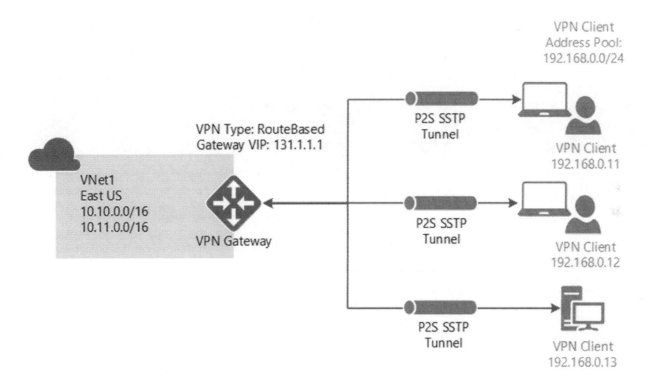

Design Nuggets P2S VPN

1. VPN Gateway is created in GatewaySubnet (Not shown above).
2. By default VPN gateway consists of two instances in an active-standby configuration.
3. On premises addresses should not overlap with VNET addresses.
4. **P2S VPN uses certificates as Authentication for client connections**.
5. Public IP is dynamically assigned. Static IP is not supported for VPN Gateway.
6. Do not assign Network Security Group (NSG) to GatewaySubnet.

Step by Step Creating Point to Site (P2S) VPN

1. Create or use existing Virtual Network.
2. Create Gateway Subnet in Virtual Network.
3. Create Virtual Network Gateway. Specify Virtual Network of step 1, Choose Gateway type as VPN, Choose VPN Type as Route Based, Gateway SKU (Basic, Standard, HighPerformance), create or choose Dynamic Public IP. It will take around 45 minutes to create Virtual Network Gateway.
4. Generate Certificates. This is done on Premises. You can use self-signed certificates or commercial PKI Certificate.
5. Add the client address pool. **Address pool** is the pool of IP addresses from which clients that connect will receive an IP address.
6. Upload the root certificate .cer file to Azure.
7. Download and install the VPN client configuration package from Azure P2S Dashboard, to the on premises Client Machine.
8. Install the client certificate on the on premises client machine.
9. Connect to Azure from your on premises client machine by clicking the VPN client installed in step 7.

VPN Gateway Redundancy

Active-Passive Azure VPN gateway with Single VPN Device

Every Azure VPN gateway consists of two instances in an active-standby configuration. This is the default configuration.

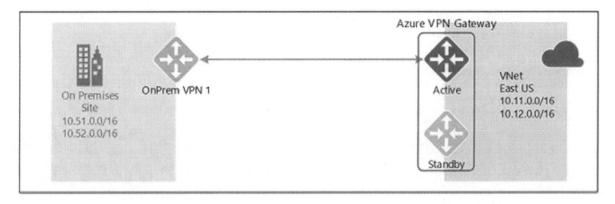

Active-Passive Azure VPN gateway with Dual VPN Device

This configuration provides multiple active tunnels from the same Azure VPN gateway to your on-premises devices in the same location.

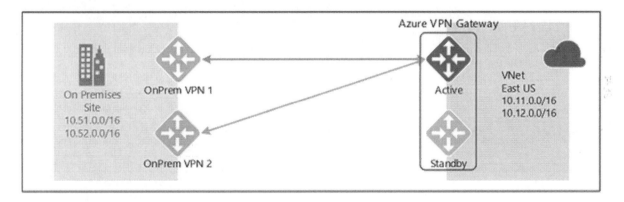

1. You need to create one local network gateway for each VPN device.
2. Each local network gateways corresponding to your VPN devices must have unique public IP addresses.
3. **BGP is required for this configuration**. Each local network gateway representing a VPN device must have a unique BGP peer IP address.

Active-Active Azure VPN gateway with Single VPN Device

In Active-Active Azure VPN gateway configuration, each Azure gateway instance will have a unique public IP address, and each will establish an IPsec/IKE S2S VPN tunnel to on-premises VPN device specified in local network gateway configuration. **Both VPN tunnels are part of the same connection.**

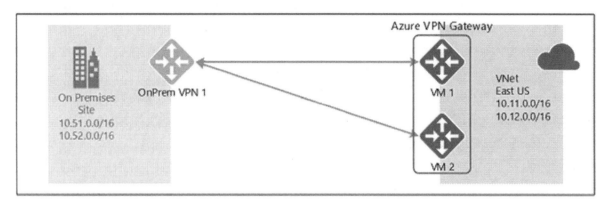

Active-Active Azure VPN gateway with Dual VPN Device

In this case both Azure VPN gateway and on premises VPN device are in active-active configuration. The result is a full mesh connectivity of 4 IPsec tunnels between your Azure virtual network and your on-premises network. **BGP is required to allow the two connections to the same on-premises network.**

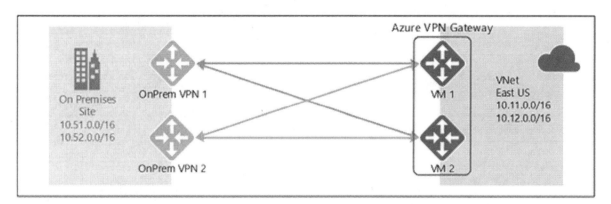

This topology will require two local network gateways and two connections to support the pair of on-premises VPN devices, and BGP is required to allow the two connections to the same on-premises network.

Border Gateway Protocol (BGP) with Azure VPN Gateways

BGP routing protocol is commonly used over Internet to exchange routing and reachability information between two or more networks.

In the context of Azure Virtual Network, BGP enables the Azure VPN Gateways and your on-premises VPN devices, called BGP peers or neighbors, to exchange "routes" that will inform both gateways on the availability and reachability for those prefixes to go through the gateways or routers involved.

BGP is an optional feature you can use with Azure Route-Based VPN gateways. Azure Route-Based VPN gateway supports both static routes (without BGP) *and* dynamic routing with BGP between your networks and Azure.

BGP Use cases

1. BGP is required to support multiple S2S VPN tunnels from the same Virtual Network Gateway.

Figure below shows multiple tunnels from same VPN gateway to on-premises VPN devices. VPN gateways are in Active-Passive setup.

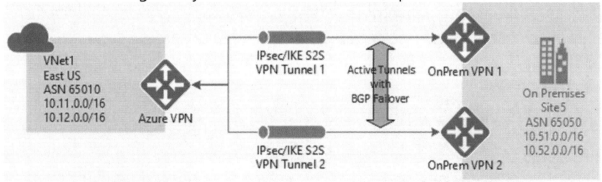

1. This configuration setup provides multiple tunnels (paths) between the two networks in an active-active configuration. If one of the tunnels is disconnected, the corresponding routes will be withdrawn via BGP and the traffic automatically shifts to the remaining tunnels.
2. Supports automatic and flexible prefix updates to BGP peer over the IPsec S2S VPN tunnel.

BGP Design Nuggets

1. You cannot use same Autonomous System Numbers (ASN) for both on-premises VPN networks and Azure VNETs.
2. You cannot use ASN reserved by Azure and IANA.
3. BGP is supported on Azure **VpnGw1**, **VpnGw2** and **VpnGw3 VPN** Gateways. Basic Gateway is not supported.
4. BGP is supported on Route-Based VPN gateways only. There is no BGP support on Policy based VPN Gateways.
5. You can mix both BGP and non-BGP connections for the same Azure VPN gateway.

Demonstration Exercise 33: Connecting VNET to on-premises Data Center using Site to Site (S2S) VPN

We will show configuration on Azure side only. IP Address of on-premises VPN Device is 128.8.8.8.

1. **Create GatewaySubnet**: Go to knet Dashboard>Click Subnet in left pane>Click +Gateway Subnet in Top Right Pane>Add Subnet Blade opens. The name of the Subnet will be Pre-populated with GatewaySubnet.

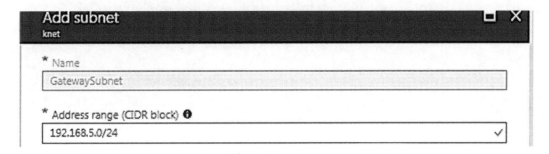

2. **Create VPN Gateway**: Click Create a resource> Networking> Virtual Network Gateway> Create Virtual Network Blade opens> Enter required information and click create.

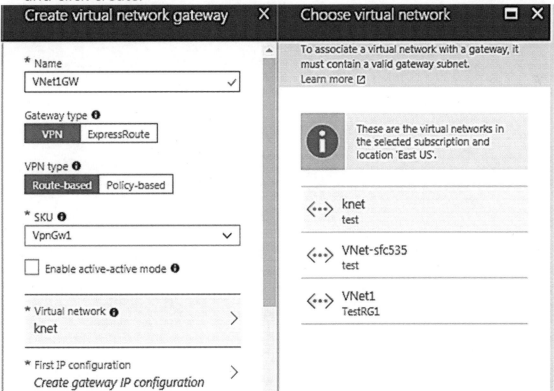

3. **Create Local Gateway**: The local network gateway refers to your on-premises location. Click +New> Networking> Local Network Gateway> Create Local Network Blade opens> Enter Public IP of on-premises VPN device and address prefixes located on your on-premises network and click create.

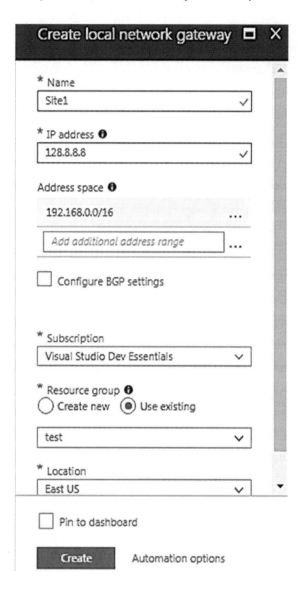

4. **Configure your on-premises VPN Device**: Configure on-premises VPN device with S2S VPN and specify Pre-Shared Key and Public IP address of Azure Virtual Network gateway.

6. **Create the VPN Connection**: Go the Virtual Network Gateway (VNet1GW) Dashboard>Click Connections>+Add>Add connection blade opens>Choose and specify following and click ok.

VPN Gateway Pricing

VPN Gateway is charged is based on the amount of time gateway is provisioned and available. VPN Gateway pricing includes upto 10 Tunnels. Additional Tunnels are charged.

VPN Gateway Type	Price	S2S TUNNELS PRICING
Basic	$0.04/hour	Included
VpnGw1	$0.19/hour	1-10 Included. 11-30: $0.015/hour per tunnel
VpnGw2	$0.49/hour	1-10 Included. 11-30: $0.015/hour per tunnel
VpnGw3	$1.25/hour	1-10 Included. 11-30: $0.015/hour per tunnel

VNET External Connectivity over Private WAN connection using ExpressRoute Gateway

ExpressRoute is an Azure Managed service, which creates dedicated private connections between Microsoft datacenters and on-premises infrastructure.

ExpressRoute connections don't go over the public internet. They offer more reliability, faster speeds, lower latencies and higher security than typical internet connections.

Azure ExpressRoute connects Virtual Network (VNET), and Azure Public Resources (Azure SQL, Azure Storage etc) to your on-premises infrastructure.

ExpressRoute, connections to Azure are established at an Exchange provider facility. Each ExpressRoute circuit consists of two connections to two Microsoft Enterprise edge routers (MSEEs) from the connectivity provider.

Figure below shows ExpressRoute Circuit Dual Connection (Primary & Secondary) between Microsoft Edge Routers and Partner Service Provider. From Service Provider to Customer Network it can be dual or Single connection.

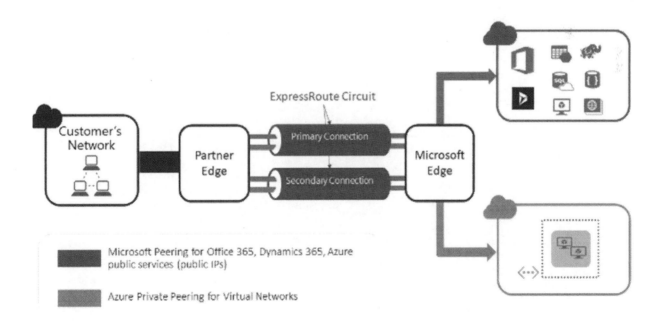

For Connecting Virtual Network (VNET) to on-premises infrastructure, ExpressRoute Gateway is created in GatewaySubnet. A GatewaySubnet is created in Azure Virtual Network (VNET). Every Azure ExpressRoute gateway consists of two instances in an active-standby configuration.

Figure Below shows Virtual Network with ExpressRoute Gateway Installed in Gateway Subnet.

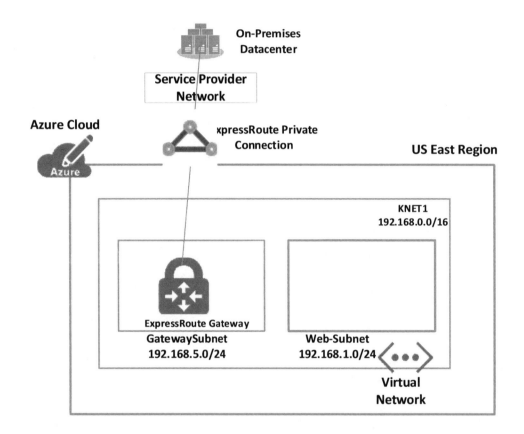

Note 1: Azure ExpressRoute Gateway consists of two instances in an active-standby or active-active configuration.
Note 2: There is dual Connectivity from Microsoft to Service Provider edge.
Note 3: Connectivity from Customer Network to Service Provider can be single or dual.

ExpressRoute Routing Domains

An ExpressRoute circuit has multiple routing domains associated with it: Azure private, Azure public, and Microsoft. In this chapter we will focus on private peering only.

Private peering domain

On premises infrastructure connects with Azure virtual network (VNET) through the private peering domain. The private peering domain is an extension of your on premises network into Microsoft Azure Virtual Network. Private peering lets you connect to virtual machines directly on their private IP addresses.

Public Peering Domain

On premises infrastructure connects with Azure Services such as Azure Storage, Azure SQL databases etc through public peering domain. Connectivity is always initiated from your WAN to Microsoft Azure services. Microsoft Azure services will not be able to initiate connections into your network through this routing domain.

Microsoft Peering

Connectivity to Microsoft online services (such as Office 365 services) will be through the Microsoft peering.
Please Note that Microsoft does not recommends creating Microsoft Peering using ExpressRoute circuit Connection. Microsoft recommends that online services like office 365 and Dynamics 365 be accessed through internet as these services were built with security and reliability over public internet.

Peering is configured through ExpressRout Circuit Dashboard (See Pg Demonstartion Exercise).

Difference between ExpressRoute Gateway and VPN Gateway

When network traffic is sent on a dedicated private connection, you use the gateway type 'ExpressRoute'. This is also referred to as an ExpressRoute gateway. When network traffic is sent encrypted across the public Internet, you use the gateway type 'Vpn'. This is referred to as a VPN gateway.

ExpressRoute Gateway SKU

Standard
HighPerformance
Ultra HighPerformance

Comparison of aggregate throughput by gateway SKU.

SKU	ExpressRoute Gateway Throughput
Standard	1000 Mbps
High Performance	2000 Mbps
Ultra High Performance	9000 Mbps

ExpressRoute Bandwidth options

ExpressRoute connection is available in multiple bandwidth options.

50 Mbps
100 Mbps
200 Mbps
500 Mbps
1 Gbps
2 Gbps
5 Gbps
10 Gbps

Dynamic scaling of bandwidth

You can increase the ExpressRoute circuit bandwidth (on a best effort basis) without having to tear down your connections.

ExpressRoute Connection Tiers

ExpressRoute Connection Circuit comes in 2 Tiers: Standard & Premium Add on.

ExpressRoute Standard Connection

The ExpressRoute Standard Connection provides the following capabilities:

1. Upto 10 VNET Links per ExpressRoute circuit.
2. An ExpressRoute circuit created in any region will have access to resources across any other region in the same Geographic region. For Example a VNET created in US East can be accessed through ExpressRoute circuit provisoned in any region in United States only. This VNET in US east cannot be accessed by ExpressRoute Circuit provisioned in Europe.
3. Supports Private and Public Peering
4. Supports upto 4000 routes for Azure Public & Private Peering.

ExpressRoute Premium Connection

The ExpressRoute premium is an add-on over the ExpressRoute circuit. The ExpressRoute premium add-on provides the following capabilities:

1. Increased route limits for Azure public and Azure private peering from 4,000 routes to 10,000 routes.
2. An ExpressRoute circuit created in any region (excluding Azure China, Azure Germany and Azure Government cloud) will have access to resources across any other region in the world. For example, a virtual network created in West Europe can be accessed through an ExpressRoute circuit provisioned in Silicon Valley.
3. Increased number of VNet links per ExpressRoute circuit from 10 to a larger limit of 100 (depending on the bandwidth of the circuit).
4. Supports Private, Public Peering & Microsoft Peering.

ExpressRoute Service Providers

Microsoft has large Service Provider partner network which provide ExpressRoute Circuit across various locations in the world. Some of the Service Provider partners include AT&, Airtel, British Telecom, China Telecom, Comcast, Colt, Equinix, MTN, NTT Communications, Sify, Singtel, Tata Communications, Telenor, Vodafone & Verizon etc.

ExpressRoute System Integrators

Microsoft ExpressRoute System Integrator Partners provide ExpressRoute circuit integration services. These partners help in connecting on-premises Data center with Azure using ExpressRoute circuit. Some of the System Integrator Partners include Avande, Equinix, Bright Skies GmbH, Orange Networks & Presidio etc.

ExpressRoute Limits

ExpressRoute circuits per region per subscription for ARM	10
Maximum number of routes for Azure private peering with ExpressRoute standard	4000
Maximum number of routes for Azure private peering with ExpressRoute premium add-on	10000
Maximum number of routes for Azure public peering with ExpressRoute standard or Premium add-on	200
Maximum number of routes for Azure Microsoft peering with ExpressRoute standard or Premium add-on	200

Number of Virtual Networks per ExpressRoute circuit

Circuit Speed	ExpressRoute Standard	ExpressRoute Premium Add-on
50 Mbps	10	20
100 Mbps	10	25
1 Gbps	10	50
10 Gbps	10	100

Connecting Virtual Networks (VNET) to ExpressRoute circuit

There are 6 steps to connecting Virtual Networks to ExpressRoute circuit. This assumes that VNET is already created.

1. Create an ExpressRoute Circuit.
2. From ExpressRoute Dashboard copy the key and send to your Service Provider.
3. After Circuit is Provisioned, Configure Routing (Private Peering) in ExpressRoute Dashboard.
4. Create GatewaySubnet in VNET.
5. Create Virtual Network Gateway of type ExpressRoute in GatewaySubnet.
6. Link VNET to an ExpressRoute Circuit.

Site-to-Site and ExpressRoute coexisting connections

In certain Scenarios you require both ExpressRoute and S2S VPN to co-exist.

Use Site-to-Site VPN as a secure failover path for ExpressRoute connection
Figure below shows S2S VPN configured as failover for ExpressRoute connection. The ExpressRoute circuit is always the primary link. Data flows through the Site-to-Site VPN path only if the ExpressRoute circuit fails.

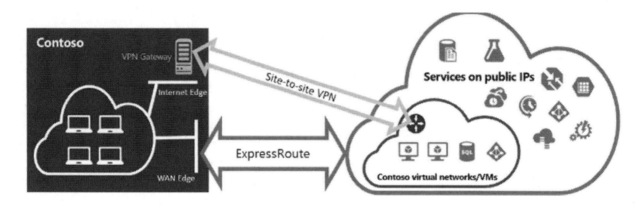

Scenario 2: Use Site-to-Site VPNs to connect to sites that are not connected through ExpressRoute connection.
Figure below shows On-premises 1 is connected to Azure Virtual Network through ExpressRoute Connection and on-premises 2 is connected through Site to Site VPN.

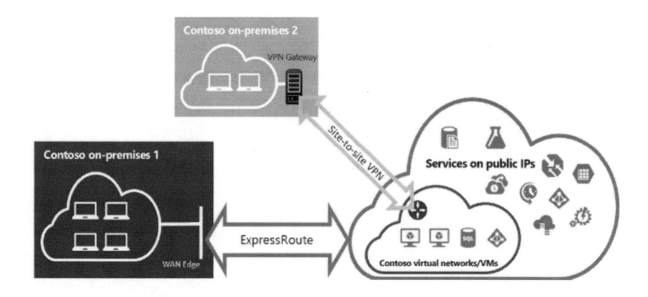

Both the above Scenarios requires two virtual network gateways for the same virtual network, one using the gateway type 'Vpn', and the other using the gateway type 'ExpressRoute'.

Figure Below shows the detailed Network diagram. On-premises HQ has ExpressRoute as Primary link and S2S VPN as failover link. On-Premises site2 has S2S VPN as the Primary link.

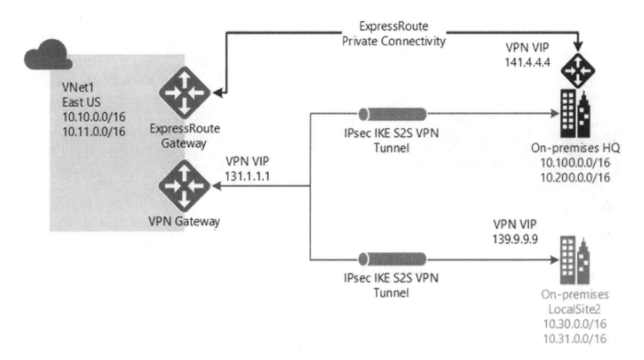

Design Nuggets for Site-to-Site and ExpressRoute co-existing connections

1. **Basic SKU gateway is not supported** for both the ExpressRoute gateway and the VPN gateway.
2. **Only route-based VPN gateway is supported.**
3. Static route should be configured for your VPN gateway if your local network is connected to both ExpressRoute and a Site-to-Site VPN.
4. ExpressRoute gateway must be configured first and linked to a circuit before you add the Site-to-Site VPN gateway.
5. **Transit routing is not supported.** You cannot route (via Azure) between your local network connected via Site-to-Site VPN and your local network connected via ExpressRoute.

ExpressRoute Gateway Pricing

ExpressRoute Gateway Type	Price
Standard ExpressRoute Gateway	$0.19/hour
High Performance ExpressRoute Gateway	$0.49/hour
Ultra Performance ExpressRoute Gateway	$1.87/hour

ExpressRoute Connection Pricing

ExpressRoute has 2 Pricing option – Metered Data Plan and Unlimited Data Plan.

Metered Data Plan

Metered Data Plan has 2 components – Fixed monthly port fee (High Availability dual ports) based on Bandwidth and outbound data charge. Figure below show ExpressRoute pricing for port speed of 50 Mbps and 100 Mbps only. Note - speed can go upto 10 Gbps.

Port Speed	Price/Month with Standard SKU	Price/Month with Premium add-on	Inbound Data Transfer	Outbound Transfer
50 Mbps	$55	$130	Unlimited	See note below
100 Mbps	$100	$200	Unlimited	See note below

Note 1 - Outbound data transfer is charged at a rate of $0.025 per GB for Zone 1, $0.05 per GB for Zone 2 and $0.14 per GB for Zone 3.

Unlimited Data Plan

With Unlimited Data Plan users are charged a single fixed monthly port fee (High Availability dual ports) based on Bandwidth. All inbound and outbound data transfer is free of charge. Figure below show ExpressRoute pricing for port speed of 50 Mbps and 100 Mbps only. Note - speed can go upto 10 Gbps.

Port Speed	Price/Month with Standard SKU	Price/Month with Premium add-on	Inbound Data Transfer	Outbound Transfer
50 Mbps	$300	$375	Unlimited	Unlimited
100 Mbps	$575	$675	Unlimited	Unlimited

Comparing ExpressRoute and VPN

	P2S VPN	S2S VPN	ExpressRoute
Bandwidth	100 Mbps, 650 Mbps, 1 Gbps & 1.25 Gbps	100 Mbps, 650 Mbps, 1 Gbps & 1.25 Gbps	5 Mbps, 100 Mbps 200 Mbps, 500 Mbps, 1 Gbps and 10 Gbps
Protocols Supported	Secure Sockets Tunneling Protocol (SSTP)	IPsec	Direct connection over VLANs
Routing	Static	policy—based (static routing) and route-based (dynamic routing VPN)	BGP
use cases	Prototyping, dev / test / lab scenarios for cloud services and virtual machines	Dev / test / lab scenarios and small scale production workloads for cloud services and virtual machines	Enterprise-class and mission critical workloads. · Backup · Big Data · Azure as a DR site

Forced Tunneling

Forced tunneling redirects all Internet-bound traffic back to your on-premises location via a Site-to-Site VPN tunnel for inspection and auditing. Without forced tunneling, Internet-bound traffic from your VMs in Azure always traverses from Azure network infrastructure directly out to the Internet.

Forced tunneling option allows you to inspect or audit the traffic. Unauthorized Internet access can potentially lead to information disclosure or other types of security breaches.

Figure below shows the Architecture of Forced Tunneling Solution.

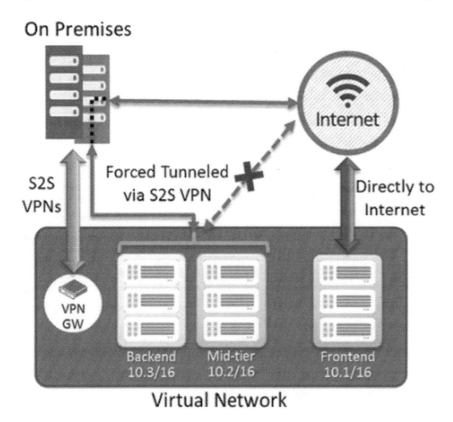

As seen in above figure the Mid-tier and Backend subnets are forced tunneled. Any outbound connections from these two subnets to the Internet are redirected back to an on-premises site via one of the S2S VPN tunnels.

Frontend subnet is not forced tunneled. The workloads in the Frontend subnet can continue to accept and respond to customer requests from the Internet directly.

Architecting Microsoft Azure Solutions Study & Lab Guide Part 1: Exam 70-535

Forced Tunneling Configuration

Forced tunneling is configured using user-defined routes (UDR). You create a Route Table and add a route which forces internet bound traffic to Virtual Network Gateway in GatewaySubnet. The Route Table will be associated with Subnet whose internet traffic you want to Force Tunnel to on-premises.

Chapter 11 Azure Active Directory

This Chapter covers following Topic Lessons

- Azure Active Directory (Azure AD)
- Azure AD Editions
- Azure AD Features
- Azure AD Users and Groups
- Azure AD licenses
- Azure AD Custom Domain
- Azure AD Connect
- AD Connect Health
- AD Federation Services (AD FS)
- SAML, OAuth 2.0 & WS-Federation Protocols
- Identity options with Azure Active Directory (Azure AD)
- Azure AD Domain Services
- Azure AD Multi Factor Authentication
- Azure AD Single sign-on

This Chapter Covers following Case Studies

- Federating On-premises Active Directory and Azure AD Directory for Authentication and Single sign-on
- Website authentication using on-premises ADFS as SAML Identity Provider

This Chapter Covers following Lab Exercises to build below topology

- Exploring Dashboard of Default Azure AD
- Create Users
- Changing Directory Role of a User
- Create a Group
- Activating Premium P2 Free Trial Licenses
- Deploying Azure AD Domain Services
- Create Authentication Provider
- Enabling MFA for Users in Classic Portal
- Azure MFA Feature settings
- Adding Applications in Azure AD Access Panel (Twitter)

Chapter Topology

In this chapter we will configure the default Azure Active Directory which was created when we signed for the Azure Subscription. We will also add Multi-Factor Authentication Service to the topology.

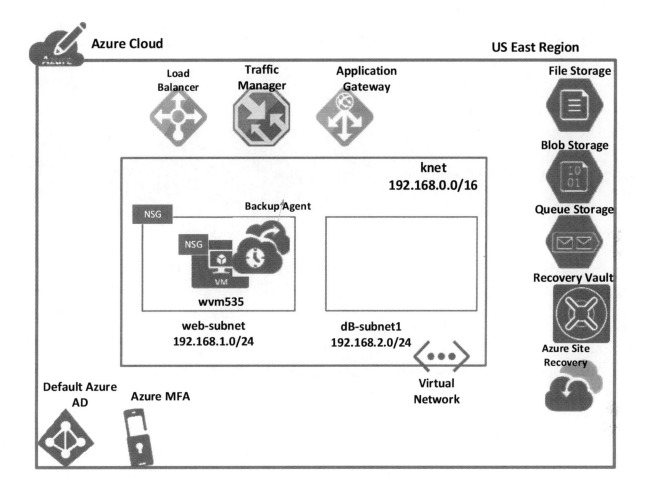

Azure Active Directory

Microsoft Azure Active Directory (Azure AD) is a Multi-tenant cloud-based directory & identity management solution that combines core directory services, application access management, and identity protection into a single solution.

Azure AD also provides enterprise service's such as multifactor authentication service, a centralized application access panel for SAAS applications, an application proxy by which you can setup remote access for your on premises applications as well as Graph API that you can use to directly interact with Azure AD objects.

One of the advantage of Azure AD is that application developers can easily integrate identity management in their application without writing complex code.

Azure AD can also act as SAML Identity provider. It Provides identity and authentication services to application using SAML, WS-Federation and OpenID connect protocols.

Azure Active Directory editions

Azure AD is offered in 4 Tiers: Free, Basic, Premium P1 and Premium P2

Azure Active Directory Free edition can manage users and groups, synchronize with on-premises directories, get single sign-on across Azure, Office 365, and thousands of popular SaaS applications.

Azure AD Basic edition adds features such as group-based access management, self-service password reset for cloud applications, and Azure Active Directory Application Proxy.

Azure Active Directory Premium P1 edition add enterprise class features such as enhanced monitoring & security reporting, Multi-Factor Authentication (MFA), and secure access for your mobile workforce.

Azure Active Directory Premium P2 edition adds Identity Protection and Privileged Identity Management features.

Architecting Microsoft Azure Solutions Study & Lab Guide Part 1: Exam 70-535

Comparing Azure AD Editions

Features	Free	Basic	Premium (P1 & P2)
Directory Objects	50000	No Limit	No Limit
User/Group Management	√	√	√
Single sign-on (SSO)	10 apps/user	10 apps/user	No limit
Self-Service Password Change for cloud users	√	√	√
AD Connect	√	√	√
Security/Usage Reports	3 Basic Reports	3 Basic Reports	Advanced Reports
Group based access Management		√	√
Self Service password reset for cloud users		√	√
Logon page customization		√	√
SLA 99.9%		√	√
Self Service Group and app management			√
Self Service Password reset with on premises write back			√
Multi Factor Authentication	√ (See note 1)	√ (See note 1)	√
Microsoft Identity Manager user CAL + MIM Server			√
Azure AD Connect Health			√
Conditional access based on group and location			√
Conditional access based on device state (allow access from managed/domain joined devices)			√
Identity Protection			Premium P2
Privileged Identity Management			Premium P2

Note 1: Multi-Factor Authentication is available for Azure AD Free and Azure AD Basic, when you create a Multi-Factor Authentication Provider by the 'per user' or 'per authentication' billing/usage model.
Note 2: A default Azure AD (Free Edition) tenant is automatically created when you sign for Azure Subscription.

Architecting Microsoft Azure Solutions Study & Lab Guide Part 1: Exam 70-535

Azure AD Identity Management Features

- **Connect on-premises Active Directory with Azure AD**: In today's scenario, Organizations have large number of on-premises Active Directory users. Using Azure AD connect synchronize on-premises directory objects (users and groups) with Azure AD. This makes users more productive by providing a **common identity** for accessing resources regardless of location. Users and organizations can then use **single sign on (SSO)** to access both on-premises resources and Azure cloud services.

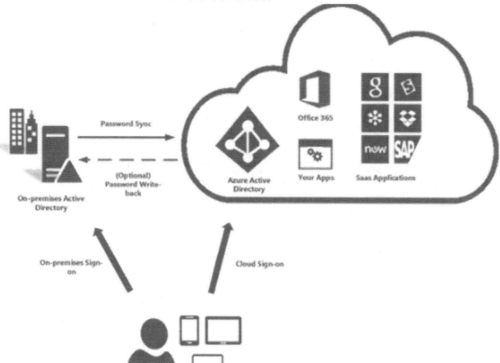

- **Manage and control access to corporate resources**: Enable application access security by using **Multi-Factor Authentication** for both on-premises and cloud applications.
- **Improve user productivity** with self-service password reset (**SSPR**).
- **Protecting Administrative Accounts**: Using Azure AD **Privileged Identity** Management you can restrict and monitor administrators and their access to resources and provide just-in-time access when needed.
- Provide **secure remote access** to on-premises application using Application Proxy without configuring VPN.

Note: These Features will be discussed in detail in Azure AD chapters.

Default Azure AD

A Default Azure AD Free Edition is automatically created with the subscription. You can upgrade Default Free edition to Basic or Premium Edition.

Domain name of the default Azure AD is in the following format:

<System generated Name>.onmicrosoft.com

System generated Name is based on the name and mail id used to create the subscription. You can check Domain of the default Azure AD by going to Azure AD Dashboard and click domain names in left pane.

Figure below shows **harikohlioutlook.onmicrosoft.com** as domain name of the default AD which I am using for this book.

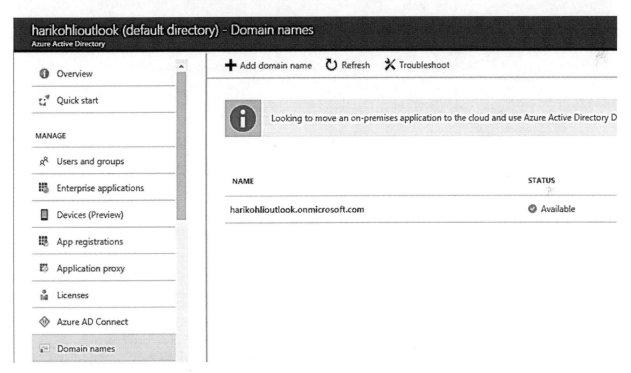

Note 1: user login name will be in following format for the above domain. xyzxyz@harikohlioutlook.onmicrosoft.com

Note 2: You can assign custom Domain to your Default Azure AD. For example you can assign test.com. User login names will be xyzxyz@test.com

Exercise 34: Exploring Dashboard of Default Azure AD

Login to Azure Portal @ https://portal.azure.com>Click Azure Active Directory in left Pane> Azure AD Tenant Dashboard Opens.

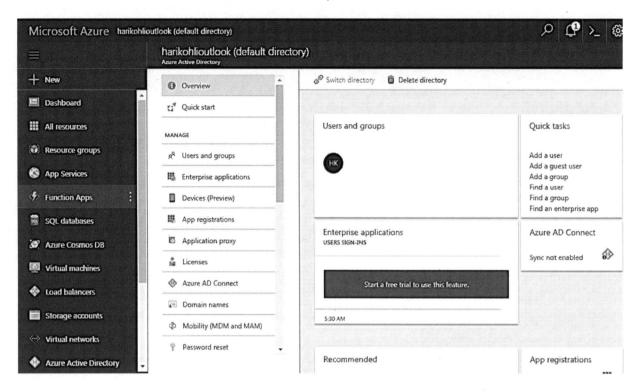

With **Users and Groups** option you can create user and Groups and Add users to groups.

With **Enterprise application** option you can provide single sign-on to SaaS and custom application.

With **License** option you can assign Basic or Premium licenses to Users.

With **domain Name** option you can assign custom Domain Names to Default Azure AD.

With **Application Proxy** option you can provide secure remote access to on-premises application.

With **AD Connect** option you can synchronize on-premises users to Azure AD.

Exercise 35: Create Users (User1 & User2)

In Azure AD Dashboard>Click Users in left pane> All Users blade open>+New User> Add user blade opens> Enter name user1. Assign Directory role of Limited admin to user1. Similarly create user2 and assign Limited admin role.

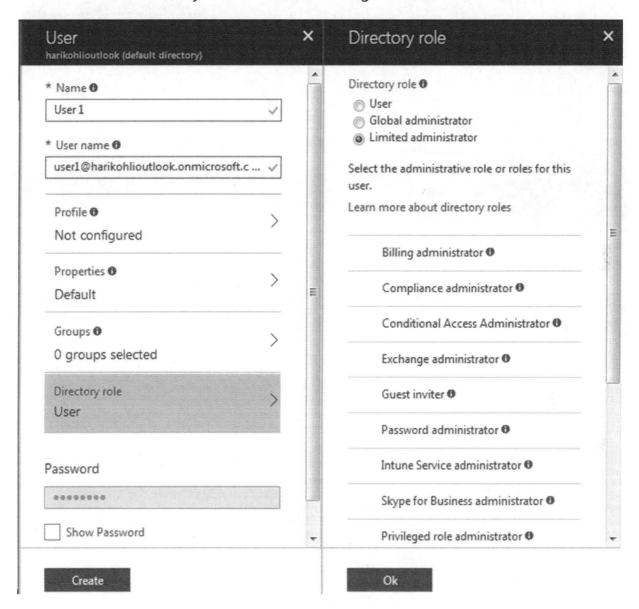

Directory Role for User: User, Global Administrator or Limited Administrator.
User Name: User name should be in email format with a verified domain. Verified domain can be default domain or custom Domain. In this case we are using default domain harikohlioutlook.onmicrosoft.com
Note 3: Password is system generated. System will ask to change in first login.

Directory Role for User

User is assigned Directory role during user creation time. If required you can change user Directory role from Azure AD Dashboard.

A user can be assigned one of the following directory roles:

User: User can login to Azure portal but cannot create a resource. For a user to view and manage a resource in Azure Portal it need to be assigned to that resource.

Global Administrator: The global administrator has access to all administrative features. Only global administrators can assign other administrator roles.

Limited Administrator: Limited administrator role has full access to particular administrative feature. Following Limited Administrative roles are available in Azure.

Billing Administrator	Exchange Service Administrator	Password Administrator / Helpdesk Administrator
Compliance Administrator	Global Administrator / Company Administrator	Power BI Service Administrator
Conditional Access Administrator	Guest Inviter	Privileged Role Administrator
Dynamics 365 service administrator	Information Protection Administrator	Security Administrator
Device Administrators	Intune Service Administrator	Service Support Administrator
Directory Readers	Mailbox Administrator	SharePoint Service Administrator
Directory Synchronization Accounts	Skype for Business / Lync Service Administrator	
Directory Writers	User Account Administrator	

Exercise 36: Changing Directory Role of a User

In Exercise 19 we assigned limited Administrative role to user2. In this exercise we will change user2 directory role to user.

1. In Azure AD Dashboard>Click Users in left pane>All Users blade open in right pane>Select user2>user2 blade opens>Click Directory role in left pane>In Right pane select user and click save.

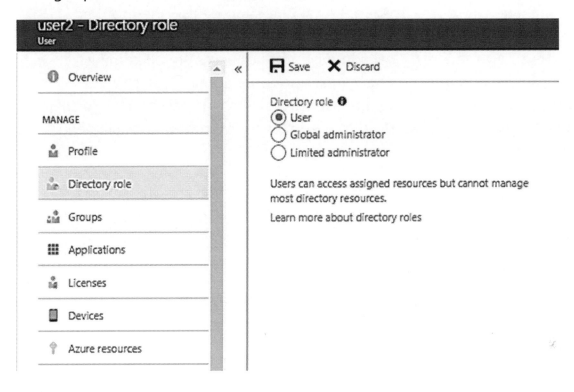

2. Log on to Azure portal with user2 email-id and password. You can see there are no resources to display for user2.

Note: In Role Based Access control topic in chapter 7 we will assign user2 to Storage account and check in Azure portal if it can manage it or not.

Azure AD Groups

Group is a collection of users. The advantage of group is that it lowers administrative overhead of managing users. For Example instead of assigning Azure AD Basic or premium licenses to individual users, assign to group.

Adding users to group: Users can be added to group by manual selection or by using dynamic membership rules. Adding users by Dynamic rules requires an Azure AD Premium P1 license for each user member added.

Creating Group and Adding members manually: In Azure AD Dashboard>Click Users and Groups >All Groups>+ New Group> Add Group Blade opens.

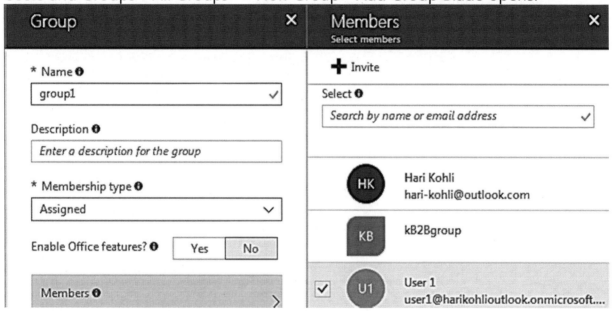

Adding members by Dynamic rules: Select membership type Dynamic user.

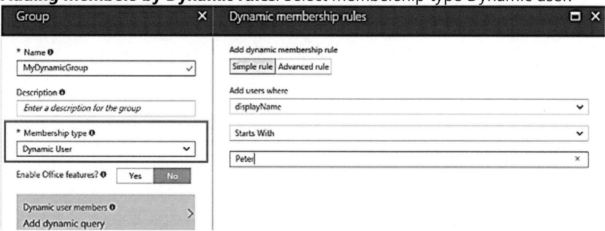

Exercise 37: Create Group and add users (user1 & user2)

In Azure AD Dashboard>Click Groups >All Groups Blade open>+ New Group>
Add Group Blade opens>Select Group type as Security>Select user1 and user2
and click select and then ok.

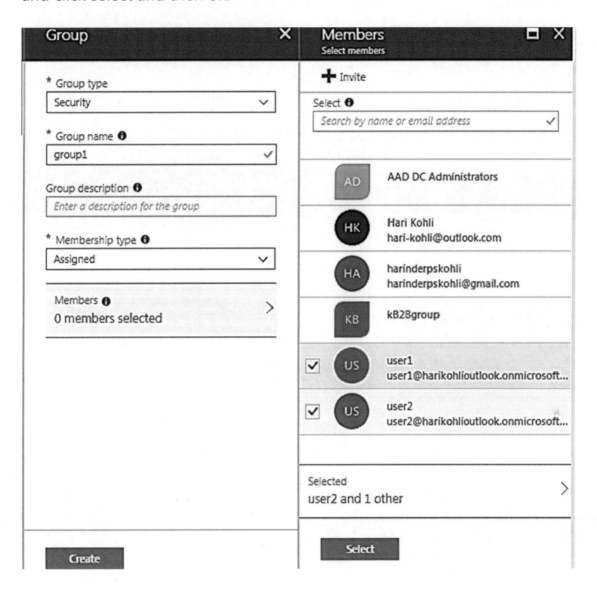

Note: In membership type dropdown box you have only Assigned as an option. If
you have Premium P1 license then you also get Dynamic user as an option

Azure AD Basic & Premium Licenses

The Basic and Premium editions Licenses are available for purchase through following options:

1. Microsoft Enterprise Agreement.
2. Open Volume License Program.
3. Cloud Solution Providers.
4. Online using credit card (Azure Subscribers only).
5. Premium P2 Free Trial licenses

After you have purchased license through one of the above method the licenses will then be available in Azure Portal after activation. You can then assign these licenses to Azure users or groups.

Exercise 38: Activating Premium P2 Free Trial Licenses

In Azure Portal you get 2 options to activate Premium P2 Free Trial Licenses.

One option is Enterprise Mobility + Security E5 option which includes Azure Active Directory Premium P2, Microsoft Intune and Azure Rights Management Trial Licenses for 250 users for 90 days.

Second is Azure AD Premium P2 trial licenses for 100 users for 30 days.

1. Go to Azure AD Admin Center @ https://aad.portal.azure.com/> Click Try Azure AD Premium.

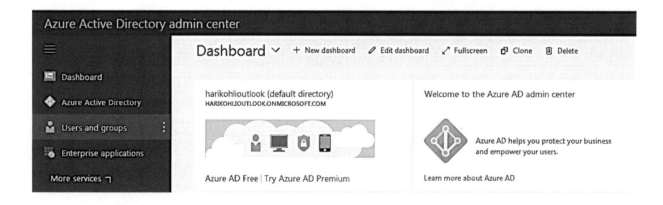

2. Activate Blade opens> Select your option> Click activate.

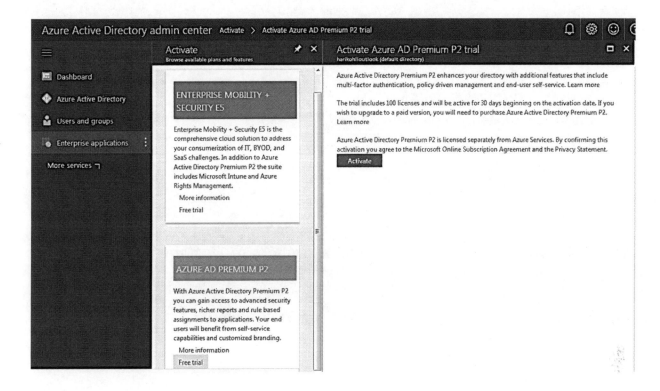

Azure AD Connect

Azure AD Connect integrates on-premises directories with Azure Active Directory. AD Connect synchronizes on-premises users in Active Directory Domain Services (AD DS) to Azure Active Directory.

The **advantage** of AD Connect is that Users can access cloud and on-premises resources with the single identity. Another advantage is that we don't have to manually create user in Azure Active Directory as they synced from on-premises AD. Third advantage is that by enabling single sign-on, users who are logged on to on-premises can access cloud resources without logging to Azure.

You need to just manage your on-premises AD and all changes are synchronized with Azure AD

AD Connect is usually installed on-premises with a service component in Azure.

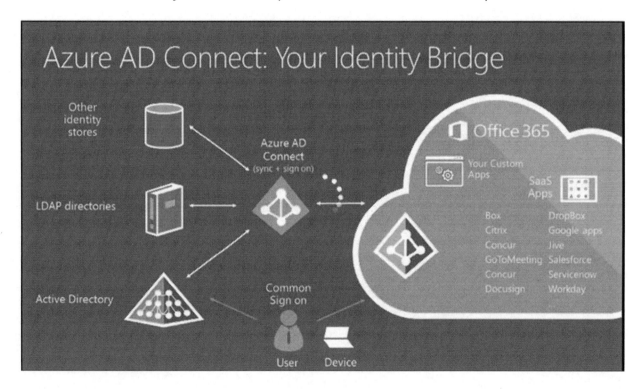

Hardware Requirement for AD Connect Server

CPU: Dual Core 1.6 GHz or Higher
Memory: 4GB or Higher (Depends on number of objects in Active Directory)
HDD: 70 GB to 500 GB (Depends on number of objects in Active Directory)

Table below shows Database, Memory and HDD requirement for AD Connect based on number of objects in Active Directory. CPU Requirement remains same - Dual Core @ 1.6 GHZ or higher

Number of objects in Active Directory	Database	Memory	HDD
Upto 50000	SQL Server Express or SQL Server	4 GB	70 GB
50,000–100,000	SQL Server Express or SQL Server	16 GB	100 GB
100,000–300,000	SQL Server	32 GB	300 GB
300,000–600,000	SQL Server	32 GB	450 GB
More than 600,000	SQL Server	32 GB	500 GB

Software Requirements for AD Connect Server

Operating System: Windows Server 2008 Standard or higher version. Recommended is to install on windows Server 2008 R2 SP1 Standard or higher version. The Azure AD Connect server must have .NET Framework 4.5.1 or later and Microsoft PowerShell 3.0 or later installed.

Database: SQL Server Express or SQL Server. By default a SQL Server 2012 Express is installed that enables you to manage approximately 100,000 objects. To manage more than 100000 objects you need SQL Server 2008 onwards. Azure SQL Database is not supported.

Note 1: Certain feature like group managed service account require Windows server 2012.

DNS Requirement

The Azure AD Connect server needs DNS resolution for both intranet and internet. The DNS server must be able to resolve names both to your on-premises Active Directory and the Azure AD endpoints.

Azure AD requirement for AD Connect Server

An Azure subscription or an Azure trial subscription.
Add and verify the custom domain you plan to use in Azure AD.

AD Connect Installation with Express Setting Option

If AD Connect is installed with Express setting option then only Password synchronization option is there to synchronize on-premises AD DS users to AAD.

Install AD Connect with Express Setting Option under following assumptions:

1. You have less than 100,000 objects in your on-premises Active Directory.
2. You have a single Active Directory forest on-premises.

Installing AD Connect with Express Setting provides following capabilities:

1. Password synchronization from on-premises to Azure AD.
2. A configuration that synchronizes users, groups, contacts, and Windows 10 computers.
3. Synchronization of all eligible objects in all domains and all OUs.
4. Does not support group-based filtering.

AD Connect Installation with Custom Setting Option

When you install AD Connect with Custom option you get to select one of the following options for user synchronization:

1. Password Synchronization
2. Pass-through Authentication
3. Federation with AD FS
4. Do not configure

Install AD Connect with custom Setting Option under following assumptions:

1. You have more than 100,000 objects and need to use a full SQL Server.
2. You plan to use group-based filtering and not only domain or OU-based filtering.
3. You have more than one forest or you plan to synchronize more than one forest in the future.
4. You plan to use federation or pass-through authentication for user sign-in.

Figure below shows AD Connect Custom Installation option Dialog Box showing options to synchronize on-premises Active Directory to Azure AD.

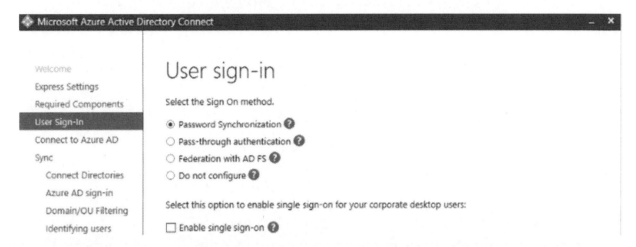

Enable Single sign-on check box is available only for Password synchronization and Pass through authentication option only. This provides seamless Single sign-on without requiring any complex on-premises infrastructure as in the case of Federation with AD FS option.

If AD connect is installed with **Password Synchronization option** then password Hash of users is also synchronized with Azure AD along with Active Directory users. User login and authentication happens in cloud.

If AD connect is installed with **Pass-through Authentication** then password Hash of users is not synchronized with Azure AD and only Active Directory users are synchronized. User login and password is entered in cloud but password is passed to the on-premises Active Directory controller to be validated.

If AD connect is installed with **federation with ADFS option** then password Hash of users is not synchronized with Azure AD and only Active Directory users are synchronized. This option also requires ADFS to be installed on-premises. User login but authentication happens on-premises by ADFS against Local Active Directory.

Components of AD Connect

Azure Active Directory Connect is made up of three components: the synchronization services, the optional Active Directory Federation Services (ADFS) component and the monitoring component named <u>Azure AD Connect Health</u>.

Synchronization Service

It synchronize's identity data between your on-premises Active Directory and Azure AD. The synchronization feature of Azure AD Connect has two components

1. The on-premises component Azure AD Connect sync, also called sync engine.
2. The service residing in Azure AD also known as Azure AD Connect sync service.

Synchronization service copies usernames and password hash from on-premises active directory to Azure AD tenant. This allows users to authenticate against Azure AD using there on-premises credentials.

AD Connect Health

Azure AD Connect Health helps you monitor and gain insight into your on-premises identity infrastructure and the synchronization services.

AD Connect Health Monitors - Active Directory Federation Servers (AD FS), Azure AD Connect servers (Sync Engine), Active Directory Domain Controllers (AD DS).

Azure Connect Health requires Azure AD Premium edition. You also require an agent on each of your on-premises identity servers.

Figure below shows Azure AD Connect Health portal which is used to view alerts, performance monitoring, usage analytics, and other information for your identity Infrastructure.

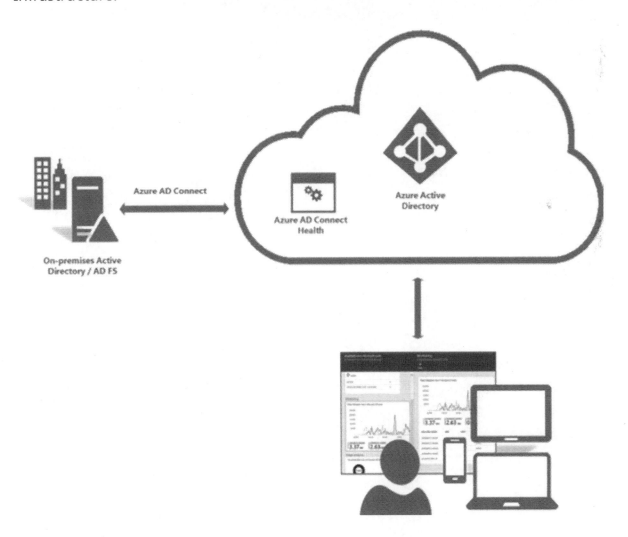

The AD Connect Health Portal URL is at https://aka.ms/aadconnecthealth. On the Portal you can see the identity services which are being monitored and the severity level of the services. You can drill down on the service further by clicking one of the tile. Figure bellows AD Connect Health Portal dashboard showing monitoring of ADFS, AD Connect & AD DS.

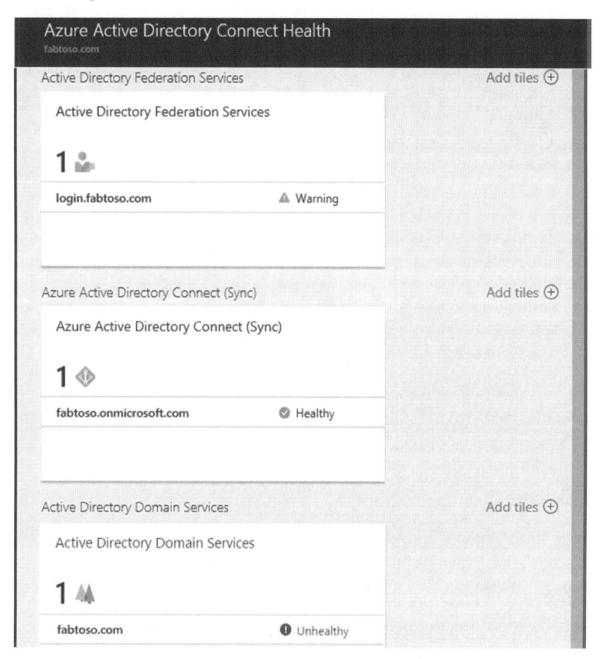

AD Federation Services (AD FS) (Explained in the context of Azure AD)

ADFS is optional Component in AD Connect. ADFS component is used only when AD Connect is installed with Federation with AD FS Option. This option also requires ADFS Server installed on-premises.

AD FS options provides Identity Federation with Single Sign-on. User Login happens in cloud but user authentication is redirected to on-premises ADFS.

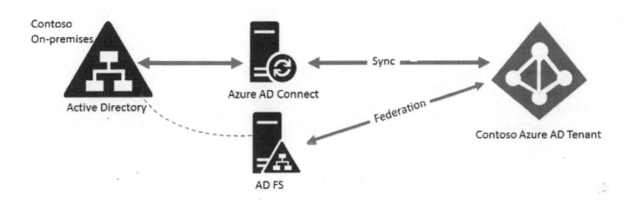

Identity Federation: ADFS creates identity federation between 2 organizations by establishing trust. Trust can be one-way or two-way trust. Federation server should be on both sides of 2 organizations.

Active Directory Federation Services (ADFS) server installed on-premises and ADFS component in AD Connect will federate the 2 directories (Azure AD and AD DS) which will results in one-way trust with Azure AD **Trusting** on-premises ADFS. User Login happens in cloud but user authentication is redirected to on-premises ADFS.

Secondly ADFS enables single sign-on. Users who are already logged on to their corporate network can sign on to Azure AD without entering there on-premises password again.

Federation can be used to configure a hybrid environment using an on-premises AD infrastructure. This can be used by organizations to address complex deployments, such as enforcement of on-premises AD sign-in policy, SSO and smart card or 3rd party MFA.

AD FS (Not in the context of Azure AD)

ADFS provides secure sharing of identity information between federated business partners.

In ADFS, identity federation is established between two organizations by establishing trust between two security realms. A federation server on one side (Account side) authenticates the users against Active Directory Domain Services and then issues a token containing a series of claims about user. On the other side, resource side another federation server validates the token and issues another for the local servers to accept the claimed identity. This allows a system to provide controlled Access to its resources to a user that belongs to another security realm without requiring the user to authenticate directly to the system and without the two systems sharing a database of user identities or passwords.

Tokens are set of claims

Trust can be one-way or two-way trust. In one-way trust, trusted organization authenticates and issues claim based token to user of trusted organization who are connecting to trusting organization for resource access. In this way trusting organization need not maintain the identity infrastructure.

ADFS can be used in following 2 ways.

One way is that ADFS federation server can be installed on both sides for identity federation between account side and resource side and one way or two way trust can be established between federations.

Second way is that ADFS will be configured as SAML identity provider on account side and other side (Resource side) will be configured to redirect user authentication to ADFS server using WS-federation, SAML, oauth2 or open-id connect protocol. Resource site is usually a website also known as service provider or relying party.

In Both cases ADFS will issue a token containing a series of claims about user.

ADFS Case Study 8: Federating On-premises Active Directory and Azure AD Directory for Authentication and Single sign-on

Organization A has application workloads running in Azure. Organization A has a security requirement that user logging to Azure AD for resource access need to be authenticated by on-premises Active Directory Infrastructure. The Solution should also provide single sign-on. Users already logged on to on-premises Active Directory should be able to access Azure cloud resource without logging again. Suggest a Solution which satisfies above requirement.

Solution

AD connect installed on-premises with Federated identity option will synchronize on-premises active directory users to Azure. This will also install a component of ADFS in AD connect. Figure below shows Architecture of the solution.

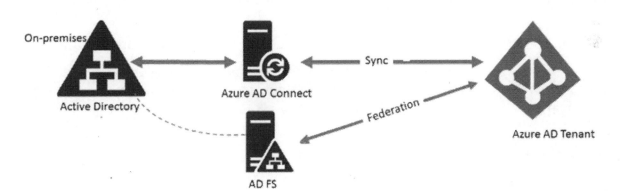

Active Directory Federation Services (ADFS) server installed on-premises and ADFS component in AD Connect will federate the 2 directories which will results in one-way trust with Azure AD **Trusting** on-premises ADFS. User Login happens in cloud but user authentication is redirected to on-premises ADFS.

ADFS also enables single sign-on. Users who are already logged on to their corporate network can sign on to Azure AD without entering there on-premises password again.

Requires AAD Subscription, AD Connect, AD DS and AD FS.

ADFS Case Study 9: Website authentication using on-premises ADFS as Identity Provider (Not in the context of Azure)

There are 2 organisations – Org A and Org B. Org B has a website which will be used by Org A users. Website requires authentication before a user can be allowed to surf. Org B does not want to maintain Authentication infrastructure. Org A already has Active Directory Infrastructure. Suggest a Solution which satisfies above requirement.

Solution

Install ADFS server in Org A as SAML Identity Provider. Website in Org B will be configured to pass user authentication to ADFS server in Org A using either WS Federation, or SAML or OAuth2 protocol.

The Org B website will be service provider or relying party. ADFS will act as identity Provider (IP). ADFS server in Org A will authenticates the users against Active Directory Domain Services and will issues a token containing a series of claims about user.

Using ADFS as an identity provider means that user accounts don't need to be set up and managed in Org B website, greatly reducing the administrative effort of maintaining user accounts.

SAML, OAuth 2.0 & WS-Federation Protocols

SAML, Oauth 2.0 & WS-Federation Protocols are sign in protocols.

I will try to explain this in the context of ADFS Case Study 9 on previous page (Website authentication using on-premises ADFS as SAML Identity Provider). Please read the ADFS Case Study 9 on previous page again.

Following 3 components are involved when Org A users access website in Org B. Org B Website is configured to allow access after authenticating users against ADFS server in Org A.

1. Sign-in Protocol
2. Authentication Protocol
3. Token Type

SAML, Oauth 2.0 & WS-Federation Protocols are sign in protocols. Users of Org A when access Org B Website they are redirected to on-premises ADFS server using one of the sign in protocols (Which can be SAML or Oauth 2.0 or WS-Federation) it has been configured with.

ADFS servers prompts you for Authentication using Authentication protocol. This Authentication protocol will be **form based** for WS-Federation and OAuth 2.0 sign in protocol. Authentication Protocol will be **kerbos based** for SAML Sign in protocol.

After authentication ADFS will issue token containing a series of claims about user. When the WS-Fed sign-in protocol is used, ADFS will always issue a **SAML 1.1 token** back to your browser. When the SAML sign-in protocol is used, ADFS will always issue a **SAML 2.0 token** back to your browser.

Identity options with Azure Active Directory (Azure AD)

Cloud Identity: Identity is maintained in cloud only. Authentication happens in cloud only. Requires Azure AD Subscription.

Following 3 identity options are available when you install AD connect to synchronize on-premises users to cloud.

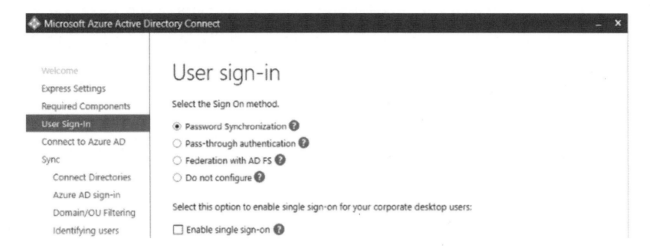

Synced Identity with Password Synchronization: Identity is maintained both in cloud and on-premises. Authentication happens in cloud.

AD Connect installed on-premises with password synchronization option, synchronizes users and password hash of on-premises Active Directory users to Azure AD. User Login and authentication happens in cloud.

Figure below shows Synced identity with Password Synchronization

Requires Azure AD Subscription, AD Connect and on-premises AD DS.

The advantage of this option is that you can access on-premises and Azure AD with same identity.

Features of Password Synchronization Option

1. Users can access on-premises and Azure AD with same identity.
2. The passwords are never sent to Azure AD or stored in Azure AD in clear text. Only Password Hash are stored in Azure AD.
3. This option also provides single sign as an option to be selected during installation of AD Connect with Password Synchronization option. Seamless single sign-on implements Single sign-on without requiring any complex on-premises infrastructure as in the case of Federation with AD FS option. Users who are already logged on to their corporate network can sign on to Azure AD without entering there on-premises password again.

Figure below shows user accessing on-premises and Azure AD with a single identity.

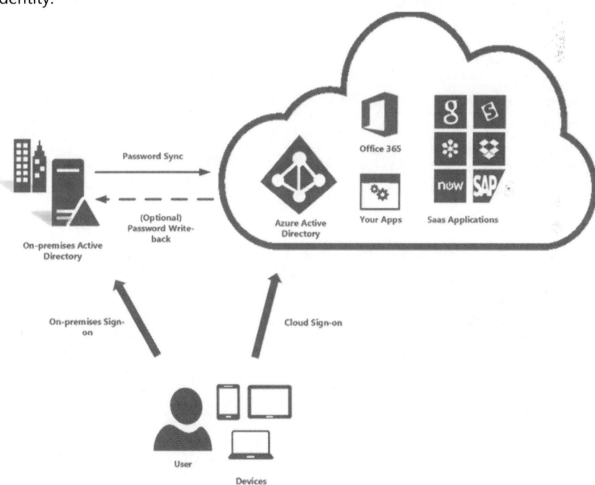

Pass-through Authentication Option: Identity is maintained in both cloud and on-premises. Authentication happens on-premises with Active Directory.

AD Connect installed on-premises with Pass-through Authentication Option, Synchronizes on premises Active Directory users to Azure AD. In this case Password Hash of users are not Synchronized.

In this case user Login and user Password are entered in cloud but password is passed to the on-premises Active Directory controller for validation. Password is never stored in cloud.

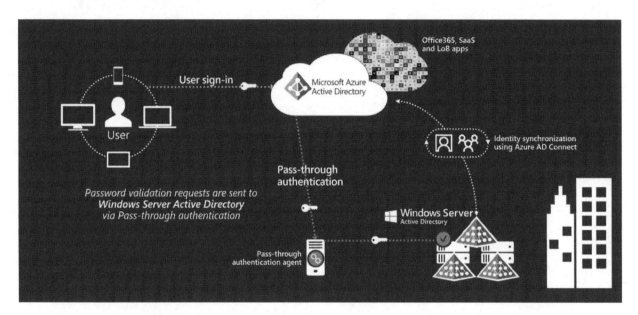

Requires AAD Subscription, AD Connect installed on-premises, A Light weight Pass through agent installed on-premises on a windows server and on-premises Active Directory Domain Services.

Brief Working

With pass-through authentication, the user's password is validated against the on-premises Active Directory controller. Pass-through authentication uses a simple agent on a Windows Server 2012 R2 domain-joined machine in the on-premises environment. This agent listens for password validation requests. It doesn't require any inbound ports to be open to the Internet.
This allows for on-premises policies, such as sign-in hour restrictions, to be evaluated during authentication to cloud services.

Features of Pass-through Authentication Option

1. Users can access on-premises and Azure AD with same identity.
2. On-premises passwords are never stored in the cloud in any form.
3. Enable seamless single sign-on for users on domain-joined machines that are on the corporate network without creating any complex on-premises deployments or network configuration as in the case of ADFS. Users who are already logged on to their corporate network can sign on to Azure AD without entering there on-premises password again.
4. The agent only makes outbound connections from within your network. Therefore, there is no requirement to install the agent in a perimeter network, also known as a DMZ.
5. Protects your user accounts by working seamlessly with Azure AD Conditional Access policies, including Multi-Factor Authentication (MFA), and by filtering out brute force password attacks.

Figure below shows user accessing on-premises and Azure AD with a single identity. All Cloud logins are redirected to on-premises for validation.

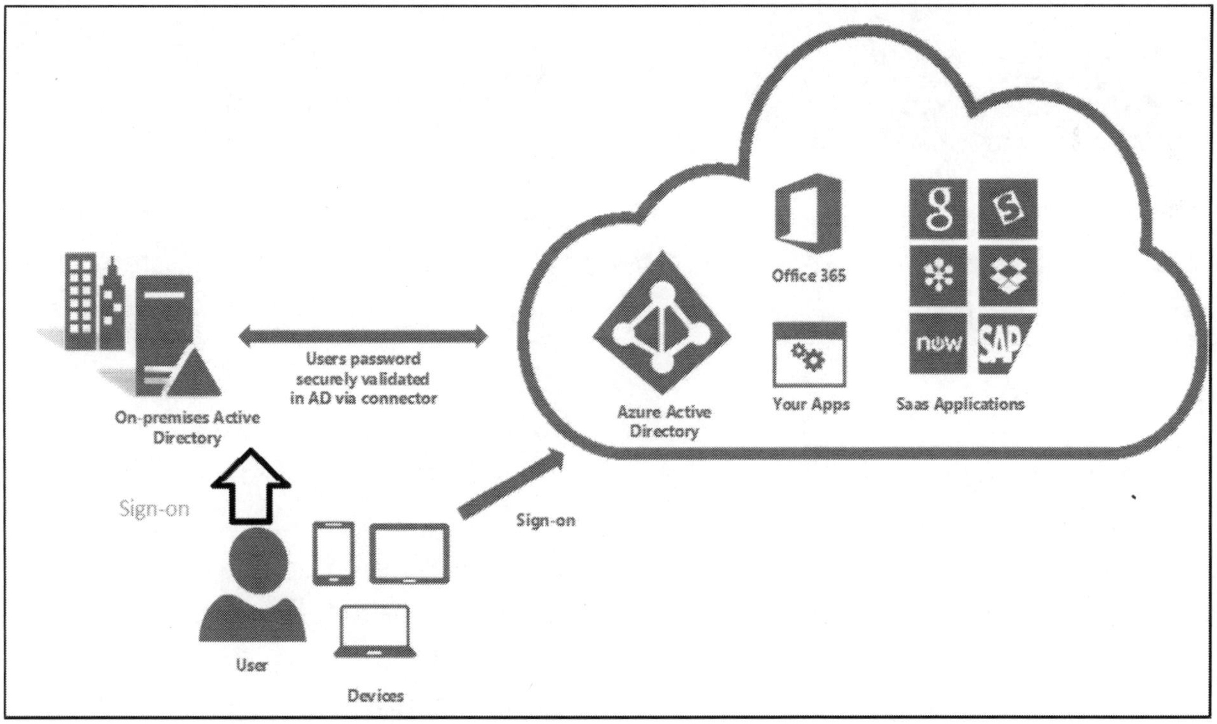

Federated Identity with ADFS: Identity is maintained in both cloud and on-premises. User Authentication happen on-premises by Active Directory Federation Services (ADFS) server against local Active Directory.

AD Connect installed on-premises with Federation with ADFS option, Synchronizes on premises Active Directory users to Azure AD. In this case Password Hash of users are not Synchronized.

Active Directory Federation Services (ADFS) server installed on-premises and ADFS component in AD Connect, federate the 2 directories which results in one-way trust with Azure AD **Trusting** on-premises ADFS. User Login happens in cloud but user authentication is redirected to on-premises ADFS.

Secondly ADFS enables single sign-on. Users who are already logged on to their corporate network can sign on to Azure AD without entering there on-premises password again.

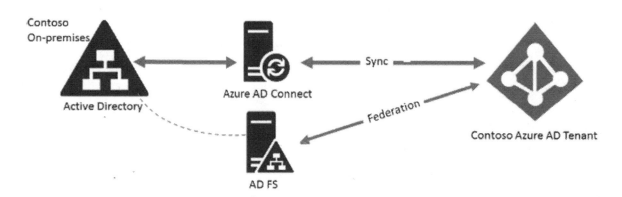

Requires AAD Subscription, AD Connect Installed on-premises, on-premises Active Directory Federation services (AD FS) server and on-premises Active Directory Domain Services (AD DS). If users are accessing resources from outside the corporate HQ then you will also require ADFS Web Application Proxy Server.

Federation can be used to configure a hybrid environment using an on-premises AD infrastructure. This can be used by organizations to address complex deployments, such as enforcement of on-premises AD sign-in policy, SSO and smart card or 3rd party MFA.

Figure below show users accessing Corporate resources and Azure AD from within or outside the Corporate Headquaters using a single identity. Single sign-on is also enabled.

Note 1: Web Application proxy server is required when users are accessing from outside the Company premises.

Note 2: AD connect is not shown in the figure but is always required.

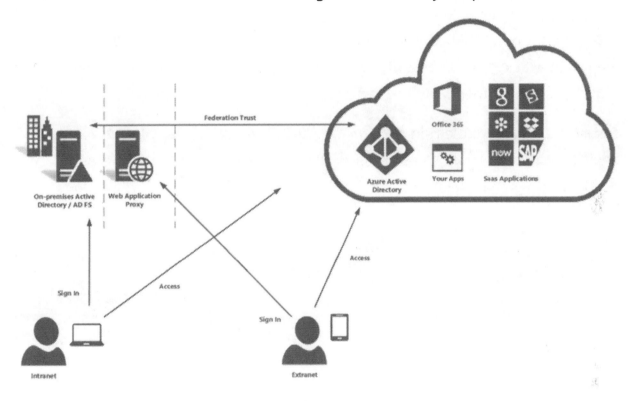

Seamless single sign-on

With seamless single sign-on users who are already logged on to their corporate network on domain-joined machines can sign on to Azure AD without entering there on-premises password again.

The advantage of this feature is that it can be enabled without creating any complex on-premises deployments and network configuration as in the case of Federation with ADFS.

Seamless Single sign-on is enabled during installation of AD Connect with either Password Hash Synchronization option or Pass-through Authentication option as shown in figure below. You to need to just check the Enable single sign-on option.

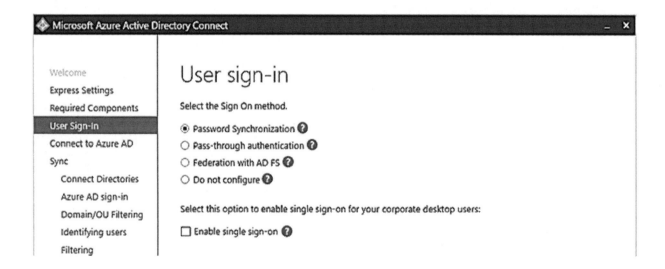

Note: Enable single sign-on option is only available for Password Hash Synchronization option and Pass-through Authentication option. It is not applicable for Federation with ADFS option.

Key Features of Seamless Single sign-on

1. Users are automatically signed into both on-premises and cloud-based applications.
2. Works with Password Hash Synchronization or Pass-through Authentication.

Architecting Microsoft Azure Solutions Study & Lab Guide Part 1: Exam 70-535

3. Register Domain joined non-Windows 10 devices with Azure AD to **enable device based conditional access.** This capability needs you to install version 2.1 or later of the workplace-join client. Version 2.1 has added support for Azure Active Directory Seamless Single Sign On (https://aka.ms/hybrid/sso).

Note: For Windows 10, the recommendation is to use Azure AD Join for the optimal single sign-on experience with Azure AD.

Figure below shows using seamless single sign-on users logged on to domain joined machines can access Azure AD application without entering there passwords.

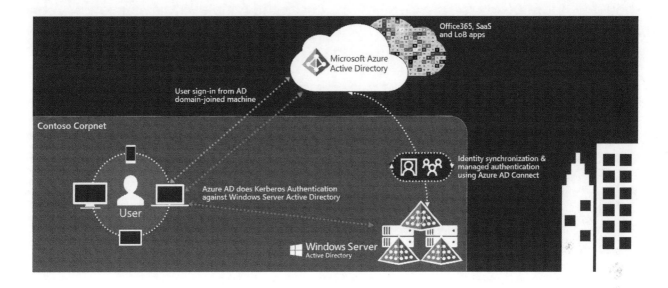

Device management in Azure AD using Registration or AD Join

In Today's scenario users are accessing corporate applications not only from on-premises but also from home using corporate owned or personal devices.

In Security paranoid world IT administrators want to make sure that devices accessing corporate resources meet their standards for security and compliance.

Device management using Azure AD is foundation for device-based conditional access. With device-based conditional access, you can ensure that access to resources in your environment is only possible with trusted devices.
To manage devices using Azure AD you have 2 options: Registration or AD Join.

Registration: Registering a device to Azure AD enables you to manage a device's identity. When a device is registered, Azure AD device registration provides the device with an identity that is used to authenticate the device when a user signs-in to Azure AD. You can use the identity to enable or disable a device.
When combined with a mobile device management(MDM) solution such as Microsoft Intune, you can create conditional access rules that enforce access from devices to meet your standards for security and compliance.

AD Join: Joining a device to Azure AD not only provides all the benefits of registering a device but also manages the local state of a device. Changing the local state enables your users to sign-in to a device using an organizational work account instead of a personal account.
AD Join requires Windows 10 Professional or Enterprise Device only.

Azure AD Join is intended for organizations that are cloud-first / cloud-only. These are typically small- and medium-sized businesses that do not have an on-premises Windows Server Active Directory infrastructure.

With Azure AD Join you can provide Single-Sign-On (SSO) to Azure managed SaaS apps and services. The SSO functionality is even when they are not connected to the domain network available.

With Azure AD Join you can Restrict access to apps from devices that meet compliance policy.

Azure AD Domain Services

Azure AD Domain Services is managed domain services in cloud which provides subset of Active Directory Domain controller functionality such as domain-join, LDAP, Kerberos, Windows Integrated authentication and group policy.

Azure AD Domain Services is installed as a Virtual Machine in Virtual Network.

Features of Azure AD Domain Services

Domain Join: You can domain-join Virtual Machines located in Virtual Networks.

Read only: Azure AD Domain Services is largely read-only except for any custom OUs you create. This feature might change in future.

Group Policy: You can use a single built-in GPO each for the users and computers containers to enforce compliance with required security policies for user accounts and domain-joined computers. You can also create your own custom GPOs and assign them to custom OUs to manage group policy.

NTLM and Kerberos authentication: With support for NTLM and Kerberos authentication, you can deploy applications that rely on Windows Integrated Authentication.

Integrated with Azure AD: User accounts, group memberships, and user credentials (passwords) from your Azure AD directory are automatically available in Azure AD Domain Services. New users, groups, or changes to attributes from your Azure AD tenant are automatically synchronized to Azure AD Domain Services. You do not need to configure or manage replication to Azure AD Domain Services.

Indirect Integration with Active Directory: On-premises Active Directory can be synchronized with Azure AD Domain Services through Azure AD. In this case AD connect Synchronizes on-premises Active Directory to Azure AD and Azure AD is automatically synchronized to Azure AD Domain Services.

High Availability: Azure AD Domain Services is highly available. Built-in health monitoring offers automated remediation from failures by spinning up new instances to replace failed instances.

Custom Domain: You can provision Azure AD Domain Services with custom domain which can be either verified or unverified domain name.

Simple Deployment: Azure AD Domain Services can be provisioned within minutes with few clicks.

Azure AD Domain Services Working

Azure AD Domain Services provides a managed AD domain to Virtual machines in an Azure virtual network. You can join machines to this managed domain using traditional domain-join mechanisms. Windows client (Windows 7, Windows 10) and Windows Server machines can be joined to the managed domain. Additionally, you can also join Linux and Mac OS machines to the managed domain.

Azure AD Domain Services is installed as a Managed Virtual Machine in a dedicated Subnet in Virtual Network.

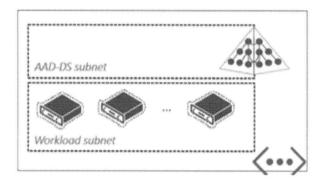

Azure AD Domain Services is largely read-only except for any custom OUs you create. **All user data is automatically synchronized from Azure AD Tenant as shown below.**

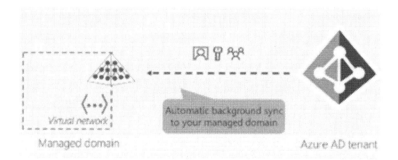

You cannot directly log on Azure AD Domain Services. You need to manage it from Domain joined machine using Server Manager or Powershell.

Domain Joined machines can be managed using Group Policy, thus enforcing compliance with your organization's security policies. You can sign in to the Domain Joined machine using your corporate credentials.

Synchronization in Azure AD Domain Services

Azure AD Domain Services is largely read-only except for any custom OUs you create. User accounts, group memberships, and credential hashes are synchronized from your Azure AD tenant to your Azure AD Domain Services managed domain.

Figure below shows synchronization in Azure AD Domain Services managed domain.

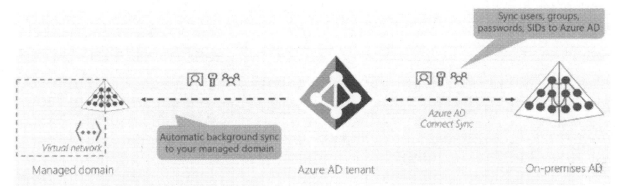

Synchronization of Azure AD tenant to Azure AD Domain Services is automatic. You do not need to configure, monitor, or manage this synchronization process. After the one-time initial synchronization of your directory is complete, it typically takes about 20 minutes for changes made in Azure AD to be reflected in your managed domain. This synchronization interval applies to password changes or changes to attributes made in Azure AD.

Synchronization process is one-way/unidirectional from Azure AD tenant. Your managed domain is largely read-only except for any custom OUs you create. As a result, there is no reverse synchronization of changes from your managed domain back to your Azure AD tenant.

Synchronization from on-premises directory to Azure AD Domain Services

On-premises Active Directory can be synchronized with Azure AD Domain Services through Azure AD. In this case AD connect Synchronizes on-premises Active Directory to Azure AD and Azure AD is automatically synchronized to Azure AD Domain Services.

Azure AD Domain Services Use Cases

Many Traditional on-premises workloads require Directory services for their working. These workloads when migrated to Azure cloud and running in Azure Virtual Machine require Directory services. Some of the workloads which require Active Directory for their working are as follows:

1. Directory-aware applications may rely on LDAP for read or write access to the corporate directory or rely on Windows Integrated Authentication (Kerberos or NTLM authentication) to authenticate end users.
2. Line-of-business (LOB) applications running on Windows Server are typically deployed on domain joined machines, so they can be managed securely using Group Policy.

Why Use Azure AD Domain Services

To provide Active Directory services to workloads in cloud you have following options:

1. Deploy a stand-alone domain in Azure using domain controllers deployed as Azure virtual machines.
2. Extend the corporate AD domain/forest infrastructure by setting up replica domain controllers using Azure virtual machines.
3. Deploy a site-to-site VPN connection between workloads running in Azure Infrastructure Services and the corporate directory on-premises.

All the above options have high administrative overhead and cost. Administrators are required to deploy domain controllers using virtual machines in Azure. Additionally, they need to manage, secure, patch, monitor, backup, and troubleshoot these virtual machines. The reliance on VPN connections to the on-premises directory causes workloads deployed in Azure to be vulnerable to transient network glitches or outages. These network outages in turn result in lower uptime and reduced reliability for these applications.

Azure AD Domain Services to provide an easier alternative to the above options. It comes as a managed service which means you don't need to patch or upgrade or troubleshoot or configure High availability. It can be deployed in minutes with few clicks.

Azure AD Domain Services v/s Active Directory Domain Services installed as VM

The following table shows comparison between Azure AD Domain Services and Active Directory infrastructure in Azure.

Feature	Azure AD Domain Services	Active Directory in Azure VM
Managed service	✓	X
Group Policy	✓	✓
Domain join	✓	✓
Custom OU structure	✓	✓
LDAP write	X	✓
Schema extensions	X	✓
Geo-distributed deployments	X	✓
AD domain/forest trusts	X	✓
Domain or Enterprise administrator privileges	X	✓
Domain authentication using NTLM and Kerberos	✓	✓
DNS server	✓	✓
LDAP read	✓	✓

Azure AD Domain Services v/s Azure AD Join

The following table shows comparison between Azure AD Join and Azure AD Domain Services.

Feature	Azure AD Join	Azure AD Domain Services
Device controlled by	Azure AD	Azure AD Domain Services
Representation in the directory	Device objects in the Azure AD directory	Computer objects in the AAD-DS managed domain.
Authentication	OAuth/OpenID Connect based protocols	Kerberos, NTLM protocols
Management	Mobile Device Management (MDM) software like Intune	Group Policy
Networking	Works over the internet	Requires machines to be on the same virtual network as the managed domain.
Use Case	End-user mobile or desktop devices	Server virtual machines deployed in Azure

Demonstration Exercise 39: Deploying Azure AD Domain Services

Deploying, using and managing Azure AD Domain Services is a 4 step process:

1. Deploy Azure AD Domain Services.
2. update DNS settings for the Azure virtual network
3. Azure AD Password Synchronization (This step is very important).
4. Manage Azure AD Domain Services from a Domain joined Azure VM.

Step 1 Deploy Azure AD Domain Services: Click create a resource> Security + Identity>Azure AD Domain Services>Enable Azure AD Domain Services Blade opens> Select your Virtual Network and Subnet (Dedicated to Domain Services) and Enter other required information and click create.

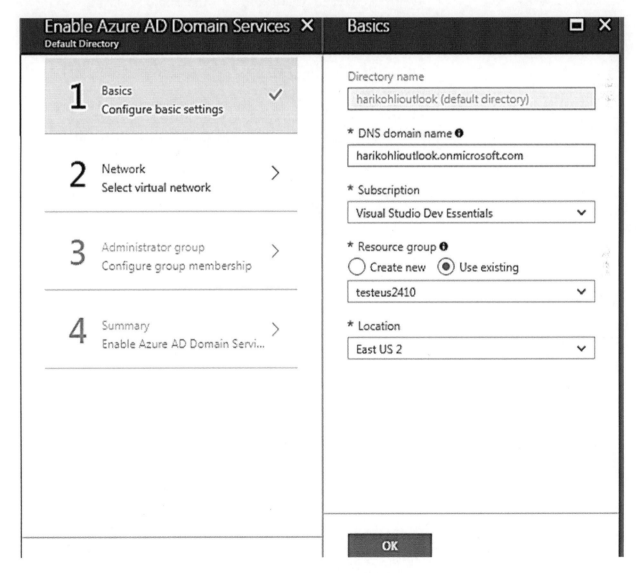

Step 2 update DNS settings for the Azure virtual network: In this step update the DNS server settings for your virtual network to point to the two IP addresses of Azure AD Domain Services controller.

Go to overview tab of Azure AD Domain Services Dashboard>Copy the IP addresses of 2 Azure AD Domain Services controller deployed from the dashboard>Click configure DNS servers> Select Custom and Add IP addresses of AD domain services> Click **Save** to update the DNS servers for the virtual network.

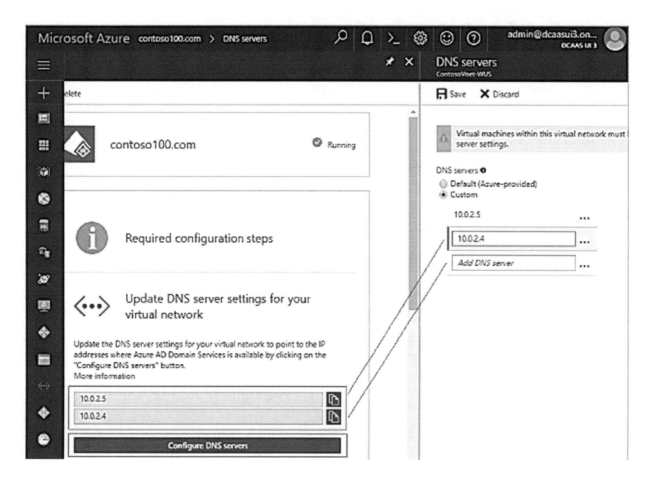

Note: Virtual machines in the network only get the new DNS settings after a restart.

Step 3: Azure AD Password Synchronization

To authenticate users on the managed domain, Azure AD Domain Services needs credential hashes in a format that's suitable for NTLM and Kerberos authentication.

Azure AD does not generate or store user credential hashes in the format that's required for NTLM or Kerberos authentication, until you enable Azure Active Directory Domain Services for your tenant.
What this means is that you need to change the password of all users in Azure AD after you have deployed Azure AD Domain Services. After Azure AD Domain Services is deployed, Azure AD will store user credential hashes in the format that's required for NTLM or Kerberos authentication.

Change password of Azure AD DC Administrator Group users. This was the group in which users were added during deployment of Azure AD Domain services.

Step 4: Manage Azure AD Domain Services

Domain Join an Azure VM to Azure AD Domain Services. Manage your Azure AD Domain Services from Domain joined VM.

You cannot directly log on Azure AD Domain Services. You need to manage it from Domain joined machine using Server Manager or Powershell.

Azure AD Domain Services Pricing

Azure Active Directory Domain Services usage is charged per hour, based on the total number of objects in your Active Directory Domain Services managed domain, including users, groups, and domain-joined computers.

NUMBER OF DIRECTORY OBJECTS	PRICE
Less than 25,000	$0.15/hour
25,001 to 100,000	$0.40/hour
100,001 to 500,000	$1.60/hour

Azure Multi Factor Authentication

Multifactor authentication (**MFA**) is a security system that requires more than one method of authentication apart from username/password.

Azure multifactor authentication (MFA) provides a second level of security when signing into cloud-based or on-premises applications apart from user password. When enabled, Azure MFA can be configured to verify a user's identity using a call to a mobile or landline phone, a text message, a mobile app notification, Mobile app verification code or 3rd party OATH tokens.

Azure Multi-Factor Authentication is available as a service in cloud or as MFA Server to be installed on-premises.

Use Case

It can be used both on-premises and in the cloud to add security for accessing Microsoft online services, Azure Active Directory-connected SaaS applications, line of business applications and remote access applications.

Versions of Azure Multi-Factor Authentication

1. **Multi-Factor Authentication for Office 365**: This version works exclusively with Office 365 applications and is managed from the Office 365 portal. So administrators can now help secure their Office 365 resources by using multi-factor authentication. This version comes with an Office 365 subscription.

2. **Multi-Factor Authentication for Azure Administrators**: The same subset of Multi-Factor Authentication capabilities for Office 365 will be **available at no cost** to all Azure administrators. Every administrative account of a Azure subscription can now get additional protection by enabling this core multi-factor authentication functionality.

3. **Azure Multi-Factor Authentication**: Azure Multi-Factor Authentication offers the richest set of capabilities. It provides additional configuration options via

the Azure Management portal, advanced reporting, and support for a range of on-premises and cloud applications. Azure Multi-Factor Authentication comes as part of Azure Active Directory Premium and Enterprise Mobility Suite. Azure Multi-Factor Authentication is available in both cloud or as MFA Server.

Note: In this chapter we will focus on 3rd option only.

Feature Comparison between various versions of Azure Multi-Factor Authentication

Feature	Multi-Factor Authentication for Office 365	Multi-Factor Authentication for Azure Administrators	Azure Multi-Factor Authentication
Protect admin accounts with MFA	√	√	√
Mobile app as a second factor	√	√	√
Phone call as a second factor	√	√	√
SMS as a second factor	√	√	√
App passwords for clients that don't support MFA	√	√	√
Admin control over verification methods	√	√	√
PIN mode			√
Fraud alert			√
MFA Reports			√
One-Time Bypass			√
Custom greetings for phone calls			√
Custom caller ID for phone calls			√
Trusted IPs			√
Remember MFA for trusted devices			√
MFA SDK			√
MFA for on-premises applications			√

Comparison between Azure Multi-Factor Authentication in the cloud and Multi-Factor Authentication Server

Features	MFA Cloud	MFA Server
Mobile app notification as a second factor	√	√
Phone call as a second factor	√	√
One-way SMS as second factor	√	√
Two-way SMS as second factor	√	√
Hardware Tokens as second factor		√
PIN mode		√
Fraud alert	√	√
MFA Reports	√	√
One-Time Bypass		√
Custom greetings for phone calls	√	√
Customizable caller ID for phone calls	√	√
Trusted IPs	√	√
Remember MFA for trusted devices	√	
Conditional access	√	√
Cache		√

Azure Multi-Factor Authentication license options

1. Purchase Azure Multi-Factor Authentication licenses and assign them to your users in Azure Active Directory.

2. Use Azure Active Directory Premium edition as they include Azure MFA Licenses.

3. Use Enterprise Mobility + Security suite as they include Azure MFA licenses.

4. Create an Azure Multi-Factor Authentication Provider within an Azure subscription. Azure MFA Providers are Azure resources that are billed against your Enterprise Agreement, Azure monetary commitment, or credit card. There are two usage models available – per user and per authentication. With this option Azure AD Free and Basic Edition users can also use MFA.

Enabling Azure MFA

Azure MFA can be enabled in 2 ways for the users.

1. If you have licenses (MFA, Azure AD Premium or EMS License) then enable MFA per user.
2. If you don't have licenses then create Authentication using per user or per authentication model and then enable MFA per user.

Azure MFA using Azure Multi-Factor Authentication Provider

Azure Multi Factor Authentication Provider enable two-step verification for your users who do not have MFA license through Azure MFA, Azure AD Premium, or Enterprise Mobility + Security (EMS). If you have licenses, then you do not need an Azure Multi-Factor Authentication Provider.

Azure MFA Authentication Providers are Azure resources that are billed against your Enterprise Agreement, Azure monetary commitment, or credit card.

There are two types of authentication provider - per user or per authentication billing/usage model.

With **Per User Billing Model** pricing is calculated based on number of individuals in your tenant who perform two-step verification in a month. Typically used in scenarios where some users have MFA licenses but need to extend MFA to more users beyond your licensing limits.

With **Per Authentication Billing Model** pricing is calculated based on number of authentications performed against your tenant in a month.
This option is best if you have a number of users authenticating only occasionally. Typically used in scenarios that use Azure Multi-Factor Authentication in a consumer-facing application.

Design Nugget

With Azure Multi Factor Authentication Provider option users with Azure AD Free and Basic license can also use MFA.

Exercise 40: Create Authentication Provider

1. Log on Azure Portal> Azure AD Dashboard>Click MFA server under security in left Pane>Click Providers>Click + Add> Add Provider Blade Opens> Enter as per your requirement and click add.

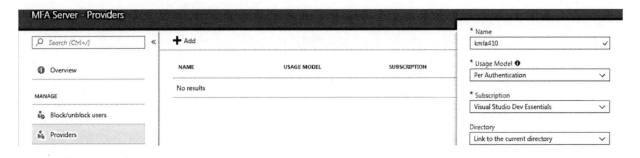

Exercise 41: Enabling MFA for Users in Classic Portal

Azure AD Dashboard> Users & Groups> All Users> click Multi factor Authentication> A new browser windows opens in Classic portal>Select a user>click enable in right pane.

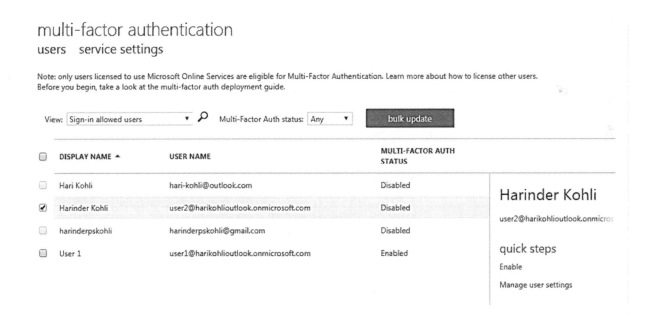

Demonstration Exercise 42: Azure MFA Feature settings

After MFA is up and running, following features can be configured. Figure below shows MFA Authentication Provider Dashboard.

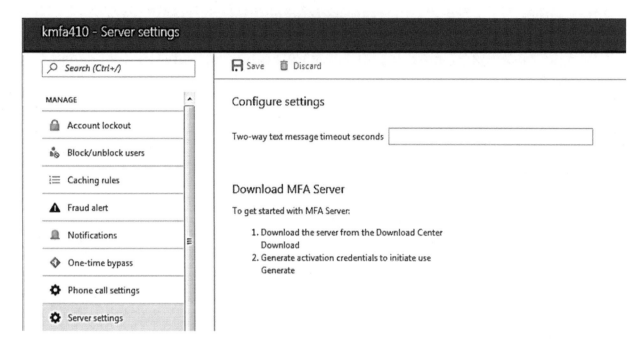

Block/Unblock Users: A blocked user will not receive Multi-Factor Authentication requests. Authentication attempts for that user will be automatically denied. A user will remain blocked for 90 days from the time they are blocked. To manually unblock a user, click the "Unblock" action.

One-time bypass: This feature is applicable for MFA Server. Allow a user to authenticate without performing two-step verification for a limited time. The bypass goes into effect immediately, and expires after the specified seconds.

Custom Voice Messages: Use the custom voice messages feature to use your own recordings or greetings with Multi-Factor Authentication. This feature is configured from Phone call settings.

Trusted IPs: Use Trusted IPs feature to bypass two-step verification for users who sign in from the company intranet.

Caching: Set up caching rules so that consecutive authentications don't require two-step verification. This feature only applies to MFA Server deployment.

Remember Multi-Factor Authentication for trusted devices and browsers:
Users can bypass subsequent verifications for a specified number of days, after
they've successfully signed-in to a device by using Multi-Factor Authentication.

The remember Multi-Factor Authentication feature sets a persistent cookie on the
browser when a user selects the **Don't ask again for X days** option at sign-in.
The user isn't prompted again for Multi-Factor Authentication from that same
browser until the cookie expires. If the user opens a different browser on the
same device or clears their cookies, they're prompted again to verify.

Selectable verification methods: You can choose the verification methods that
are available for your users by using the selectable verification methods feature.

1. Azure AD Dashboard> Users & Groups> All Users> click Multi factor
    Authentication> A new browser windows opens in Classic portal>Select
    Service Settings>Select app password, Verification options as per your req.

multi-factor authentication
users   service settings

app passwords

- ◉ Allow users to create app passwords to sign in to non-browser apps
- ○ Do not allow users to create app passwords to sign in to non-browser apps

verification options

Methods available to users:
- ☑ Call to phone
- ☑ Text message to phone
- ☑ Notification through mobile app
- ☑ Verification code from mobile app

remember multi-factor authentication

- ☐ Allow users to remember multi-factor authentication on devices they trust
  Days before a device must re-authenticate (1-60): 14

Enable Azure MFA with a conditional access policy

Enabling Azure MFA with a conditional access policy gives you the ability to specify exactly when two-step verification is required. For example, you can make a policy such as this one: When contractors try to access our procurement app from untrusted networks on devices that are not domain-joined, require two-step verification.

Step by Step Enabling Azure MFA with a conditional access policy

1. Sign in to the Azure portal as an administrator.
2. Go to Azure Active Directory > Conditional access.
3. Select New policy.
4. Under Assignments, select Users and groups. Use the include and Exclude tab to specify which users and groups the policy manages.
5. Under Assignments, select Cloud apps. Choose to include All cloud apps.
6. Under Access controls, select Grant. Choose Require multi-factor authentication.
7. Turn Enable policy to On, and then select Save.

Note: Conditional Access will be discussed in Chapter 13

Multi-Factor Authentication Pricing

Azure Multi-Factor Authentication is bundled free of cost with Azure Active Directory Premium edition, Enterprise Mobility & Security Suite (EMS) and Enterprise Cloud Suite.

Azure Multi-Factor Authentication is also available as a stand-alone service with per user or per authentication billing options. This requires Creation of Azure Multi-Factor Authentication Provider within an Azure subscription. It's a consumption-based resource that's billed against the organization's Azure subscription, just like virtual machines or websites.

Billing Model	Price
Per user	$1.40 per month (unlimited authentications)
Per authentication	$1.40 per 10 authentications
Per user annual model	$1.40 per month (unlimited authentications)
Per user annual model (Volume Licensing)	Part of MS Enterprise licensing agreement
License as part of Azure AD Premium edition, Enterprise Mobility Suite.	Included

Azure AD Single sign-on for Applications

Azure AD enables single sign-on for users to access their all applications based on their organizational account in Azure AD. Once they have logged-in to Azure AD they can access SaaS application without signing again.

Using Azure AD Single Sign-on you get single page for all Applications which is available at Azure AD Access Panel @ https://myapps.microsoft.com.
Important Note: You need to add applications for users in Access panel.

Figure below shows Access Panel for an Azure AD user. As shown in figure below Access panel has all the applications for user in a single page.

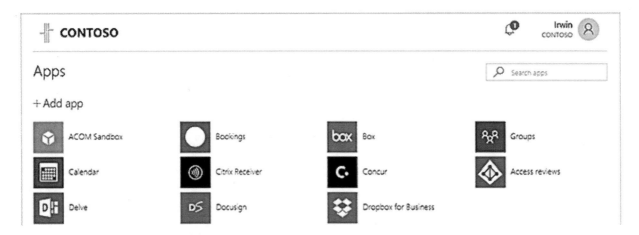

Azure AD Access panel

The Access Panel at https://myapps.microsoft.com is a web-based portal that allows an end user with an organizational account in Azure Active Directory to view and launch cloud-based applications to which they have been granted access by the Azure AD administrator. If you are an end user with Azure Active Directory Premium, you can also utilize self-service group management capabilities through the Access Panel.
Number of application which can be made available in Access Panel will depend upon Azure AD license assigned to user.

Features	Free	Basic	Premium (P1 & P2)
Single sign-on (SSO) for SaaS Apps	10 apps/user	10 apps/user	No limit

Types of application which can be added in Azure AD Access Panel

1. Applications which are featured in Azure gallery
2. Application not in Azure gallery. Requires Azure AD Premium License.
3. On-Premises application published through Azure AD Application Proxy. Requires AD Premium or Basic license.
4. Custom Application. Application need to be first registered in Azure AD.

Exercise 43: Adding Applications in Azure AD Access Panel (Twitter)

1. Go to Azure AD Dashboard>Enterprise Application in left pane> +New Application in top right pane>Add an Application Blade opens> Enter twitter in search panel>In search result click Twitter> Add Twitter app blade opens in Right pane> Click Add.

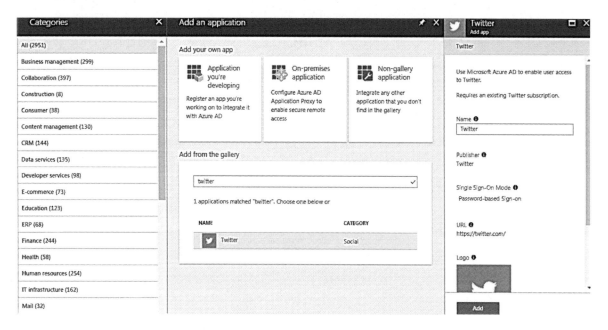

Enable Single sign-on for Twitter App. In Azure AD Dashboard click Enterprise Application in left pane>In Right Pane click Twitter Application>Twitter Enterprise Application Dashboard opens>Click single sign-on in left pane>In Right pane select password based sign on from drop down box> Click save in Top.

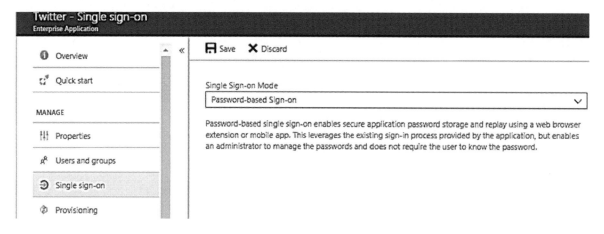

2. **Assign a user to the Twitter App**. In Twitter App Dashboard in Azure AD Click Users and groups in left pane>In Right pane click +Add User>Add Assignment blade opens> Select user2 and click select> Click Assign.

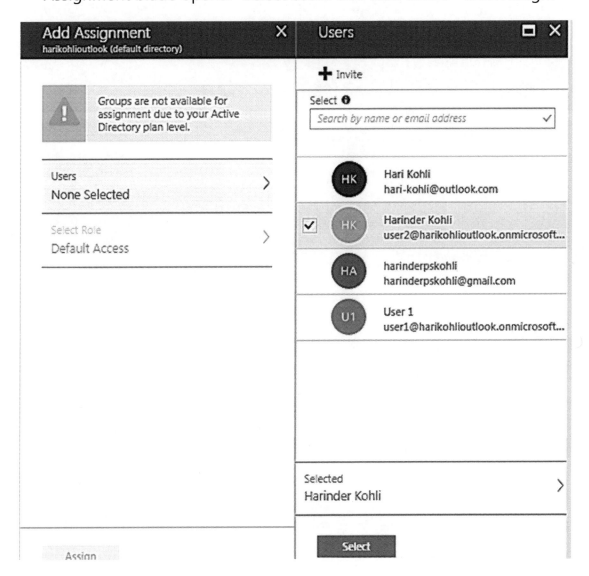

3. Sign-on to https://myapps.microsoft.com with user2 and you can see twitter.

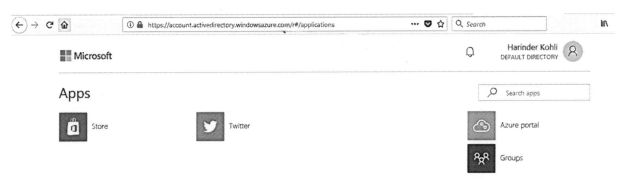

Chapter 12 Azure Active Directory Identity Providers

This Chapter covers following Topic Lessons

- Azure Active Directory B2C
- Azure Active Directory B2C Pricing
- Azure Active Directory B2B
- Azure Active Directory B2B License Pricing
- Comparing B2C and B2B

This Chapter Covers following Case Studies

- Identity Management
- Licensing Case Study 1
- Licensing Case Study 2

This Chapter Covers following Lab Exercises to build below topology

- Create Azure AD B2C Tenant and Link it to Azure Subscription
- Adding support for Local account (email & Password)
- Adding support for Social Account in your App (Facebook)

Azure Active Directory B2C

Azure Active Directory B2C is a cloud based identity and access management solution for consumer-facing web and mobile applications.

It can be easily integrated with mobile and web applications. Your customers can log on to your applications by using their existing social accounts or by creating new credentials (email & Password).

With Azure Active Directory B2C, consumers can sign up for applications by using following methods:

1. Using their Social Accounts such as Facebook, Microsoft, Google, Amazon, Linkedin etc.
2. Local Accounts by creating new credentials which can be combination of email and password or username and password.
3. Enterprise Accounts.

Design Nugget 1: Consumer/User authentication by application is redirected to Social accounts or Enterprise Accounts using industry standard sign-in protocols such as Oauth, WS-Federation or SAML.
Design Nugget 2: Consumer facing Applications are called as Service Provider or Relying party and Social Accounts or Enterprise Accounts are called as Identity Providers.

Features and Advantages of Azure AD B2C

1. Azure Active Directory B2C is capable of supporting millions of users and billions of authentications per day.
2. Protects Consumer identities.
3. Advantage of Azure AD B2C is that it allows users to gain access to web applications and services while allowing the features of authentication and authorization to be factored out of the application code.
4. Advantage for application owner is that they don't have to create and manage infrastructure (Hardware & Software) for managing large database of B2C users.
5. Advantage for consumers is that they don't have to go through lengthy process of sign up.

Exercise 44: Create Azure AD B2C Tenant and Link it to Azure Subscription

1. Go to Azure portal @https://portal.azure.com
2. Click +New> In search box type **Azure Active Directory B2C** and press enter>In the search result click Azure Active Directory B2C> Click create> Create new B2C Tenant or Link to existing Tenant Blade opens>Select create new B2C Tenant and enter the required information and click create.

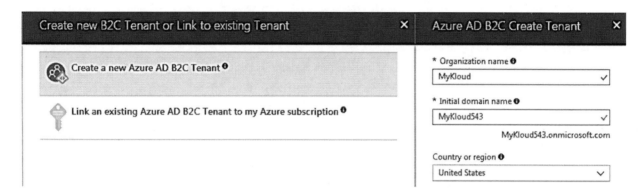

3. In the Create new B2C Tenant or Link to existing Tenant Blade which is still opens>Select Link existing Azure AD B2C Tenant to Azure Subscription> select AD B2C Tenant from Drop down box, Select Subscription and select or create Resource group>Select Pin to dashboard and click create.

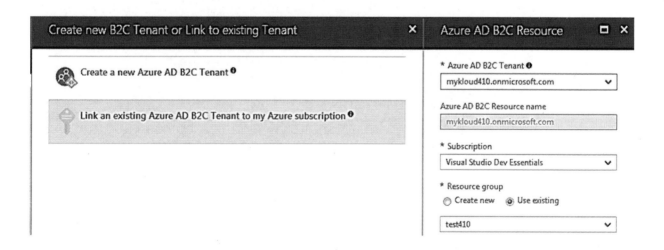

Note: mykloud410.onmicrosoft.com is B2C Tenant Domain name.

B2C Tenant Dashboard

Click Azure B2C Tenant in Azure Portal> Click Azure AD B2C setting> A new browser window will open as shown below.

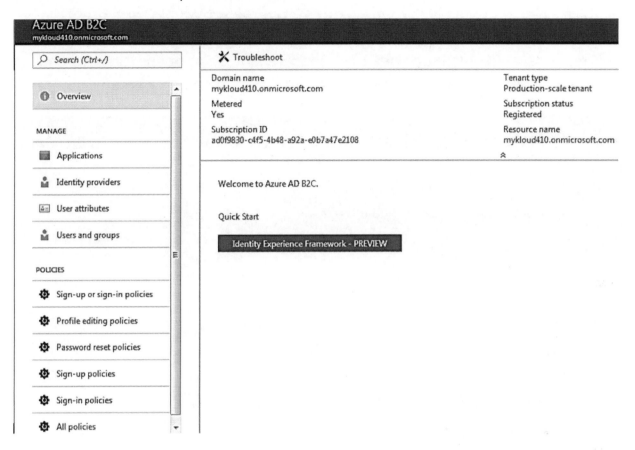

Here you can Add application if you want to add support for local accounts.

If you want to add support for Social account then register application with the Social Account Developer portal.

You can customize consumer sign-up or sign-in when they register with the application.

With User Attributes you can specify **Sign-up attributes** which you want to collect from the consumer during sign-up.

<u>To understand all the above options we will use 2 examples – one adding support for Local Accounts and other adding support for Facebook Social Account.</u>

Architecting Microsoft Azure Solutions Study & Lab Guide Part 1: Exam 70-535

Exercise 45: Adding support for Local account (email & Password)

1. **Register your application with B2C directory**. Go to B2C Dashboard >Click Applications>Click + Add. New Application Dialog Box Opens> Enter the information and click create.

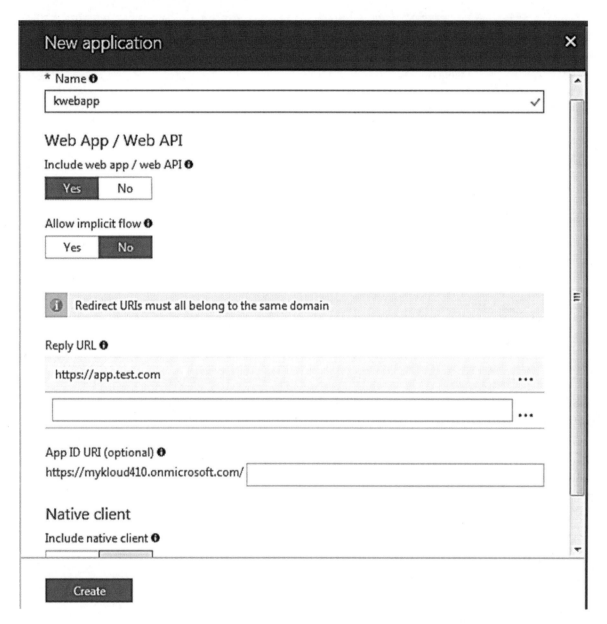

Redirect URI: Reply URLs are endpoints where Azure AD B2C returns any tokens that your application requests.

App ID URI: The App ID URI is the identifier used for your web API. The full identifier URI including the domain is generated for you.

Note 1: You need to select yes in web App as it is a Web application.

2. After App is registered>Click Application in B2C Dashboard>Click the app you registered>App properties blade opens>Note down the **application id.**

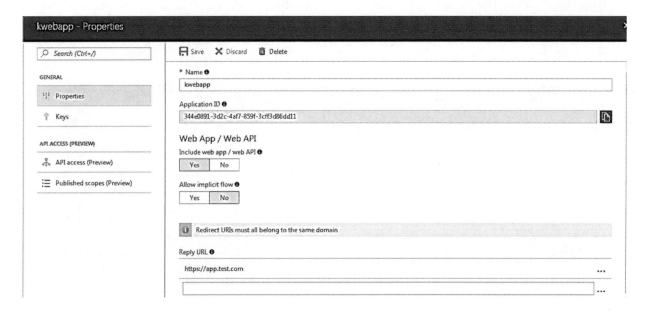

3A. Configure sign-in or sign up policies. This policy handles both consumer sign-up & sign-in with a single configuration. Click sign-up or sign-in policies in B2C Tenant dashboard>Click Add> Add Policy Blade opens> Enter name, identity Providers (**email signup**), sign up attribute, application claims information & Optional MAF.

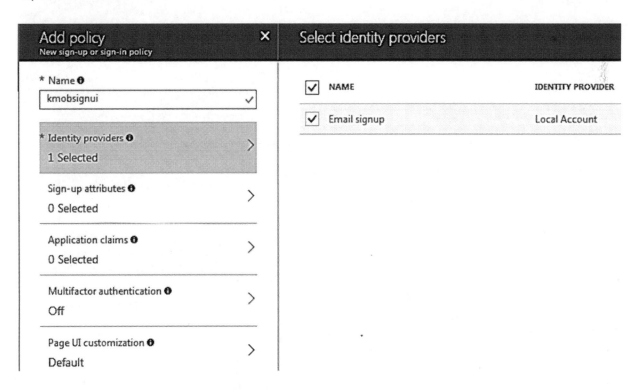

3B. Select **Sign-up attributes**. Choose attributes you want to collect from the consumer during sign-up. For example, check City, **Country/Region**, **Display Name &** Click **OK**.

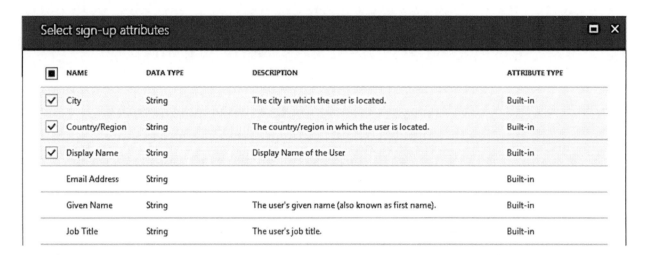

3C.   Select **Application claims**. Choose claims you want returned in the authorization tokens sent back to your application after a successful sign-up or sign-in experience. For example, select Country/Region, **Display Name and click ok.**

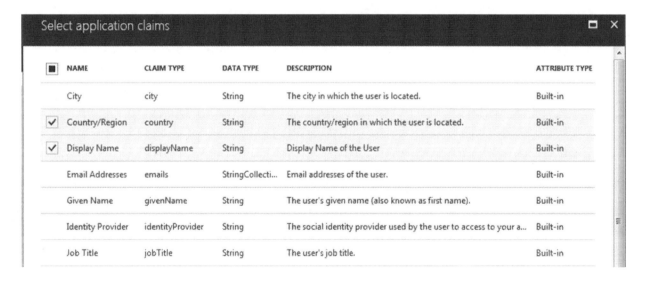

4. **Similarly Create Password Reset policy by clicking Password Reset Policies in left pane.**
5. Configure your application for email & Password sign-up and add information about B2C tenant name, Application id, sign-up or sign-in policy name & Reset Password Policy name.

Exercise 46: Adding support for Social Account in your App (Facebook)

Register your application with facebook @ https://developers.facebook.com/ and generate app id and secret key. Here you have to also specify the **Valid OAuth redirect URIs in the form of** https://login.microsoftonline.com/te/{tenant}/oauth2/authresp. Replace Tenant with B2C Tenant Domain name

1. **Configure Facebook as an identity provider**. In B2C Tenant Dashboard> Click identity providers>Click +Add> Add Identity Provider blade opens> Enter name> Click Identity Provider Type> Select Social Identity Provider Blade opens> Select Facebook as identity Provider>click ok.

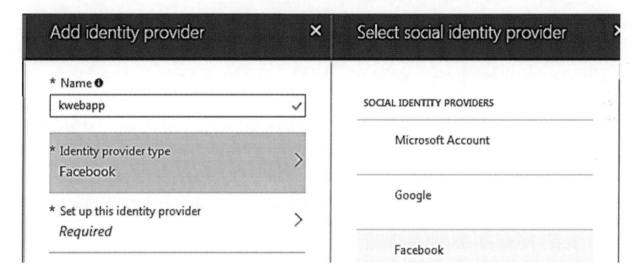

2. Click Set up this identity provider and enter the app ID and app secret (of the Facebook application that you created earlier in step 1) in the Client ID and Client secret fields respectively>click ok>click create.

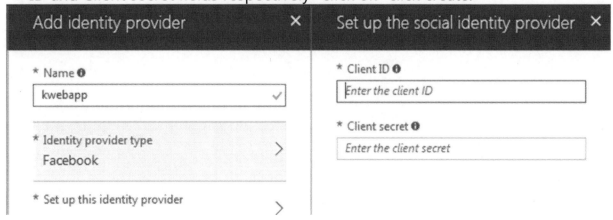

3. **Create or use existing sign-in or sign up policies**. This policy handles both consumer sign-up & sign-in with a single configuration. Here you can add depending upon your requirement single or Multiple identity Providers.

If sign-up or sign-in policy is already created then add Facebook as identity provider.

Create Sign-up or sign-in Policies: Click sign-up or sign-in policies in B2C Tenant dashboard>Click Add> Add Policy Blade opens> Enter name, Select Facebook as identity Provider, sign up attribute, application claims information & Optional MAF. (**These steps were shown in previous exercise**).

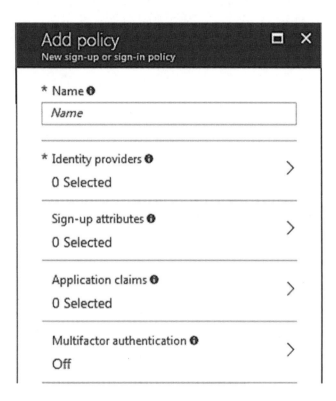

6. Configure your application for facebook sign-up and add information about B2C tenant name, Application id & Client secret, sign-up or sign-in policy name & Reset Password Policy name.

Azure Active Directory B2C Pricing

Azure Active Directory (Azure AD) B2C usage will be billed monthly based on the total number of **stored users and authentications.**

Stored Users: Users stored in the Azure AD B2C directory.

Authentications: Tokens issued either in response to a sign-in request initiated by a user or initiated by an application on behalf of a user (e.g. token refresh, where the refresh interval is configurable).

STORED USER/MONTH	Price
First 50,000	Free
Next 9,50,000	$0.0011
Next 90,00,000	$0.00094
Next 400,00,000	$0.00078
Greater than 500,00,000	$0.00063

AUTHENTICATIONS/MONTH	Price
First 50,000	Free
Next 9,50,000	$0.0028
Next 90,00,000	$0.0021
Next 400,00,000	$0.0014
Greater than 500,00,000	$0.0007

Case Study 10: Identity Management

A major cricket franchise of Indian Premier League (IPL) wants to engage its fans and monetize its website. The website has details of IPL matches, interview with cricket players, video highlights of the matches, Analysis by cricket experts, off field entertainment gossips, Sale of Merchandise and advertisement by their sponsors.

Fans who register with website, get access to additional contents, can post comments and are eligible for Prices.

They want fans to register with their social accounts – Facebook, Linkedin or Twitter or by registering with their email-id and password. They expect 250000 fans to register.

There requirement is that they do not want to maintain user accounts details. Another requirement is that user registration with the website should be very simple.

Suggest a solution which satisfies the above requirement.

Solution

We will use Azure Active Directory B2C for user identity Management.

With Azure Active Directory B2C, fans can sign up with website by using their existing social accounts (Facebook, Google or Linkedin etc) or by creating new credentials (email address and password, or username and password).

One of the advantage of B2C is that you need not maintain user account and password details and associated infrastructure (Like hardware, Databases and Directory services).

Advantage for consumers is that they don't have to go through lengthy process of sign up.

Sign-in Protocol: IPL Website will redirect user authentication to Facebook, Google or Linkedin using Sign-in protocols such as oauth2 or SAML or WS-Federation.

Step by Step Implementing identity management for IPL Franchise Web Application with Azure AD B2C

Step 1: Create Azure AD B2C Tenant.

Step 2: Add support for Local account (Email & Password sign-up)

1. Register your application with B2C directory. In B2C Dashboard>Click Applications>Add>Add Application blade Opens> Enter the information and click create.
2. In B2C dashboard go to the properties of Application registered in step 1 and note down Application Client ID that was generated.
3. In B2C dashboard create sign-up and sign-in policy. Select email as sign-up option. Also Configure sign up attribute, application claims information.
4. Configure your Website application for email & Password sign-up. In your website application code add information about B2C tenant name, Application id, sign-up or sign-in policy name & Reset Password Policy name.

Step 3: Adding support for Social Account – Facebook

1. Register your application with facebook. Go to facebook for developers @ https://developers.facebook.com/ and register your application and generate app id and secret key. Here you have to also specify the **Valid OAuth redirect URL in the form of** https://login.microsoftonline.com/te/{tenant}/oauth2/authresp. Here tenant is your B2C tenant name.
2. In B2C dashboard add Facebook as an identity provider and add App id and app secret created in step 1 in the Client ID and Client secret fields respectively.
3. In B2C dashboard create or use existing sign-up policy. Select Facebook as identity provider in sign-up option. Configure sign up attribute, application claims information.
4. Configure your Website application for Facebook sign-up. In your website application code add information about B2C tenant name, Application id, sign-up or sign-in policy name & Reset Password Policy name.

Note: For details about each step refer to Chapter

Azure Active Directory B2B

Azure Active Directory (Azure AD) B2B collaboration enables enterprises to grant access to corporate resources and applications for partner employees by using partner-managed identities.

B2B collaboration enables partners manage their own accounts and enterprises can apply security policies to partner access.

There's no need to add external users to your directory, sync them, or manage their lifecycle; IT can invite collaborators to use any email address—Office 365, on-premises Microsoft Exchange, or even a personal address (Outlook.com, Gmail, Yahoo!, etc.)—and even set up conditional access policies, including multi-factor authentication.

Developers can use the Azure AD B2B APIs to write applications that bring together different organizations in a secure way—and deliver a seamless and intuitive end user experience.

Advantages of B2B

1. Your business partners use their own sign-in credentials, which frees you from managing an external partner directory, and from the need to remove access when users leave the partner organization.
2. You manage access to your apps independently of your business partner's account lifecycle. This means, for example, that you can revoke access without having to ask the IT department of your business partner to do anything.

Easy Azure AD B2B Setup

Easy for admin of inviting organization to send invite.
No sign-up required only sign-in for partner employee.

Secure

Azure AD security features such as MFA, conditional access, identity protection and other security feature can be extended to partner identities.

Azure AD B2B Capabilities

1. Azure AD admins can invite external users.
2. Non admins like application owner can invite external users from Access panel @ https://myapps.microsoft.com
3. Support for Security features like MFA, Conditional Access for external users.
4. External users onboarding can be customized using **B2B Invitation API.**
5. For each paid license of Azure AD (Basic or Premium) you can add 5 B2B Users.

B2B Users

An Azure Active Directory (Azure AD) business-to-business (B2B) collaboration user is a user with UserType = Guest. This guest user typically is from a partner organization and has limited privileges in the inviting directory, by default. Note: If required you can change the privileges of guest users.

In some cases UserType = members. In this case users are from Same Azure AD tenant. For example supply chain depart of a contoso company has a app which is accessed by specific workers in supply chain department and invited employees of there vendors. A contoso worker in finance department also need to access to the app. Application owner of the app can send the invite to the worker in finance department using the Azure AD B2B Invitation Manager APIs to add or invite a user from the partner organization to the host organization as a member.

B2B users sign-in options

B2B collaborators can sign in with an identity of their choice. If the user doesn't have a Microsoft account or an Azure AD account – one is created for them seamlessly at the time for offer redemption.

1. With Microsoft account like outlook/Hotmail.com
2. Gmail/yahoo mail account
3. Partner domain account (testuser@contoso.com)
4. Azure AD account (If partner has its own Azure AD tenant)

Admin Adding B2B Users

1. Go to Azure AD Dashboard>Users and Groups>All Users>**Click +New Guest User**>Invite a Guest Blade opens>Enter Data as per your requirement> Click Invite (Not shown).

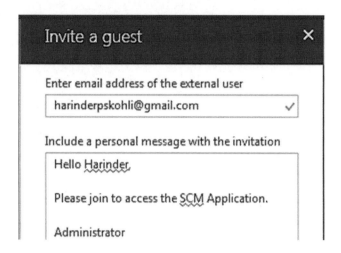

Figure below show harinderpskohli added as user type guest

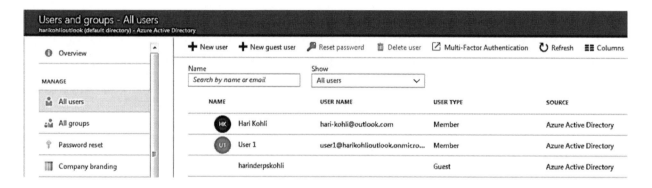

Adding B2B users directly at application level by application owner

Admins can delegate permission to add B2B users to non-admins. Non-admins can use the Azure AD Application Access Panel (https://myapps.microsoft.com) to add B2B collaboration users to applications. For this application must be enrolled for single sign-on in Azure AD Application Access Panel.

B2B License Pricing

For each paid license of Azure AD (Basic or Premium) you can add 5 B2B Users.

You can also add B2B users with Azure AD free edition without requiring any license. But in this case B2B users will be limited to features of Azure AD Free edition.

There is no need to assign licenses to B2B user accounts. Based on the 5:1 ratio, licensing is automatically calculated and reported.

If a B2B collaboration user already has a paid Azure AD license from their organization, they do not consume one of the B2B collaboration licenses of the inviting tenant.

Case Study 11: Licensing Case Study 1

A customer wants to invite 50 B2B collaboration users to its Azure AD tenant. B2B users require features of Azure AD Basic edition only. How many licenses customer should have for 50 B2B Collaboration users.

Solution: B2B licensing states that for each paid license of Azure AD (Basic or Premium) you can add 5 B2B Users.
Based on 5:1 Ratio you will require 10 licenses of Azure AD Basic Edition.

Case Study 12: Licensing Case Study 2

A customer wants to invite 100 B2B collaboration users to its Azure AD tenant. 50 of the B2B users require features of Basic edition. 30 users require MFA feature. 20 Users require both MFA & identity protection feature. How many licenses customer should have for above 100 B2B Collaboration users.

Solution: MFA feature require Azure AD Premium P1 license. Identity Protection feature requires Azure AD Premium P2 License.
Using 5:1 ratio you will require 10 licenses of Azure AD Basic, 6 licenses of Azure AD Premium P1 and 4 licenses of Azure AD Premium P2.

Comparing B2C and B2B

Both Azure Active Directory (Azure AD) B2B collaboration and Azure AD B2C allow you to work with external users in Azure AD. Table below shows difference between B2B and B2C.

Azure AD B2B collaboration	Azure AD B2C
Intended for Organizations that want to authenticate users from a partner organization, regardless of identity provider.	**Intended for** customers of your mobile and web apps, whether individuals, institutional or organizational customers into your Azure AD.
Identities supported: Employees with work or school accounts, partners with work or school accounts, or any email address.	**Identities supported**: Consumer users with local application accounts (any email address or user name) or any supported social identity with direct federation.
Directory: users from the external organization are managed in the same directory as employees, but added as guest users.	**Directory**: Managed separately from the organization's employee Directory.
Single sign-on (SSO) to all Azure AD-connected apps is supported.	**Single sign-on (SSO)** to customer owned apps within the Azure AD B2C tenants is supported.
Partner lifecycle: Managed by the host/inviting organization.	**Customer lifecycle**: Self-serve or managed by the application.
Security policy and compliance: Managed by the host/inviting organization.	**Security policy and compliance**: Managed by the application.
Branding: Host/inviting organization's brand is used.	**Branding**: Managed by application.

Chapter 13 Administering and Protecting Resources with Azure AD

This Chapter covers following Topic Lessons

- Role Based Access Control
- Azure AD Privileged Identity Management
- Azure AD Managed Service Identity (MSI)
- Azure Active Directory (AD) Application Proxy
- Conditional Access in Azure AD
- Azure Active Directory Identity Protection

This Chapter Covers following Case Studies

- Secure Remote Access to on-premises Application

This Chapter Covers following Lab Exercises to build below topology

- Assigning Backup Contributor role to user2 at Resource Level (Storage Account sa535)

Role Based Access Control

Before going into RBAC let's discuss why we need it in first place. Unlimited access to users in Azure can be security threat. Too few permissions means that users can't get their work done efficiently.

Azure Role-Based Access Control (RBAC) helps address above problem by offering fine-grained access management for Azure resources. With RBAC users are given amount of access based on their Job Roles. For example, use RBAC to let one employee manage virtual machines in a subscription, while another can manage SQL databases.

Role Based Access Management in Azure

You can assign roles to users, groups, and applications at a certain level. The level of a role assignment can be a subscription, a resource group, or a single resource.

Figure below shows RBAC can be assigned to User, Group & Application and can be applied at Subscription or Resource Group or single resource level.

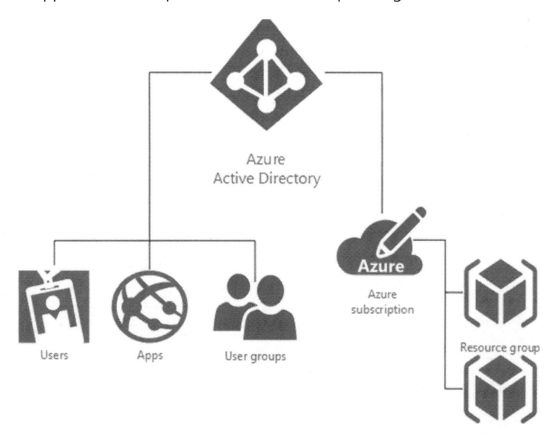

Azure RBAC Built-in roles

Owner has full access to all resources including the right to delegate access to others.
Contributor can create and manage all types of Azure resources but can't grant access to others.
Reader can view existing Azure resources.

Azure RBAC Scope and Assignment

Scope: RBAC role assignments are scoped to a specific subscription, resource group, or resource.
A user given access to a single resource cannot access any other resources in the same subscription.
A role assigned at a parent scope also grants access to the children contained within it. For example, a user with access to a resource group can manage all the resources it contains, like websites, virtual machines, and Virtual Networks etc.

Role: Within the scope of the assignment, access is narrowed even further by assigning a role. Roles can be high-level, like owner, or specific, like virtual machine reader.

Following is a **partial list** of built-in roles available.

RBAC Built in Roles	Description
Backup Contributor	Can manage backup in Recovery Services vault.
Backup Operator	Can manage backup except removing backup, in Recovery Services vault.
Backup Reader	Can view all backup management services.
BizTalk Contributor	Can manage BizTalk services.
Azure Cosmos DB Account Contributor	Can manage Azure Cosmos DB accounts.
Network Contributor	Can manage all network resources.
SQL DB Contributor	Can manage SQL databases, but not their security-related policies.
User Access Administrator	Can manage user access to Azure resources.
Virtual Machine Contributor	Can create and manage virtual machines, but not the virtual network or storage.

Custom Roles

Custom Roles in Azure Role Based Access control (RBAC) are created and used when none of the built-in roles meet user's specific access needs.

Just like built-in roles, you can assign custom roles to users, groups, and applications at subscription, resource group, and at individual resource level.

Custom Roles can be created by using Azure PowerShell, Azure Command-Line Interface (CLI) and REST API. Custom roles are stored in an Azure AD tenant and can be shared across subscriptions. Each tenant can create up to 2000 custom roles.

Following example shows a custom role for monitoring and restarting virtual machines:

```
{
  "Name": "Virtual Machine Operator",
  "Id": "cadb4a5a-4e7a-47be-84db-05cad13b6769",
  "IsCustom": true,
  "Description": "Can monitor and restart virtual machines.",
  "Actions": [
    "Microsoft.Storage/*/read",
    "Microsoft.Network/*/read",
    "Microsoft.Compute/*/read",
    "Microsoft.Compute/virtualMachines/start/action",
    "Microsoft.Compute/virtualMachines/restart/action",
    "Microsoft.Authorization/*/read",
    "Microsoft.Resources/subscriptions/resourceGroups/read",
    "Microsoft.Insights/alertRules/*",
    "Microsoft.Insights/diagnosticSettings/*",
  ],
  "NotActions": [
  ],
  "AssignableScopes": [
    "/subscriptions/c276fc76-9cd4-44c9-99a7-4fd71546436e",
    "/subscriptions/e91d47c4-76f3-4271-a796-21b4ecfe3624",
  ]
}
```

The **Actions** property of a custom role specifies the Azure operations which can be performed by custom role. **NotActions** property of a custom role specifies operations that are to be excluded. The **AssignableScopes** property of the custom role specifies the scopes (subscriptions, resource groups, or resources) within which the custom role is available for assignment.

The access granted by a custom role is computed by subtracting the **NotActions** operations from the **Actions** operations.

Exercise 47: Assigning Backup Contributor role to user2 at Resource Level (Storage Account sa535)

1. **Checking various Roles Available in a Resource using IAM functionality:**
   Go to Storage Account (sa535) Dashboard>Click Access Control (IAM) in left Pane > Click +Add in right pane> Add permission blade opens>Click the dropdown box in Role>you can see various roles available. Scroll down to see more roles.

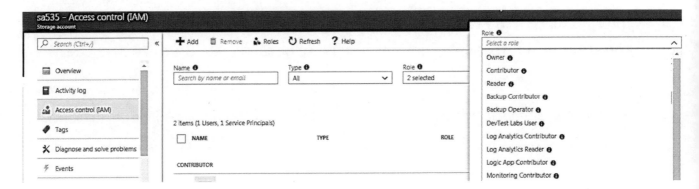

2. **Assigning Backup Contributor Role**: Choose Backup Contributor role from role dropdown box>Select User2>click save.

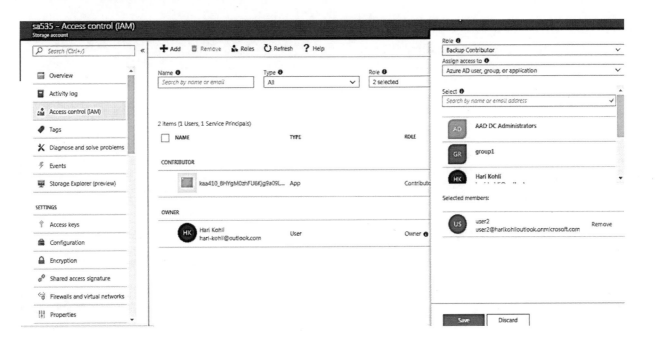

3. Log on to Azure portal with user2 email-id and password. Email-id of user2 is: user2@harikohlioutlook.onmicrosoft.com.

You can see that user2 has only one resource which is Storage account sa535 to manage.

Additional Exercise

As an exercise to readers assign role to user2 at resource group level and check in portal what resources it can manage.

Note: In this case user2 can manage all resources created under resource group.

Azure AD Privileged Identity Management

Azure Active Directory Privileged Identity Management is a feature of the Azure AD Premium P2 edition. Azure AD comes in four editions – Free, Basic, Premium P1 and Premium P2.

Before going into Privileged Identity Management let's discuss why we need it in first place. Organizations want to minimize the number of people who have access to secure information or resources, because that reduces the chance of a malicious user getting that access, or an authorized user inadvertently impacting a sensitive resource.

Azure AD Privileged Identity Management helps you manage and protect **privileged/Administrative accounts** so that you can restrict and monitor administrators and their access to resources and provide just-in-time access when needed.

Managing & Monitoring Administrative access with Privileged Identity Management

1. See which users are Azure AD administrators.
2. Enable on-demand, "just in time" administrative access using the concept of an **eligible admin**.
3. Get reports about administrator access history and changes in administrator assignments.
4. Get alerts about access to a privileged role.

Just in time administrator access with Eligible Admin

Azure AD Privileged Identity Management introduces the concept of an **eligible admin. Eligible admin is given just in time administrative access** for a predetermined amount of time.

Eligible admin role is inactive until the user needs access. When they need access they need to complete an activation process and become an active admin for a predetermined amount of time.

Enable Privileged Identity Management for your directory

1. https://portal.azure.com
2. Click +Create a Resource> Identity>Azure AD Privileged Identity Management> Privileged Identity Management Blade opens>Click Create.

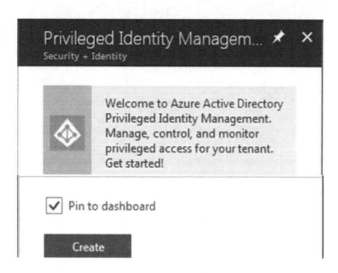

Privileged Identity Management dashboard

Azure AD Privileged Identity Management dashboard provides following information:

1. Alerts that point out opportunities to improve security.
2. The number of users who are assigned to each privileged role.
3. The number of eligible and permanent admins.
4. Ongoing access reviews.

Figure below shows Privileged Identity Management dashboard.

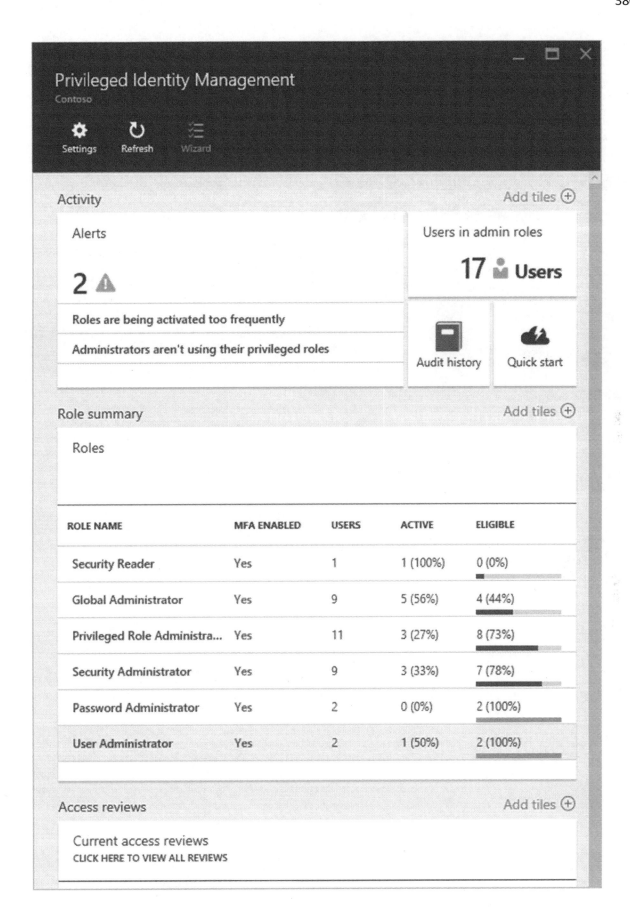

Roles managed in PIM

With Privileged Identity Management you can assign following administrator roles to users:

1. **Global administrator** has access to all administrative features. You can have more than one global admin in your organization.
2. **Privileged role administrator** manages Azure AD PIM and updates role assignments for other users.
3. **Billing administrator** makes purchases, manages subscriptions, manages support tickets, and monitors service health.
4. **Password administrator** resets passwords, manages service requests, and monitors service health. Password admins are limited to resetting passwords for users.
5. **Service administrator** manages service requests and monitors service health.
6. **User management administrator** resets passwords, monitors service health, and manages user accounts, user groups, and service requests. The user management admin can't delete a global admin, create other admin roles, or reset passwords for billing, global, and service admins.
7. **Exchange administrator** has administrative access to Exchange Online through the Exchange admin center (EAC), and can perform almost any task in Exchange Online.
8. **SharePoint administrator** has administrative access to SharePoint Online through the SharePoint Online admin center, and can perform almost any task in SharePoint Online.
9. **Skype for Business administrator** has administrative access to Skype for Business through the Skype for Business admin center, and can perform almost any task in Skype for Business Online.

Azure AD Managed Service Identity (MSI)

Before going into Managed Service Identity (MSI) let's discuss why we need it in first place. A common challenge when building cloud applications is how to securely manage the credentials that needs to be in your code for authenticating to cloud services. Adding security credentials in application code or applying to Azure VM is not only a security problem but also an operational & Administrative Overhead.

For Example you want to mount Azure File share on Azure Windows VM. When running net use command on Azure windows VM to mount File share you will also need to enter storage account access keys. Entering Storage Account key in Azure Windows VM is a security loophole as well as administrative overhead. Shown below is net use command entered in Azure windows VM command line:

net use Z: \\kstor.file.core.windows.net\kfs /u:kstor <**Storage Account Access Key**>. Here kstor is Storage Account name and kfs is Azure file share name.

Managed Service Identity (MSI) solves this problem by giving Azure services an automatically managed identity in Azure Active Directory (Azure AD). You can use this identity to authenticate to any service that supports Azure AD authentication, including Key Vault, without having any credentials in your code or in your Azure Virtual Server.

Azure Services on which MSI can be enabled

Azure Virtual Machines
Azure App Services
Azure Functions

Azure services that support Azure AD authentication

The following services support Azure AD authentication request from Azure client services that use Managed Service Identity.

Azure Resource Manager
Azure Key Vault
Azure Data Lake | Azure SQL | Azure Storage

Enabling MSI on Azure VMs

1. Log on to Azure Portal @ https://portal.azure.com
2. Go to Azure VM Dashboard on which you want to enable MSI>Click Configuration under services in left panel>Click yes to enable MSI on the VM.

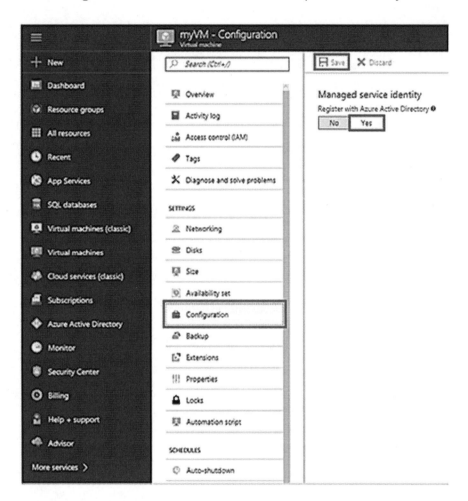

Result of Enabling MSI on Azure VM

When MSI is enabled on Azure VM, Azure Resource Manager creates a Service Principal in Azure AD to represent the identity of the VM.

Azure Resource Manager also configures the Service Principal details of the MSI VM Extension in the VM by configuring client ID and certificate used by the extension to get access tokens from Azure AD.

Step By Step Azure AD MSI Working

Figure below shows working of MSI.

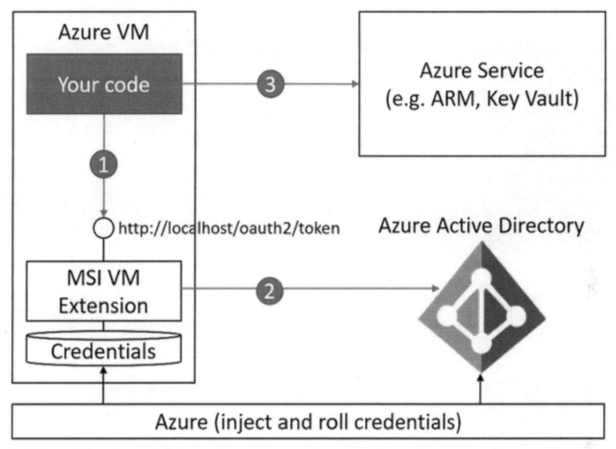

1. When The Azure VM needs to authenticate to Azure Resource, Your code running on the VM requests a token from a local endpoint that is hosted by the MSI VM extension by sending request @ http://localhost/oauth2/token
2. The MSI VM Extension uses its configured client ID and certificate to request an access token from Azure AD. Azure AD returns a JSON Web Token (JWT) access token.
3. Your code sends the access token on a call to a service that supports Azure AD authentication.

Managed Service Identity Pricing

MSI is part of Azure AD. There is no additional cost for Managed Service Identity.

Azure AD Application Proxy

Azure Active Directory (AD) Application Proxy publishes on-premises applications to be accessed over the internet by the remote users.

Application Proxy provides Remote Access as a Services (RASaaS).

Remote users access on-premises application through internet via Application Proxy service running in Azure cloud. Application Proxy service obviates the need to setup VPN on-premises.

Figure below shows internet users accessing on-premises application through Application Proxy service.

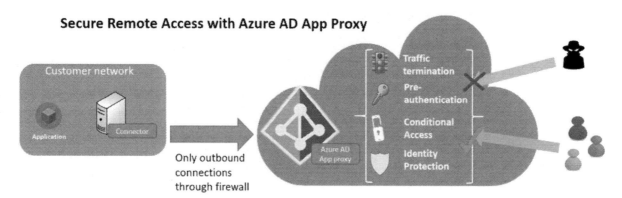

Advantages of Application Proxy

The biggest advantage of application proxy is that you don't need to configure any VPN on-premises for remote users to access the applications. Installing & Configuring VPN is a complex job and requires professional services from the system integrator.

Secondly user authentication is integrated very easily.

Thirdly application proxy solution provides enhanced security as all external user connects to on-premises application through application proxy service.

You no longer need DMZ on premises to publish your application to internet.

Azure AD Application Proxy Components

Azure AD Application Proxy consists of two components.

1. Cloud based application proxy service.
2. The Azure AD Application Proxy connector which is installed on-premises on a windows server.

Application Proxy prerequisites

1. Azure AD with Basic or Premium Subscription.
2. On-premises windows server.

Application Proxy Security Features

Authenticated access: Only authenticated connections can access the on prem network.

Conditional access: With conditional access, it is possible to further define restrictions on what traffic is allowed to access your back-end applications. You can define restrictions based on location, strength of authentication, and user risk profile.

Traffic termination: All traffic is terminated in the cloud. Back-end servers are not exposed to direct HTTP traffic.

All access is outbound: You don't need to open inbound connections to the corporate network. Azure AD connectors maintain outbound connections to the Azure AD Application Proxy service, which means that there is no need to open firewall ports for incoming connections.

Conditional Access in Azure AD

Azure Conditional Access is a feature of the Azure AD Premium P2 edition.

Before going into Conditional Access in Azure AD let's discuss why we need it in first place. In today's Cloud and Mobile era users are accessing corporate applications & services not only from on-premises but also from home or anywhere in world using corporate owned or personal devices.

Corporate IT Administrators are faced with two opposing goals:

1. Empower the end users to be productive wherever and whenever.
2. Protect the corporate assets.

With Conditional Access you can balance both the above goals.

Conditional access is a capability of Azure Active Directory that enables you to enforce controls on the access to apps in your environment based on specific conditions.
With controls, you can either **block access** or **allow access** or **allow access with additional requirements**. The implementation of conditional access is based on policies.

Figure below shows that upto 6 conditions can be applied before access to cloud apps is allowed or blocked.

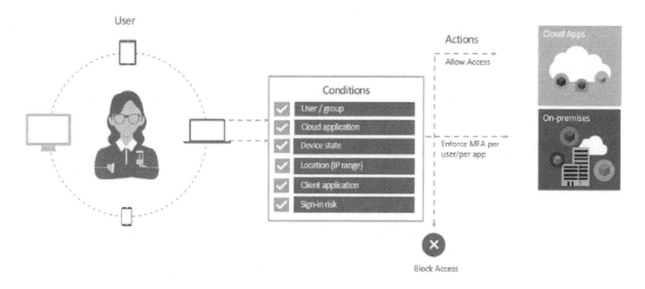

Conditional Access Policy

The combination of a condition statement with controls represents a conditional access policy. Figure below shows components of conditional access policy.

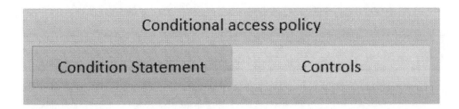

Based on the result of condition statement, controls are applied.

Condition Statements

In a conditional access policy, condition statements are criteria that need to be met for your controls to be applied.

You can include the **following 3 criteria's** into your condition statement:

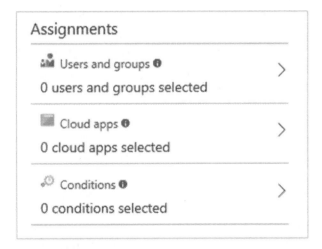

1. **Users & Groups**: In conditional access policy, you need to select the users or groups your policy applies to.

2. **Cloud Application**: In conditional access policy, you need to select the cloud application your policy applies to.

Conditions: In conditional access policy, you can define 4 conditions:

Sign-in risk | Device platforms | Locations | Client application

3. **Sign-in risk**: Sign-in risk level is used as a condition in a conditional access policy.

4. **Device Platform**: In a conditional access policy, you can configure the device platform condition to tie the policy to the operating system on a client. Azure AD conditional access supports the following device platforms:

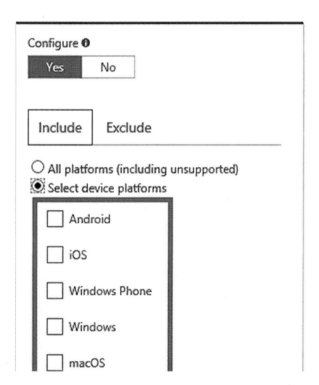

5. **Location**: In a conditional access policy, you can define conditions that are based on where a connection attempt was initiated from. The entries in the locations list are either **named locations** or **MFA trusted IPs**.

Named locations is a feature of Azure Active Directory that allows you to define labels for the locations connection attempts were made from. To define a location, you can either configure an IP address ranges or you select a country / region.

MFA trusted IPs is a feature of multi-factor authentication that enables you to define trusted IP address ranges representing your organization's local intranet. When you configure a location condition, Trusted IPs enables you to distinguish between connections made from your organization's network and all other locations.

6. **Client Apps**: The client apps condition allows you to apply a policy based on Client application type – Browser, Mobile apps or Desktop client.

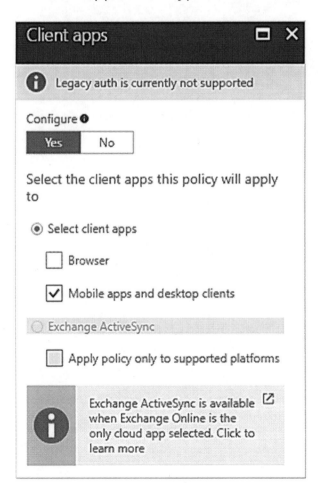

Controls

In a conditional access policy, controls define what it is that should happen when a condition statement has been satisfied.
With controls, you can either **block access** or **allow access** or **allow access with additional requirements**. When you configure a policy that allows access, you need to select at least one requirement.

There are two types of controls: Grant Control and Session Control.

Grant Control: Grant controls govern whether or not a user can complete authentication and reach the resource that they're attempting to sign-in to. Azure AD enables you to configure the following grant control requirements:

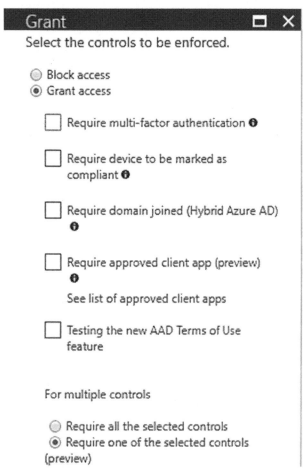

Session Control: Session controls enable limiting experience within a cloud app. The session controls are enforced by cloud apps and rely on additional information provided by Azure AD to the app about the session.

Azure Active Directory Identity Protection

Before going into Azure AD Identity Protection let's discuss why we need it in first place. The vast majority of security breaches take place when attackers gain access to an environment by stealing a user's identity.

<u>Azure AD Identity Protection helps in detecting and remediating compromised user identities by configuring risk-based policies that automatically respond to detected issues when a specified risk level has been reached.</u>

Azure Active Directory Identity Protection provides risk-based conditional access to your applications and critical company data. Identity Protection uses adaptive machine learning algorithms and heuristics to detect anomalies and risk events that may indicate that an identity has been compromised. Using this data, Identity Protection generates reports and alerts that enable you to investigate these risk events and take appropriate remediation or mitigation action.

Azure Active Directory Identity Protection is a feature of the Azure AD Premium P2 edition.

Azure AD Identity Protection Function

1. Get a consolidated view of flagged users and risk events detected using machine learning algorithms.
2. Improve security posture by acting on vulnerabilities.
3. Set risk-based Conditional Access policies to automatically protect your users from impending security breaches. Identity protection offers 3 Risk based policies to configure - Azure **Multi-factor Authentication registration policy, User risk policy & sign-in risk policy.**

Enabling Azure Active Directory Identity Protection

1. Log on to Azure Portal @ **https://portal.azure.com**
2. Click +Create a resource> Identity>Azure AD Identity Protection> Privileged Identity Management Blade opens>Click Create.

Azure AD Identity Protection Dashboard

Figure below show Identity Protection dashboard. It has 3 Mini Dashboards – **Users flagged for Risk, Risk Events and Vulnerabilities**.

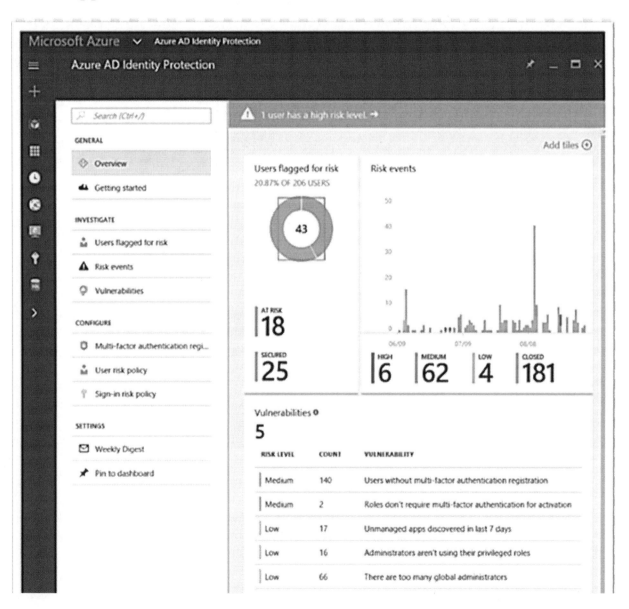

Users Flagged for Risk: These are users in your directory whose credentials might be compromised based on observed patterns of behavior. The chart shows you the number of users who are currently at risk as well as users who had risk events that were already remediated.

Clicking on the chart opens a blade which gives the list of users and the reason why they're flagged. From there, you can further investigate individual users by clicking on their names. Identity Protection provides you the IP address, location, timestamp of the sign-in and all other relevant information.

Remediating Risk: After you have investigated, you can remediate risk events by resetting the user's password—this takes control away from any attacker who had the previous password.

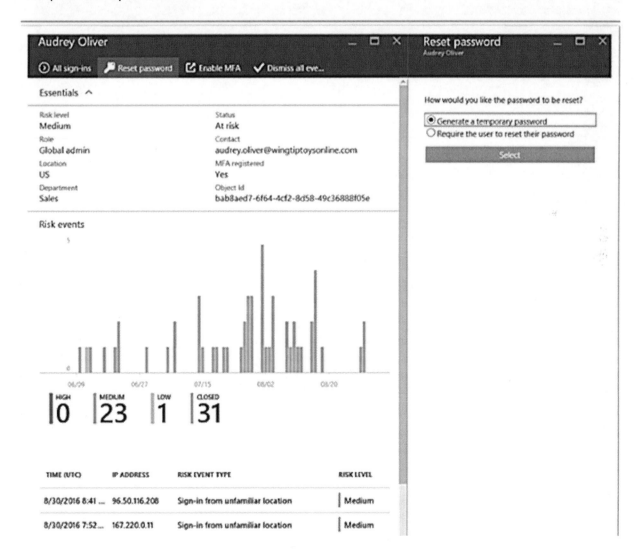

Risk events

These are events that Identity Protection has flagged as high risk and indicate that an identity may have been compromised. Currently, Identity Protection flags six types of risk events.

1. Users with leaked credentials
2. Irregular sign-in activity
3. Sign-ins from possibly infected devices
4. Sign-ins from unfamiliar locations
5. Sign-ins from IP addresses with suspicious activity
6. Sign-ins from impossible travel

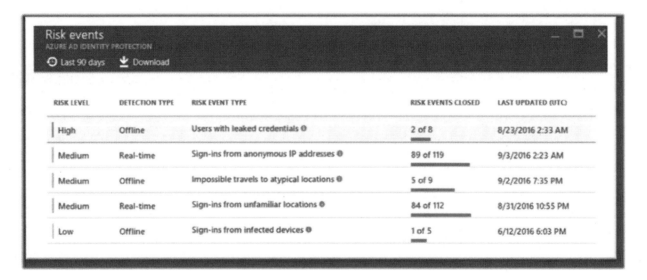

Vulnerabilities

These are weaknesses in your environment that can be exploited by an attacker. It is recommended that you address these vulnerabilities to improve the security posture of your organization and prevent attackers from exploiting these vulnerabilities. Identity Protection detects the following types of vulnerabilities.

1. Users not registered for multi-factor authentication
2. Unmanaged apps discovered in last 7 days
3. Security Alerts from Privileged Identity Management

Security Policies

Identity Protection offers 3 types of security policies to help protect your organization.

Azure Multi-factor Authentication registration policy: Azure **Multi-factor Authentication registration policy** helps you manage and monitor the roll-out of multi-factor authentication registration by enabling you to define which employees are included in the policy, configure how long they are allowed to skip registration, and view the current registration state of impacted users.

User risk policy: This is a Conditional Access policy which helps block risky users from signing in, or forces them to securely change their password. You can control which action (block or secure password change) is triggered at different risk levels depending your organization's risk tolerance.

Sign-in risk policy: This is a Conditional Access policy to automatically mitigate sign-in risk. You can configure a sign-in risk policy to block user sign-in or require multi-factor authentication at different risk thresholds (high/medium/low). Similar to user risk policy, the policy blade provides an estimated policy impact.

Case Study 13: Secure Remote Access to on-premises Application

A regional confectionary company in USA manufactures and sells its products like cookies, cakes & chocolates to consumers in the state of California. Products are sold to consumer's indirectly through retailers.

There sales people visit the retailer for order booking every week. The stock is then delivered directly to retailers by the company. To clear the stock they also offer promotional schemes to retailers.

They have custom developed core business application which shows the stock position, retailer payment due & promotions. The application is hosted in on-premise Data Center. On-premise Data Center has one Cisco firewall.

All IT Resources are accessed from within the internal network except for core business application and Mail which accessed by sales reps and top management both on desktop & mobile (Android & Apple) from internet. To provide access to Business application from internet, SSL VPN has been setup on Cisco ASA Firewall. Total 15 users access the Business application from outside the corporate network.

Recently they had a security breach where in excel worksheet containing details of retailers and inventory was downloaded.

They don't have big IT budget. They have one system admin who manages everything. There VAR is small time IT Company which lacks skills to implement security solutions.

They recently got a quote from a big IT VAR for implementing security solutions. It consists of new firewall, IPS and identity management and cost was around 40000 USD. This was beyond their budget.

They are looking for a solution to protect their applications from security breaches. They want a simple and cost effective solution. They also don't want skilled resources and administrative overheads of managing the security solution.

Suggest a solution which satisfies above requirement with cost breakup.

Solution

We will use Azure Active Directory (AD) Application Proxy for protecting on-premises Business application.

With Azure Active Directory (AD) Application Proxy all access to Business application will happen through Application Proxy service running in Azure cloud. Application Proxy service obviates the need to setup VPN on-premises.

Figure below shows internet users accessing on-premises application through Application Proxy service.

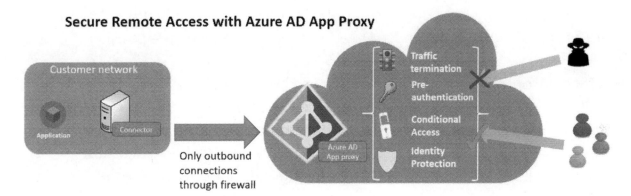

Application Proxy Security Features

Traffic termination: All traffic is terminated in the cloud. Back-end servers are not exposed to direct HTTP traffic.

All access is outbound: You don't need to open inbound connections to the corporate network. Azure AD connectors maintain outbound connections to the Azure AD Application Proxy service, which means that there is no need to open firewall ports for incoming connections.

Authenticated access: Only authenticated connections can access the on premises network. We will configure only 15 users who can access Business application from outside the corporate network.

Conditional access: With conditional access, it is possible to further define restrictions on what traffic is allowed to access your back-end applications. You can define restrictions based on location, strength of authentication, and user risk profile.

Cost of the Solution

We will use Azure AD Basic or Premium P1 Licenses or Premium P2 License. All the 3 license options provide Application Proxy feature. Azure AD Premium P1 license provides additional capability of conditional Access. Azure AD Premium P2 license provides additional capability of identity protection.

License	License cost (USD)/Month	Number of users	Total Cost/Month (USD)	Total Cost/Year (USD)
Basic	1	15	15	180
Premium P1	6	15	90	1350
Premium P2	9	15	135	2025

The above costing was submitted to the company management and they decided to go with Premium P1 License.

Advantages of the solution

The biggest advantage of application proxy is that we don't need to configure any advanced firewall & IPS features and VPN on-premises for remote users to access the applications. Installing & Configuring VPN is a complex job and requires professional services from the system integrator.

Solution is very cost effective as compared to on-premises cost of implementing the solution which was USD 40000.

You also don't require skilled resources to manage the solution.

Chapter 14 Azure Key Vault

This Chapter covers following

- Azure Key Vault
- Software and HSM Protected Keys
- Step by Step creating and using Azure Key Vault with Application
- SQL Server Transparent Data Encryption using Azure Key Vault
- Using Key Vault Secret with ARM Templates
- Using Certificates with Key Vault
- Securing Azure Key Vault Management and Data Plane
- Key Rotation
- Key Logging
- Soft Delete

This Chapter Covers following Lab Exercises to build below topology

- Step by Step creating and using Azure Key Vault with Application

Chapter Topology

In this chapter we will add Key Vault to the topology.

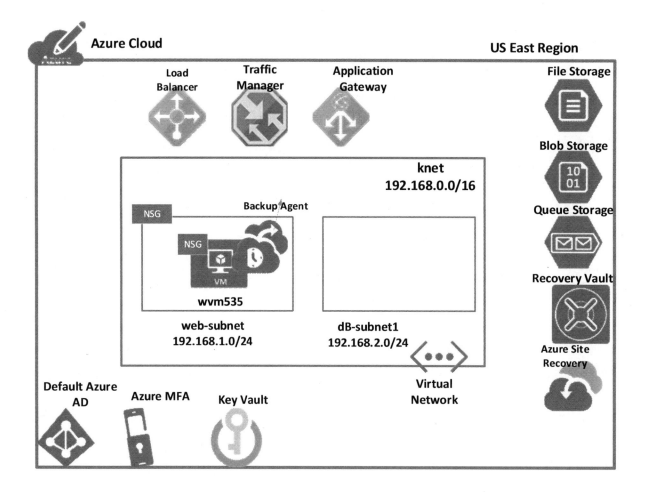

Azure Key Vault

Before going into Key Vault, lets discuss why we need it in first place. A common challenge when building cloud applications is how to securely manage the Security Keys or secret that needs to be in your code for authenticating to another application or service. Adding security credentials in application code is not only a security problem but also an operational & Administrative Overhead.

Azure Key Vault provides key management as a service.

Azure Key Vault stores and safeguard cryptographic keys, secrets and certificates used by cloud applications and services for authentication and encryption of data.

Keys are stored in a Key vault and invoked by URL when needed by applications. Keys are safeguarded by Azure, using industry-standard algorithms, key lengths, and hardware security modules (HSMs).

Key Vaults provides following 3 options to protect your sensitive data:

Keys: Keys are RSA 2048 bit asymmetric keys. Keys can be generated by the Key Vault or can be imported. Keys can be software-protected or HSM- Protected. RSA 3072 bit and 4096 bit keys are in preview.

Secrets: Key Vault accepts any value as a secret, and these are stored in binary.

Certificates: You can create self-signed or signed by a supported certificate authority or you can import a certificate.

Design Nugget

Azure key vault works on a per region basis. What this means is that an Azure key vault resource should be provisioned at the same region where the application and service is deployed. If a deployment consists of more than one region and needs services from Azure key vault, multiple Azure key vault instances should be provisioned.

Key Vault Advantages

1. When you change the security key or secret you not need redeploy application as application get the updated key or secret from the Azure Key Vault automatically.

2. You can separate the application administration function and security administration function. Security can now be centrally managed by the Security operations team.

3. Azure Key vault provides additional security ability by granting access to keys only to application which are registered with Azure AD.

Key Vault Features

1. **Encrypt keys and small secrets** like passwords using keys in Hardware Security Modules (HSMs).
2. **Import or generate your keys in HSMs certified to FIPS 140-2 level 2 standards** for added assurance, so that your keys stay within the HSM boundary.
3. **Simplify and automate tasks** for SSL/TLS certificates, enroll and automatically renew certificates from supported public certification authorities(CA).
4. **Manage and automatically rotate** Azure Storage account keys, and use shared access signatures to avoid direct contact with the keys.
5. **Provision and deploy new vaults and keys in minutes** without waiting for procurement, hardware, or IT, and centrally manage keys, secrets, and policies.
6. **Maintain control over encrypted data**—grant and revoke key use by both your own and third-party applications as needed.
7. **Segregate key management** duties to enable developers to easily manage keys used for dev/test, and migrate seamlessly to production keys managed by security operations.
8. **Rapidly scale** to meet the cryptographic needs of your cloud applications and match peak demand.
9. **Achieve global redundancy** by provisioning vaults in Azure datacenters worldwide, and keep a copy in your own HSM for added durability.

Software-Protected and HSM-Protected Keys

Key Vault stores Secrets, Keys and Certificated in Hardware Security Module (HSM).

With **Software-Protected keys**, Secrets, Keys and Certificates are stored in Hardware Security Module (HSM) but cryptographic operations (encryption and decryption) are performed in software.

With **HSM-Protected Keys** not only Secrets, Keys and Certificates are stored in Hardware Security Module (HSM) but cryptographic operations (encryption and decryption) are also performed directly on Hardware Security Module (HSM). Using Azure Key Vault, you can import or generate keys in hardware security modules (HSMs) that never leave the HSM boundary.

Use case for Software-Protected keys: Software-protected keys are used for test & development workloads.

Use case for HSM-Protected keys: HSM-Protected keys are preferred for production workloads.

Design Nugget 1: Azure Key Vault uses Thales nShield family of HSMs to protect your keys.
Design Nugget 2: To generate HSM-Protected keys you need Azure Key Vault Premium Tier.
Design Nugget 3: Software keys can be exported from key Vault whereas HSM keys can never be exported.

Hardware Security Module (HSM)

A **hardware security module** (**HSM**) is a physical computing device that safeguards and manages digital keys for strong authentication and provides cryptoprocessing.
HSMs possess controls that provide tamper evidence such as logging and alerting and tamper resistance such as deleting keys upon tamper detection. Each module contains one or more secure cryptoprocessor chips to prevent tampering and bus probing.

Exercise 48: Step by Step creating and using Azure Key Vault with Application

1. Create Azure Key Vault and note down the URL of Key vault DNS name.
2. Create a secret using key vault Dashboard.
3. Register the application with Azure AD. Note down the client id and client secret generated.
4. Authorize the application registered with Azure AD in step 3 to access key vault data plane using access policies.
5. In your application code add URL of the key vault generated in step 1 and client id and client secret generated in Step 3.

Step 1 - Creating Key vault

1. In Azure Portal Click +New> Click Security + Identity> Click Key Vault>create key vault blade open> Enter the information as per your req>click create.

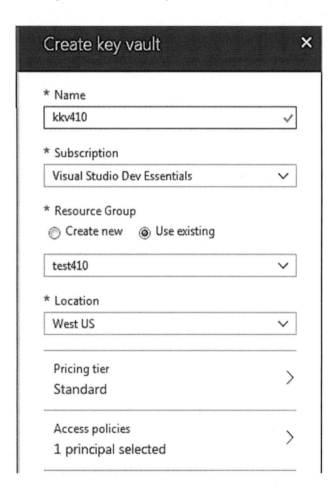

Step 2 - Create a secret or a key using key Vault Dashboard

You have the option here to use keys, secret or certificate with your application to encrypt or decrypt the data. Here you can generate a key, certificate or secret or import a key or certificate. Figure below shows Key vault Dashboard. **Note here the DNS name of the Key Vault.**

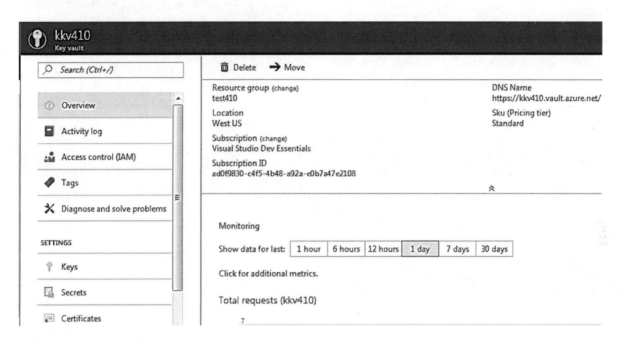

Lets generate secret here to be used with our application> Click secret on left pane>click + Add>Create a secret dashboard opens>select manual from drop down box and enter information as per your requirement and click create.

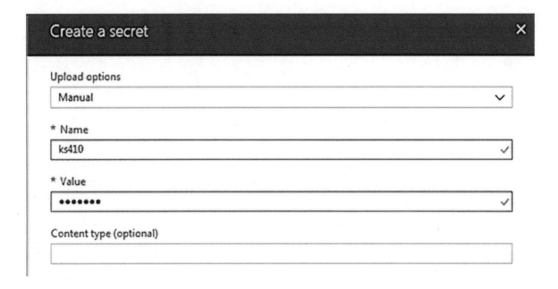

Step 3 - Register your application with Azure AD to generate Application ID and Client secret.

Applications that use a key vault must authenticate to Key Vault by using a token from Azure Active Directory. To do this, application must first register the application in their Azure Active Directory. At the end of registration, the application owner gets the following values:

- An **Application ID**
- An **authentication key** (also known as the shared secret).

The application must present both these values to Azure AD to get a token.

1. In Azure AD dashboard >Click App Registration>Click +New Application Reg >Create Blade opens>enter your application URL and click create.

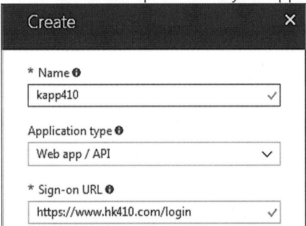

2. Figure below shows the **application id** of our application kapp410. Application id is also known as **client id.**

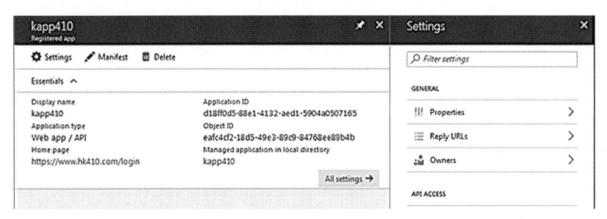

3. In your registered app > Click on All settings> Click on keys>enter key Description and select duration and click save and a Key value generated. Note down the value. This will be your **client secret.**

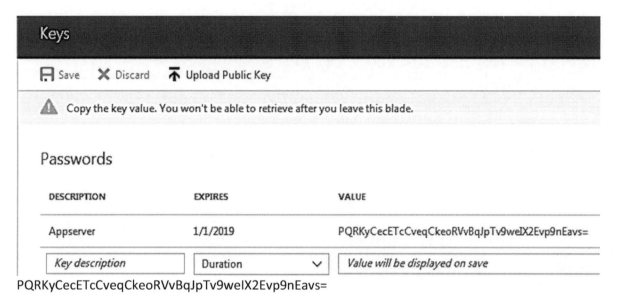

PQRKyCecETcCveqCkeoRVvBqJpTv9welX2Evp9nEavs=

Step 4 - Authorize the Application to access Key Vault Data Plane

1. In Azure Key Vault Dashboard click **Access Policies**> Click +New> Add Access Policy Blade opens>Select Your Application you registered with Azure AD in Step 3.

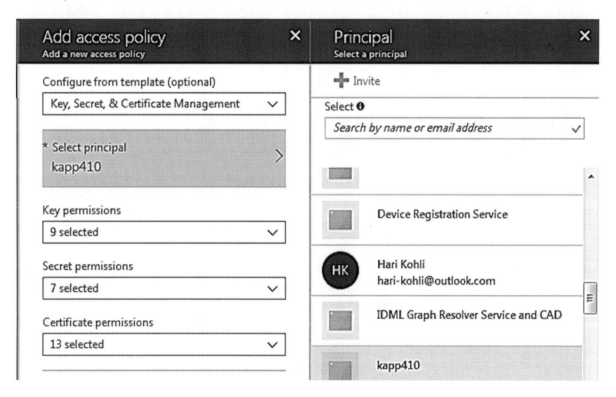

Step 5 - In your application add URL of the key vault, client id and client secret

In your application add **URL of the key vault** https://kkv410.vault.azure.net (See Key Vault Dashboard in Step 2)and **client id/application id** and **client secret** generated in Step 3.

Example: SQL Server Transparent Data Encryption using Azure Key Vault

SQL Server Transparent Data Encryption feature encrypts Data at rest. Figure below show encrypting SQL server Instance Data using Azure Key Vault. The data is encrypted using a symmetric data encryption key (DEK). The symmetric data encryption key is further protected by encrypting it with an asymmetric key stored outside of SQL Server in Azure Key Vault.

The SQL Server Connector for Microsoft Azure Key Vault enables SQL Server encryption to use the Azure Key Vault service as an <u>Extensible Key Management (EKM)</u> provider to protect SQL Server encryption keys.

The SQL Server Extensible Key Management (EKM) enables third-party EKM/HSM vendors to register their modules in SQL Server. When registered, SQL Server users can use the encryption keys stored on EKM modules. This enables SQL Server to access the advanced encryption features these modules support such as bulk encryption and decryption, and key management functions such as key aging and key rotation.

Using azure key Vault separates Database administration and Security Function. Security can now be now centrally managed by the Security team.

Architecting Microsoft Azure Solutions Study & Lab Guide Part 1: Exam 70-535

Using Key Vault Secret with ARM Templates

ARM Templates are infrastructure as code which can deploy multiple Azure resources. For example with ARM template you can deploy Azure Virtual Network, Storage Account and Virtual Machine simultaneously.

Same Azure ARM template can be used multiple times by different departments or organisations. This means we cannot reference the key vault secret in the template itself. Azure template will refer to a parameter file. Parameter file will have reference to Key Vault.

Figure below shows how the parameter file references the secret and passes that value to the template.

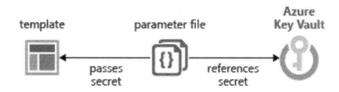

Step By step adding Support for Azure Key Vault secret in ARM Templates

1. Create a Key Vault for the secrets you want to use with Template deployment.
2. Put secrets into the vault.
3. Set advanced Access Policies on the Key Vault to allow Azure Resource Manager to retrieve secrets during deployment.
4. Edit or Author a ARM template with reference to the parameter file for login and Password.
5. Create a parameter file for the preceding template. In the parameter file, specify Key Vault Subscription ID and Secret Name.
6. Deploy the template with the Parameter file specified in step 5.

Note: Same template can be used by different organisation. You need to create separate parameter file. ARM template remains the same.

Using Certificates with Key Vault

Certificates are commonly used with web servers and application for secure communication and authentication. For example a website with address https://www.test.com indicates that traffic is encrypted with certificate.

Certificate can be a self-signed certificate or issued by a Certificate Authority (CA).

Azure key vault can generate, import and store certificates. Key vault can generate a self-signed certificate. Self-signed certificate is not recommended for production workloads. For Production workload it is recommended to import certificate from trusted Certificate Authority (CA) and then issue it.

Using Key vault you can inject stored certificate in Azure Virtual Machine. Applications running on Virtual Machine can access and use the certificate.

Securing Azure Key Vault Management and Data Plane

Access to a key vault is controlled through two separate interfaces: Management Plane and Data Plane.

The management plane and data plane access controls work independently. For example, if you want to grant an application access to use keys in a key vault, you only need to grant data plane access permissions using key vault access policies and no management plane access is needed for this application. Whereas Management plane interface is used to manage key vault.

For authentication both management plane and data plane use Azure Active Directory. For authorization, management plane uses role-based access control (RBAC) while data plane uses key vault access policies.

Granting Access to Key Vault Data Plane using Access Policies

Key Vault Data plane access is granted by access policies. Using Access Policies a user, group, application or Azure services is authorized to access Key Vault.

1. In key vault dashboard click access Policies in left pane>

2. **Granting Key Vault Access to Custom Applications, Azure AD users or Azure Services.** Click **+Add new** in Access Policies>Add Access Policy blade opens> Here we can add Application registered with Azure AD, Azure AD users or Azure Services.

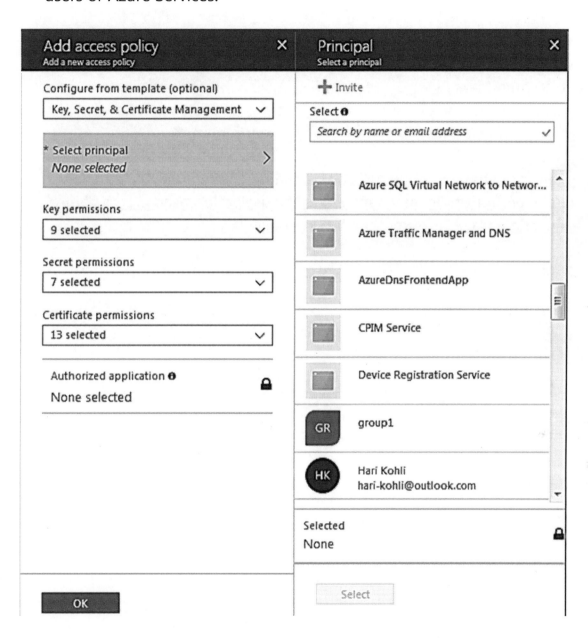

Key Vault Advance Access Policies

Following 3 advance access Policies can be enabled from Key Vault Dashboard.

1. **Enable access to Azure Virtual Machines for deployments**: Specifies whether Azure Virtual Machines are permitted to retrieve certificate stored as secrets from the Key Vault.

2. **Enable access to Azure Resource Manager for template deployments**: Specifies whether Azure Resource Manager is permitted to retrieve secrets from the Key Vault.

3. **Enable access to Azure Disk Encryption for volume encryption**: Specifies whether Azure Disk Encryption is permitted to retrieve secrets from the Key Vault.

In Key Vault Dashboard Click Access Policies in left pane> In right pane choose and Enable Advance access policies as per your requirement.

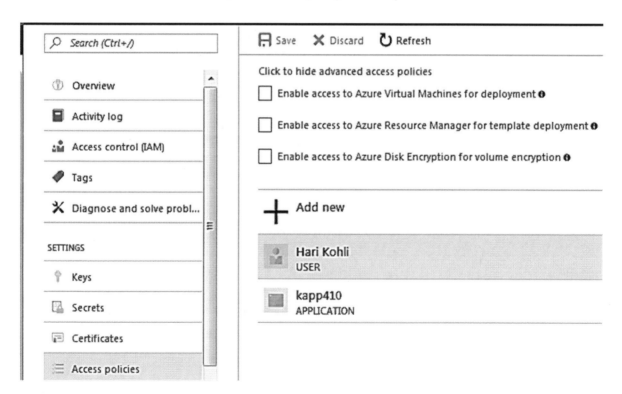

Key Rotation

One of the advantages of using Key Vault is the ability to change keys without affecting the application.

Each key or secret can have one or more versions associated with it.

1. **Changing Keys**: In the Key vault Dashboard click keys in left pane>In the right pane select your key>Key Blade opens and you can see your first version of the key as shown in the figure below.

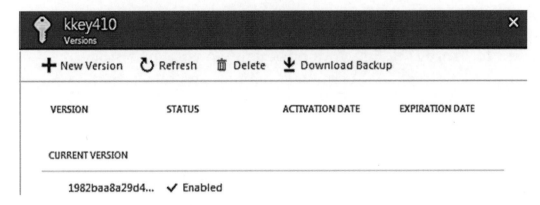

2. Click + New Version>Create a key Blade opens>Enter required information> Click Generate. A new version is of the key is created as shown below. Applications querying the key will now retrieve new version.

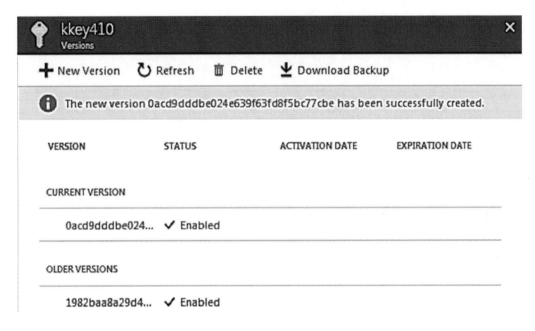

Key Logging

Access to Key Vault can be monitored by enabling logging. Following types of logs are generated:

1. Key Vault operation to create delete or change settings.
2. Key Vault operations that involve Keys, Secrets and Certificates.
3. Rest API requests.

Soft Delete

Key Vault's soft delete feature allows recovery of the deleted vaults and vault objects.

Why do we need Soft Delete Feature

Accidental or intentional delete of Key Vault or Key Vault objects can cause Business disruptions.

Scenario 1: A user may have inadvertently deleted a key vault or a key vault object.
Scenario 2: A rogue user may attempt to delete a key vault or a key vault object.

By enabling Soft Delete feature you can separate the deletion of the key vault or key vault object from the actual deletion of the underlying data. Soft Delete feature allows recovery of deleted vaults and vault objects. Soft Delete feature can be used as a safety measure.

Enabling Soft Delete Feature

You can enable Soft Delete feature through Powershell or CLI.

Azure Key Vault Tiers

Azure Key Vault is offered in two service tiers—standard and premium. Table below shows comparison between the tiers.

Features	Standard	Premium
Secrets operations	Yes	Yes
Certificate operations	Yes	Yes
Software-protected keys	Yes	Yes
HSM-protected keys	No	Yes

Azure Key Vault Pricing

Table shows the pricing of Azure key vault standard and Premier Tiers.

	Standard	Premium
Key Vault	Free	Free
Secrets operations	$0.03/10,000 request	$0.03/10,000 request
Certificate operations	$3 per renewal request	$3 per renewal request
Software-protected keys	$0.03/10,000	$0.03/10,000
HSM-protected keys	NA	$1 per key per month

Chapter 15 Azure Content Delivery Networks (CDN)

This Chapter covers following

- Azure Content Delivery Networks (CDN)
- Azure CDN Working
- Azure CDN Architecture
- Azure CDN Tiers
- Dynamic Site Acceleration (DSA) or Acceleration Data Transfer
- CDN Limits
- CDN Pricing

This Chapter Covers following Lab Exercises

- Step by Step Implementing Azure CDN

Chapter Topology

In this chapter we will add Azure CDN to the topology.

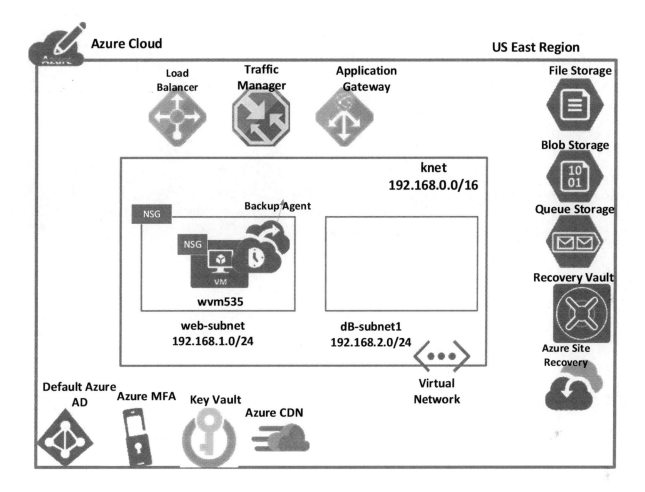

Azure Content Delivery Networks (CDN)

A content delivery network (CDN) is a distributed network of servers that deliver web content to users faster than the origin server. The Azure Content Delivery Network (CDN) caches web content from origin server at strategically placed locations to provide maximum throughput for delivering content to users.

Figure below shows Cached image being delivered to users by CDN server which is faster than the origin server.

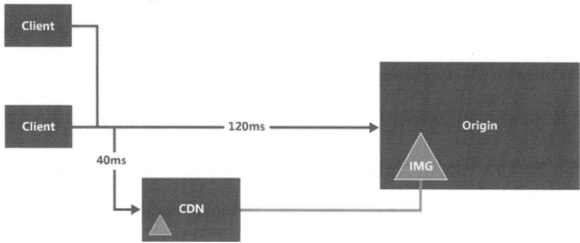

Use Cases

1. Azure CDNs are typically used to deliver static content such as images, style sheets, documents, client-side scripts, and HTML pages.

2. Streaming Video benefits from the low latency offered by CDN servers. Additionally Microsoft Azure Media Services (AMS) integrates with Azure CDN to deliver content directly to the CDN for further distribution.

Benefits of Azure CDN

1. CDN provides lower latency and faster delivery of content to users.
2. CDNs help to reduce load on a web application, because the application does not have to service requests for the content that is hosted in the CDN.
3. CDN helps to cope with peaks and surges in demand without requiring the application to scale, avoiding the consequent increased running costs.
4. Improved experience for users, especially those located far from the datacenter hosting the application.

Azure CDN Working

Figure below shows the working of Content Delivery Networks.

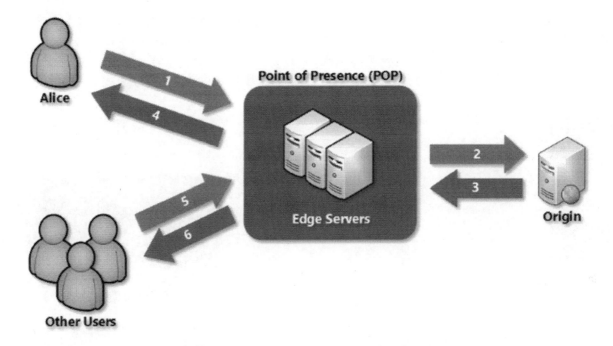

1. User Alice requests a file using URL (*<endpoint name>*.azureedge.net) in a browser. DNS routes the request to the CDN edge server Point-of-Presence (POP) location that is geographically closest to the user.

2. If the edge servers in the POP has file in their cache, it returns the file to the user Alice.

3. If the edge servers in the POP do not have the file in their cache, the edge server requests the file from the origin server. The origin server returns the file to the edge server, including optional HTTP headers describing the file's Time-to-Live (TTL). The edge server caches the file and returns the file to the user Alice. The file remains cached on the edge server until the TTL expires. If the origin didn't specify a TTL, the default TTL is seven days.

4. Additional users who request same file as user Alice and are geographically closest to the same POP will be get the file from Cache of the edge server instead of the origin server.

5. The above process results in a faster, more responsive user experience.

Azure CDN Architecture

Azure CDN Architecture consists of Origin Server, CDN Profile and CDN endpoints.

Origin Server

Origin server holds the web content which is cached by CDN Endpoints geographically closest to the user based on caching policy configured in CDN endpoint.

Origin Server type can be one of the following:

Storage
Web App
Cloud Service
Publically Accessible Web Server

CDN Profile

A CDN profile is a collection of CDN endpoints. Each profile can contain one or more CDN endpoints.
CDN pricing is applied at the CDN profile level. Therefore, to use a mix of Azure CDN pricing tiers, you must create multiple CDN profiles.

CDN Endpoints

CDN Endpoint caches the web content from the origin server. It delivers cached content to end users faster than the origin server and is located geographically closest to the user. CDN Endpoints are distributed across the world.

The CDN Endpoint is exposed using the URL format .azureedge.net by default, but custom domains can also be used.

A CDN Endpoint is an entity within a CDN Profile containing configuration information regarding caching behaviour and origin Server. Every CDN endpoint represents a specific configuration of content deliver behaviour and access.

Azure CDN Tiers

Azure CDN comes in Standard and Premium tiers. Azure CDN Standard Tier comes from Akamai and Verizon. Azure Premium Tier is from Verizon. Table below shows comparison between Standard and Premium Tiers.

	Standard Akamai	Standard Verizon	Premium Verizon
Performance Features and Optimizations			
Dynamic Site Acceleration	✓	✓	✓
Dynamic Site Acceleration - Adaptive Image Compression	✓		
Dynamic Site Acceleration - Object Prefetch	✓		
Video streaming optimization	✓	Note 1	Note 1
Large file optimization	✓	Note 1	Note 1
Global Server Load balancing (GSLB)	✓	✓	✓
Fast purge	✓	✓	✓
Asset pre-loading		✓	✓
Cache/header settings (using caching rules)	✓	✓	
Cache/header settings (using rules engine)	✓		✓
Query string caching	✓	✓	✓
IPv4/IPv6 dual-stack	✓	✓	✓
HTTP/2 support	✓	✓	✓
Security			
HTTPS support with CDN endpoint	✓	✓	✓
Custom domain HTTPS		✓	✓
Custom domain name support	✓	✓	✓
Geo-filtering	✓	✓	✓
Token authentication			✓
DDOS protection	✓	✓	✓
Analytics and Reporting			
Core reports from Verizon		✓	✓
Custom reports from Verizon		✓	✓
Advanced HTTP reports			✓
Real-time stats			✓
Edge node performance			✓
Real-time alerts			✓

Dynamic Site Acceleration (DSA) or Acceleration Data Transfer

Dynamic Site Acceleration (DSA), accelerates web content that is not cacheable such as shopping carts, search results, and other dynamic content.

Traditional CDN mainly uses caching to improve website and download performance. DSA accelerates delivery of dynamic content by optimising routing and networking between requester and content origin.

DSA configuration option can be selected during endpoint creation.

DSA Optimization Techniques

DSA speeds up delivery of dynamic assets using the following techniques:

Route optimization chooses the most optimal and the fastest path to the origin server.

TCP Optimizations: TCP connections take several requests back and forth in a handshake to establish a new connection. This results in delay in setting up the network connection.
Azure CDN solves this problem by optimizing in following three areas:
Eliminating slow start
Leveraging persistent connections
Tuning TCP packet parameters (Akamai only)

Object Prefetch (Akamai only): *Prefetch* is a technique to retrieve images and scripts embedded in the HTML page while the HTML is served to the browser, and before the browser even makes these object requests. When the client makes the requests for the linked assets, the CDN edge server already has the requested objects and can serve them immediately without a round trip to the origin.

Adaptive Image Compression (Akamai only): End users experience slower network speeds from time to time. In these scenarios, it is more beneficial for the user to receive smaller images in their webpage more quickly rather than waiting a long time for full resolution images. This feature automatically monitors network quality, and employs standard JPEG compression methods when network speeds are slower to improve delivery time.

Exercise 49: Step by Step Implementing Azure CDN

Implementing Azure CDN is a 2 step process – Create CDN profile and add CDN endpoints to the profile.

A CDN profile is a collection of CDN endpoints. Each profile can contain one or more CDN endpoints.
CDN pricing is applied at the CDN profile level. Therefore, to use a mix of Azure CDN pricing tiers, you must create multiple CDN profiles.

A CDN Endpoint is the entity within a CDN Profile containing configuration information regarding caching behaviour and origin Server. The CDN Endpoint is exposed using the URL format .azureedge.net by default, but custom domains can also be used.

Creating CDN Profile: In Azure portal click create a resource>Web + Mobile> CDN> Create CDN profile blade opens>Enter information a per your requirement and click create.

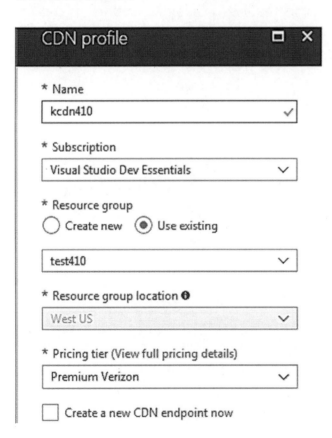

2. **Add CDN endpoint**: Go to CDN profile dashboard>Click +Endpoint>Add an endpoint blade opens> enter information as per your req and click add. For this example we have selected Storage Account as origin type.

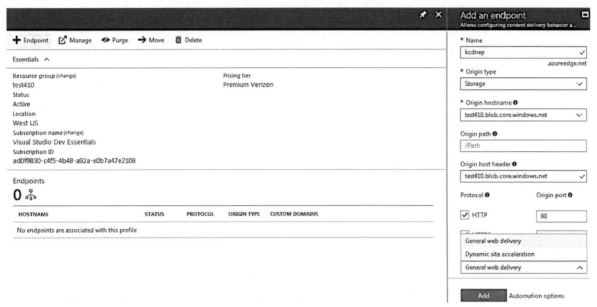

Note the General web delivery and Dynamic Site acceleration option.
Use General Web delivery for Caching Static and Dynamic content.
Use DSA option for delivering content that is not cacheable.

Figure below shows the dashboard of the endpoint created in step 2.

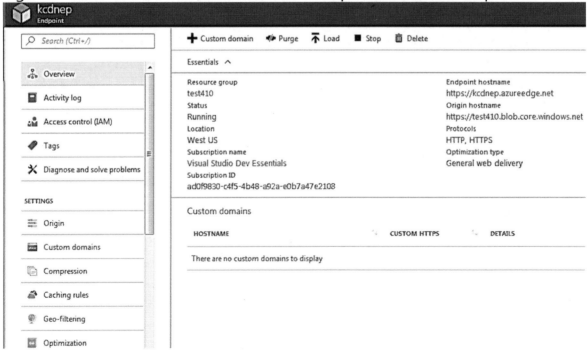

From Endpoint Dashboard as shown in previous page you can enable following features:

Adding Custom Domain to CDN Endpoint: By default endpoint is in format xyz.azuredge.net. Azure CDN provides the option of associating a custom domain (www.test.com) with your endpoint.

Compression: Compression is used to reduce the bandwidth used to deliver and receive an object. By enabling compression directly on the CDN edge servers, CDN compresses the files and serves them to end users.

Caching Rules: Control how CDN caches your content including deciding caching duration and how unique query strings are handled.

Geo-Filtering: By creating geo-filtering rules on specific paths on your endpoint, you can block or allow content in the selected countries.

Token authentication: Allows you to validate requests at the CDN edge to prevent serving assets to unauthorized clients.

Custom rules engine: Allows you to customize how HTTP requests are handled, such as blocking the delivery of certain types of content, defining a caching policy, or modifying HTTP headers.

Mobile device rules: Allows you to customize rules to deliver content optimized for mobile devices.

Edge performance analytics: Provides granular information traffic and bandwidth usage for the CDN which can be used to generate trending statistics and gain insight on how your assets are being cached and delivered to your clients.

Realtime analytics: Provides real-time data, such as bandwidth, cache statuses, and concurrent connections to your CDN profile when delivering content to your clients.

CDN Limits

Resource	Default limit	Maximum limit
CDN profiles	25	25
CDN endpoints per profile	10	25
Custom domains per endpoint	10	25

CDN Pricing

Azure CDN comes in Standard and Premium tiers. Azure CDN Standard Tier comes from Akamai and Verizon. Azure Premium Tier is from Verizon only.

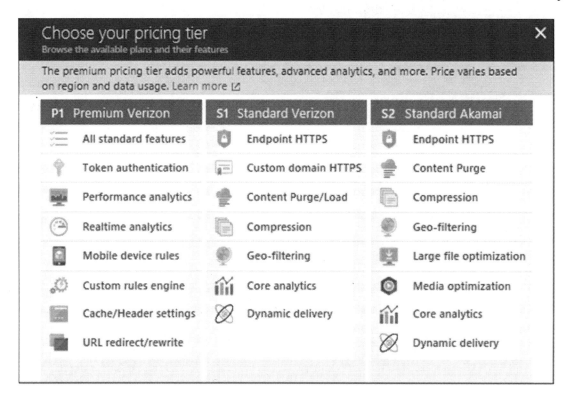

CDN pricing is applied at the CDN profile level.
CDN pricing is based on outbound Data transfer from the CDN edge servers.

Azure Content Delivery Network Standard from Verizon (S1) and Akamai (S2) outbound data transfers

OUTBOUND DATA TRANSFERS	Zone 1	Zone 2	Zone 3	Zone 4	Zone 5
First 10 TB /Month	$0.087 per GB	$0.138 per GB	$0.25 per GB	$0.14 per GB	$0.17 per GB
Next 40 TB (10–50 TB)/Month	$0.08 per GB	$0.13 per GB	$0.20 per GB	$0.135 per GB	$0.13 per GB
Next 100 TB (50–150 TB)/Month	$0.06 per GB	$0.12 per GB	$0.18 per GB	$0.12 per GB	$0.11 per GB

Azure Content Delivery Network Premium from Verizon (P1) and outbound data transfers

OUTBOUND DATA TRANSFERS	Zone 1	Zone 2	Zone 3	Zone 4	Zone 5
First 10 TB /Month	$0.17 per GB	$0.25 per GB	$0.50 per GB	$0.28 per GB	$0.34 per GB
Next 40 TB (10–50 TB)/Month	$0.15 per GB	$0.22 per GB	$0.425 per GB	$0.24 per GB	$0.29 per GB
Next 100 TB (50–150 TB)/Month	$0.13 per GB	$0.19 per GB	$0.36 per GB	$0.20 per GB	$0.245 per GB

- Zone 1—North America, Europe, Middle East and Africa
- Zone 2—Asia Pacific (including Japan)
- Zone 3—South America
- Zone 4—Australia
- Zone 5—India

Chapter 16 Azure Media Services

This Chapter covers following

- Azure Media Services
- Architecture of Azure Media Services (On-Demand Streaming)
- Architecture of Azure Media Services (Live-Streaming using on-premises encoder)
- Architecture of Azure Media Services (Live-Streaming using Cloud encoder)
- Azure Media Services Account
- Encoders
- Publish your encoded Asset using Streaming or Progressive Locators
- Streaming Endpoint
- Live Channel (For Live Streaming)
- Content Protection
- Media Analytics

This Chapter Covers following Lab Exercises to build below topology

- Create AMS Account
- Step by Step Creating Video on Demand Streaming
- Demonstration Exercise: Creating Channel and Live event

Chapter Topology

In this chapter we will add Azure Media Services to the topology.

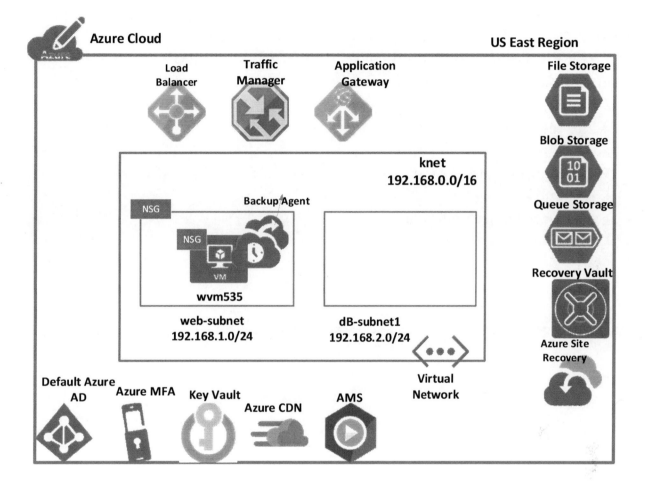

Azure Media Services

Media Services enables you to securely upload, store, encode and package video or audio content for **on-demand streaming**, **live streaming** & **Progressive download** to various clients (for example, TV, PC, and mobile devices (IOS, Android & Windows)).

Streaming Video or Live Streaming or download to users is a 2 step process.

1. Using Azure Media Services Encoder, Encode your source stream to a multi-bitrate (adaptive bitrate) video stream. This will take care of quality and network conditions while delivery content to end users.

2. Using on-demand streaming server deliver your adaptive (Multi) bitrate MP4 encoded content in streaming formats (MPEG DASH, Apple HLS or Microsoft Smooth Streaming) requested by end user. As a result, you only need to store and pay for the files in single storage format and Media Services service will build and serve the appropriate content based on requests from end user.

The following diagram shows the dynamic packaging workflow.

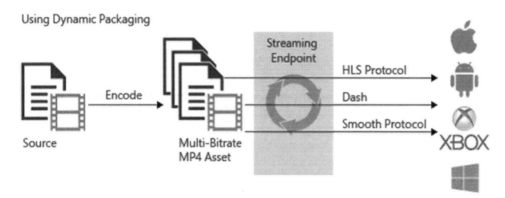

HTTP Streaming Technologies

Apple HLS, MPEG-Dash and Microsoft Smooth Streaming Protocols are HTTP Streaming Technologies.

Common to all streaming protocols is to generate multiple versions of the same content with different bitrates and chop these versions into segments (e.g., two seconds).The segments are provided on a web server and can be downloaded through HTTP standard compliant GET requests.

Architecting Microsoft Azure Solutions Study & Lab Guide Part 1: Exam 70-535

The adaptation to the bitrate or resolution is done on the client side for each segment, e.g., the client can switch to a higher bitrate – if bandwidth permits – on a per segment basis.

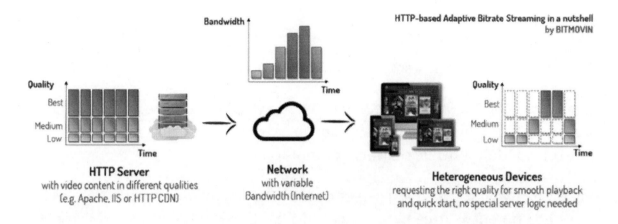

Apple HTTP Live Streaming (Apple HLS) adaptive HTTP streaming protocol is mainly targeted towards mobile devices such as iPhone, iPad or AppleTV, Android Browser and Safari and Chrome Browsers.

MPEG-DASH (Dynamic Adaptive Streaming over HTTP) is a vendor independent Streaming protocol. MPEG-DAS is an adaptive bitrate streaming technique that enables high quality streaming of media content over the Internet delivered from HTTP web servers to mobile and Desktop Browsers.

Microsoft Smooth Streaming is an IIS Media Services extension delivering adaptive streaming of media to Silverlight and other clients over HTTP.

Architecture of Azure Media Services (On-Demand Streaming)

The Figure below shows the Architect & Components of Azure Media Services for delivering Video on-demand streaming.

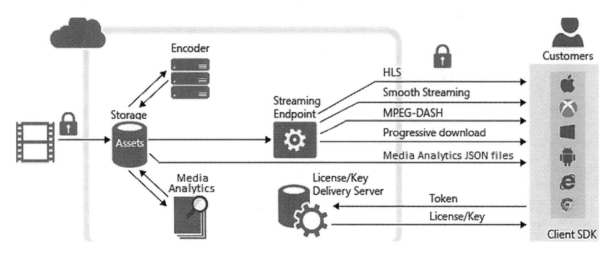

Azure Media Services (On-Demand Streaming) Components
Azure Media Services Account with Associated Storage
Encoder
Streaming Endpoint
Media Analytics (Optional)
Licence Server (used when user has to be authenticated to access content)

Brief Working

1. Create Azure Media Services Account with Associated Storage Account.
2. Upload your Video or Audio Files into Associated Azure Storage Account. The uploaded file will appear as Asset in AMS account.
3. Using Cloud Encoder convert your uploaded single bit rate files to a set of adaptive Multi Bit rate MP4 files.
4. Publish your uploaded and encoded Asset using Streaming or Progressive locator. Locators create URL for end users to access the streaming content or download the content.
5. Enable the default Streaming Endpoint or create a new Streaming Endpoint. Stream published content when requested using Streaming endpoint. Streaming Endpoint dynamically package the asset to support multiple devices and multiple Streaming protocols (HLS for IOS/Android, MPEG-Dash for Modern Browsers and Smooth Streaming for old browsers).

Architecture of AMS (Live-Streaming using on-premises encoder)

The Figure below shows the Architect & Components of Azure Media Services.

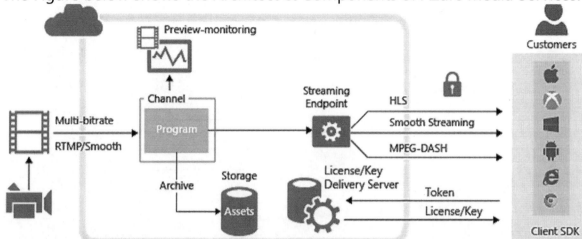

Azure Media Services has following Components:
Azure Media Services Account
Live feed from on-premises using On-premises Encoder
Live Channel (pass-through mode)
Streaming Endpoint
Preview Monitoring & Storage
Licence Server (used when delivery encrypted content to the user)

Brief Working

1. Create Azure Media Services Account.
2. Create Live Channel in pass-through mode and copy ingest URL.
3. On-premises encoder will convert live feed into multi bit rate and will input multi bit rate live feed into ingest URL of live channel in Cloud.
4. Create a live event and Preview your live stream using Preview URL.
5. Create a Program for the Live Channel created in Step 2.
6. Publish the Program using Streaming locator.
7. Enable the default Streaming Endpoint or create a new Streaming Endpoint. Stream published program when requested using Streaming endpoint. Streaming Endpoint Dynamically package the live feed to support multiple devices and multiple Streaming protocols (HLS for IOS/Android, MPEG-Dash for Modern Browsers and MS Smooth Streaming.
8. Record and store the ingested content in order to be streamed later.

Architecture of AMS (Live-Streaming using Cloud encoder)

The Figure below shows the Architect & Components of Azure Media Services.

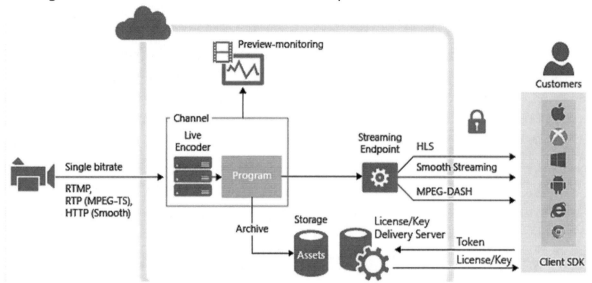

Azure Media Services has following Components:

Azure Media Services Account

Channel (Live-encoding mode)

Streaming Endpoint

Preview Monitoring

Storage

Licence Server (used when user has to be authenticated to access content)

Brief Working

1. Create Azure Media Services Account.
2. Create Live Channel in Live-encoding mode and copy ingest URL.
3. Input on-premises single bit rate live feed into ingest URL of live channel. Cloud encoder will convert single bit rate live feed into Multi Bit rate.
4. Create live event and Preview your live stream in Preview Monitoring.
5. Create a Program for the Live Channel created in Step 2.
6. Publish the Program using Streaming locator.
7. Enable the default Streaming Endpoint or create a new Streaming Endpoint. Stream published program when requested using Streaming endpoint. Streaming Endpoint Dynamically package the live feed to support multiple devices and multiple Streaming protocols (HLS for IOS/Android, MPEG-Dash for Modern Browsers and MS Smooth Streaming.

Azure Media Services Account

Azure Media Services (AMS) Account is required to access Media Services that enable you to store, encrypt, encode, manage, and stream media content in Azure. You also require associated Storage account in the same region as AMS account.

Exercise 50: Create AMS Account

1. Log on to Azure Portal> Click +Create a resource> Mobile> Media Services> Create Media Services Blade opens>For Storage Account I selected create new>Gave a name and selected all default values and clicked ok>Click create.

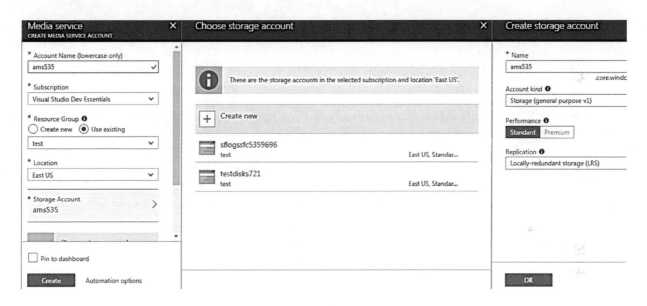

When your AMS account is created a default streaming endpoint is added to your account in the Stopped state. To start streaming your content and take advantage of dynamic packaging and dynamic encryption, the streaming endpoint from which you want to stream content has to be in the Running state.

Encoders

An **encoder** is a device, circuit, transducer, software program, algorithm or person that converts information from one format or code to another, for the purposes of standardization, speed or compression.

Azure encoder converts source file into a set of adaptive (Multi) bitrate MP4 files or adaptive bitrate Smooth Streaming files. It also provides extensive Audio and Video Processing capabilities to source files during encoding.

When you are streaming your VOD to end users, end users can have varying Bandwidth.
Adaptive bitrate streaming is a technique used in streaming multimedia over computer networks. It works by detecting a user's bandwidth and CPU capacity in real time and adjusting the quality of a video stream accordingly. It requires the use of an **encoder** which **can encode** a single source video at multiple **bit rates**.

Azure supports following two types of encoders: Standard Encoder and Premium Encoder.

1. **Standard Encoder** transcodes video and audio input files into output formats suitable for playback on a variety of devices, including smartphones, tablets, PCs, gaming consoles, and televisions.
2. **Premium Encoder** transcodes formats common to broadcast and movie applications, and supports video workflows that require complex logic.

Figure below shows Source Single bit rate Files are converted into Multi bit rate file using Azure Encoder.

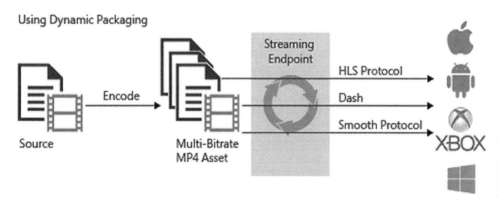

Comparison of Video and audio processing capabilities of Azure Standard and Premium media encoders

Capabilities	Standard	Premium
Apply conditional logic while encoding (for example, if the input is HD, then encode 5.1 audio)	No	Yes
Closed captioning	No	Yes
Dolby Professional Loudness Correction with Dialogue Intelligence	No	Yes
De-interlacing, inverse telecine	Basic	Broadcast
Detect and remove black borders (pillarboxes, letterboxes)	No	Yes
Thumbnail generation	Yes	Yes
Clipping/trimming and stitching of videos	Yes	Yes
Overlays of audio or video	Yes	Yes
Overlays of graphics	From image sources	From image and text sources
Multiple audio language tracks	Limited	Yes

Managing Encoder's Concurrent tasks: Number of media tasks that can be processed concurrently by the encoder depends upon the number of Media Reserved units Provisoned. For example, if your account has three reserved units, then three media processing tasks can run concurrently as long as there are tasks to be processed.

Configuring Concurency: In AMS Account Dashboard >Click Media Reserved Unit in left Pane> In Right Pane either use slider or put the number in the box to configure concurrent jobs which can run simultaneously.

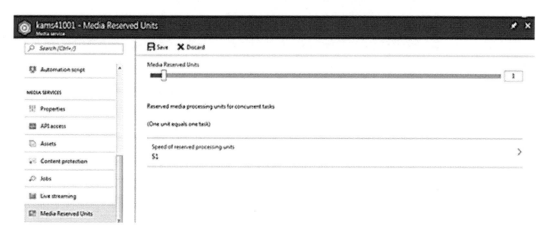

Managing Encoding Speed: In Azure Media Services, Media Reserved Unit type determines the speed with which your media processing tasks are processed by the Cloud Encoder. There are types of Media Reserved Unit: S1, S2 & S3.

Configuring and Comparing Media Reserved Unit: In AMS Dashboard > Click Media Reserved Unit in left Pane> In Right Pane click Speed of Processing units Box>Choose your pricing tier blade opens>Choose your Media Reserved Unit type and click select.

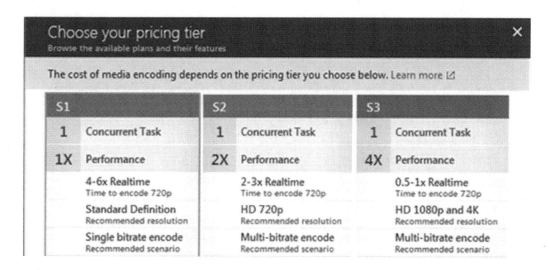

Publish your encoded Asset

To Stream your content to users or provide download option for the content to users you must publish your asset using Streaming or Progressive locator. Locators create URL for end users to access the streaming content or download the content.

Azure Media Services supports following two types of locators:

Streaming locators: Streaming locators are used to deliver Streaming Video. Examples of streaming locators include Apple HTTP Live Streaming (HLS), Microsoft Smooth Streaming, and Dynamic Adaptive Streaming over HTTP (MPEG-DASH).

Progressive (shared access signature) locators: Progressive locators are used to deliver video via progressive download.

Publishing Asset using Azure Portal

In AMS dashboard Click Assets in left Pane>Select Asset which was encoded to Multi Bit rate using encoder>Asset blade opens>click Publish>Publish the asset blade opens> Select the Locator Type (Streaming or Progressive)>click add.

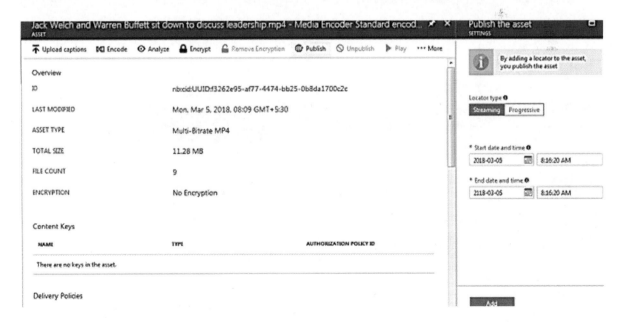

Streaming Endpoint

A Streaming Endpoint represents a streaming service that can deliver content directly to a client player application, or to a Content Delivery Network (CDN) for further distribution.

Streaming Endpoint deliver your content to virtually every device (IOS/Android, Windows) through dynamic packaging into HLS, MPEG-DASH, and Smooth Streaming as well as provide dynamic encryption for Microsoft PlayReady, Google Widevine, Apple Fairplay, and AES128.

The outbound stream from a streaming endpoint service can be a live stream, or a video on-demand Asset in your Media Services account.

When AMS account is created a default streaming endpoint is added to your account in the stopped state. To start streaming your content, the streaming endpoint from which you want to stream content has to be in the running state.

Enabling Default Streaming Endpoint: Log on to Azure Portal> Go to AMS Account Dashboard>Click Streaming endpoints in left Pane. You can see that status is stopped> In the right pane Click on the Row containing Default Streaming Endpoint> Default Streaming detail pane opens>Click start in Top left.

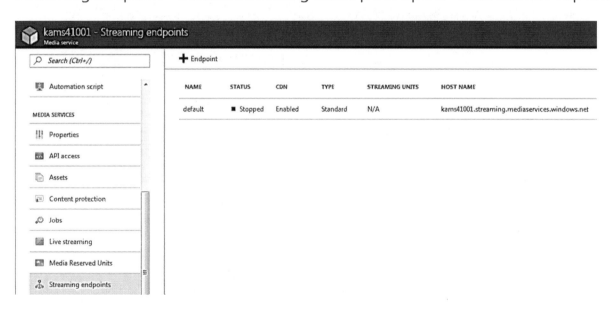

Design Nugget: you can have up to 2 streaming endpoints in your Media Services account.

Architecting Microsoft Azure Solutions Study & Lab Guide Part 1: Exam 70-535

Streaming Endpoint type

Media Services customers can choose either a **Standard** streaming endpoint or one or more **Premium** streaming endpoints.

Standard Streaming Endpoints deliver your content to virtually every device through dynamic packaging into HLS, MPEG-DASH and Smooth Streaming as well as dynamic encryption for Microsoft PlayReady, Google Widevine, Apple Fairplay, and AES128.

Premium Streaming Endpoint can provide additional Streaming units upto 10 to handle growing bandwidth needs. This option is not available in Standard Streaming Endpoint.

Figure Below shows Streaming endpoint of Premium Type. Note that you can add additional streaming units upto 10.

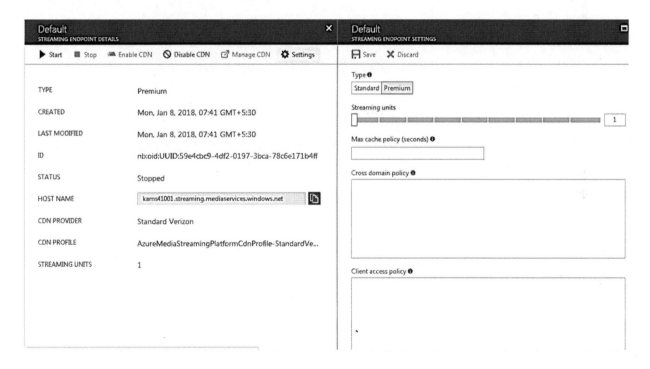

Exercise 51: Step by Step Creating Video on Demand Streaming

1. **Go Media Services Account** ams535 dashboard created in Exercise 50.
2. **Start the Default Streaming Endpoint**: In AMS dashboard Click Streaming Endpoints in left Pane>Select the Default Streaming endpoint in right pane>Default Streaming Endpoint pane opens>Click Start Button on top.

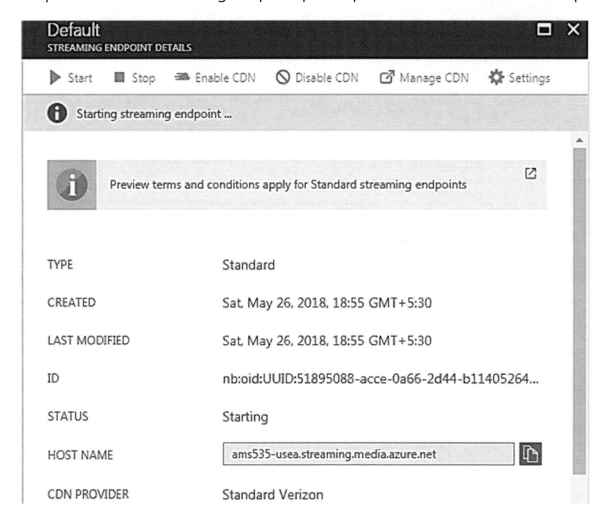

3. **Upload File**: In ams535 dashboard Click Assets in left Pane>Click Upload >Upload a Video asset blade opens> Upload your file from your desktop.

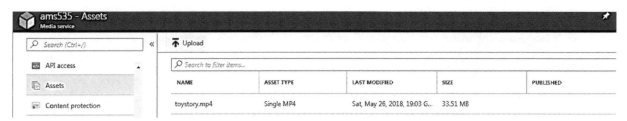

4. **Encode Uploaded File (Asset)**: In AMS dashboard Click Assets in left Pane>Select the file you uploaded in step 2>Asset Blade opens>Click encode in top> Encode an asset blade opens>Select your options and click create.

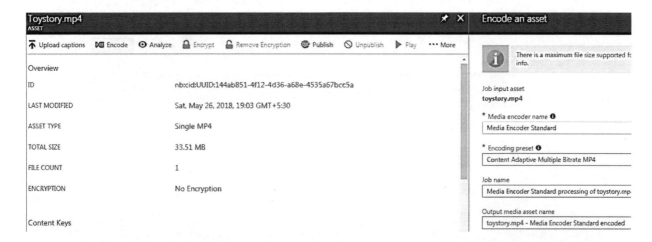

5. To view the **Progress of the encoding Job**> Click Jobs in left Pane> Start next step only when status shows finished.

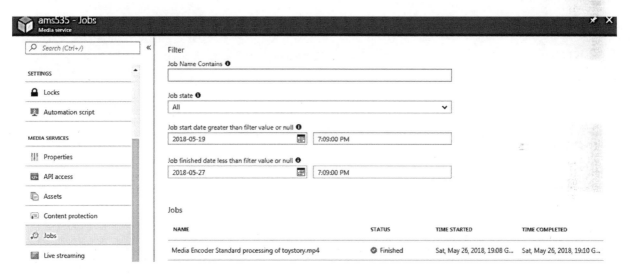

6. To see the **encoded File**>click Assets in left Pane> Note that encoded file is converted into Multi Bit rate from single Bit Rate.

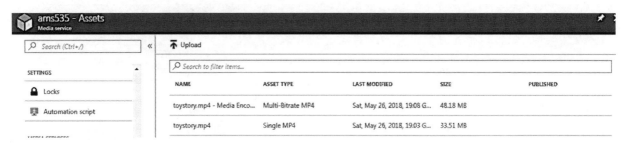

7. **Publish Content**: In AMS dashboard Click Assets in left Pane>Select Asset which was encoded to Multi Bit rate in step 3>Asset blade opens>click Publish>Publish the asset blade opens> Select the Locator Type> Which in this case is Streaming and click add.

8.

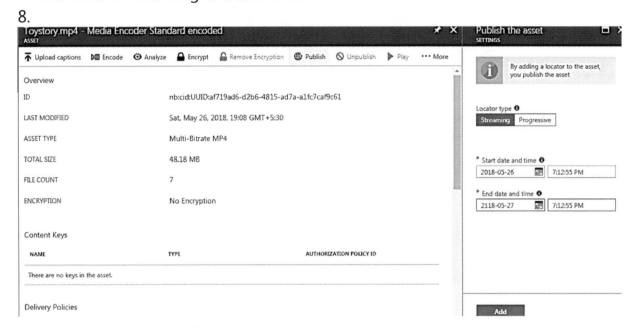

9. To **Play Content** in Azure Portal> Click Play button in the above screen.

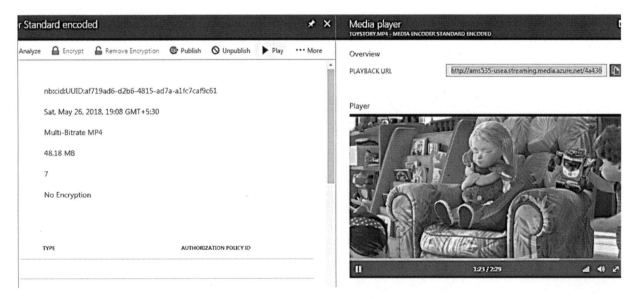

Live Channel (For Live Streaming)

A **Channel** processes on-premises live streaming content. A Channel can be configured in pass-through or live-encoding mode.

Figure below show channel configured in **pass-through mode**. In this mode channel receives multi bit rate stream from on-premises encoder.

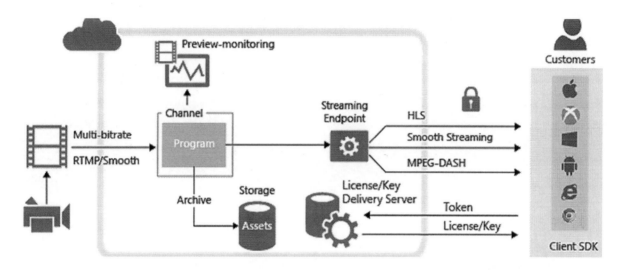

Figure below show channel configured **in Live-Encoding mode**. In this mode Channel receives single bit rate stream from on-premises. Using Live encoder (Standard or Premium) it converts single bit rate into multi bit rate stream.

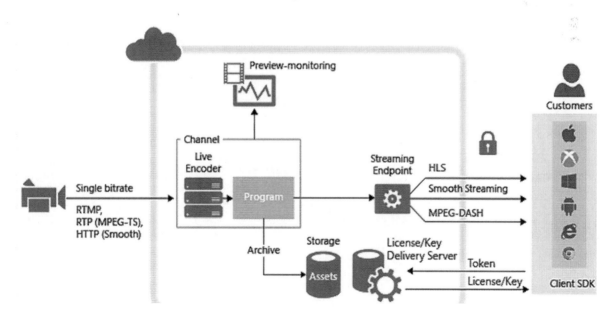

Demonstration Exercise 52: Creating Channel and Live event

1. In Azure Portal go to AMS Account Dashboard>Click Live Streaming in left Pane> Click +Quick to create channel in pass-through mode> Create Channel Blade opens> Enter information and click create.
Note: You can also use custom create to create channel in pass-through or Live encoding mode.

2. **Start the channel and copy the ingest URL**. Click the Channel in Right pane>Channel Dashboard Opens>Click Start and copy ingest URL.

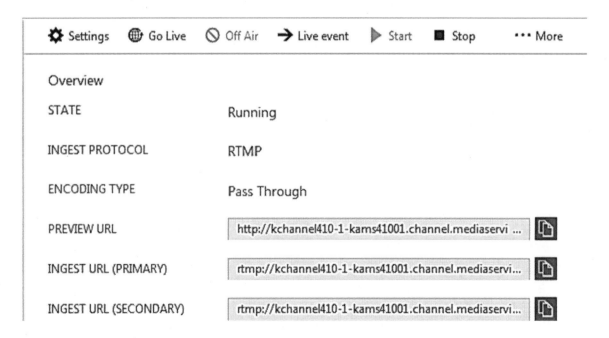

3. **Configure on Premises encoder** to send Multi Bit rate live Stream to ingest URL from step 2.

4. **Previewing the live Stream**. From the channel dashboard copy the preview URL to verify that your channel is properly receiving the live stream.

5. **Creating Live Event**. From the Channel Dashboard Click Live event in top pane> click ok to create event>Click Go Live.

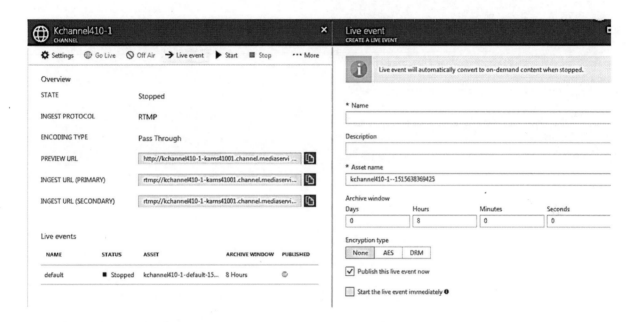

Note: Encryption Type: None, AES or DRM in Right pane.

Encryption Type AES: AES clear key encryption will be enabled on all streaming protocols: Smooth Streaming, HLS and MPEG-DASH.

Encryption Type DRM: With DRM choosen you get following options.

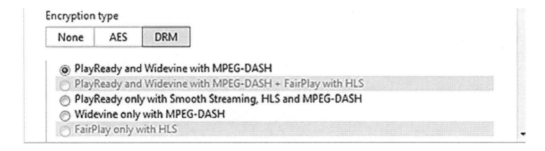

We will discuss AES & DRM Encryption later in Content Protection.

Architecting Microsoft Azure Solutions Study & Lab Guide Part 1: Exam 70-535

Content Protection

You can deliver your live and on-demand content encrypted dynamically with Advanced Encryption Standard (AES-128) or with any of the three major digital rights management (DRM) systems: Microsoft PlayReady, Google Widevine, and Apple FairPlay.

Currently, you can encrypt the HTTP Live Streaming (HLS), MPEG DASH, and Smooth Streaming protocol formats. Encryption on progressive downloads is not supported.

AES: MPEG-DASH, Smooth Streaming, and HLS
Microsoft PlayReady: MPEG-DASH, Smooth Streaming, and HLS
Google Widevine: MPEG-DASH
Apple FairPlay: HLS

AES-128 clear key vs. DRM

With AES encryption the content key is transmitted to the client in an unencrypted format.
With DRM content key is transmitted in an encrypted format.

AES-128 clear key encryption is suitable for use cases where the viewer is a trusted party.
DRM is recommended for use cases where the viewer might not be a trusted party and you require the highest level of security.

Types of encryption

AES-128 clear key encryption utilizes envelope encryption.
PlayReady and Widevine utilize common encryption (AES CTR mode). FairPlay utilizes AES CBC-mode encryption.

Architecture and Components of Content Protection

The Figure below how Content protection is implemented in AMS.

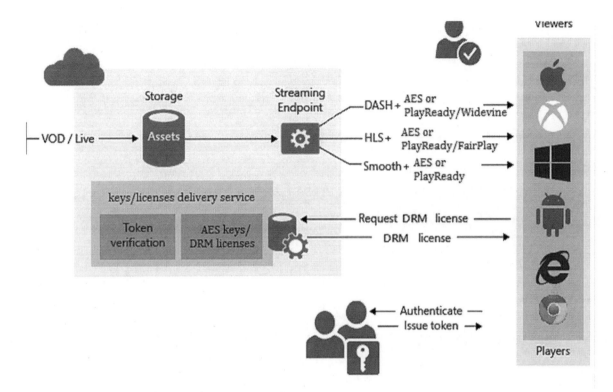

Components of Content Protection

Key/license delivery service
Encrypting the Asset

Brief Working

Create a key Authorization policy for the encryption key. Encrypt your asset using AES or DRM Key. Your assets will be configured for dynamic encryption based on the rules set in the Key Authorization policy.

When a stream is requested by a player, Media Services uses the specified key to dynamically encrypt your content by using AES clear key or DRM encryption. To decrypt the stream, the player requests the key from Media Services key delivery service. To decide whether or not the user is authorized to get the key, the service evaluates the authorization policies that you specified for the key.

Media Analytics

Azure Media Services Analytics is a collection of speech and vision components that make it easier to derive actionable insights from video files.

You Process uploaded Video files with Media Analytics media processors (MPs).

Azure Media Indexer media processor: Azure Media Indexer can make content searchable and generate closed-captioning tracks. Azure Media Indexer makes video files and media content searchable by extracting the speech content.

Azure Media Hyperlapse media processor (MP): Azure Media Hyperlapse provides video stabilization and time-lapse capability. With Hyperlapse you can create quick, consumable videos from your long-form content. **With** Hyperlapse you can also create stable videos from shaky videos captured via cell phones and camcorders.

Azure Media Face Detector media processor (MP): Media Face detection service provides two features: Face Detection and Emotion Detection. By using Face Detector, you can detect people's faces and their emotions, including happiness, sadness, and surprise.

Azure Media Motion Detector media processor (MP): Motion Detector detects motion in a video with stationary backgrounds. This makes it possible to check for false positives on motion events detected by surveillance cameras such as shadows and lighting changes.

Azure Media Redactor media processor: Azure Media Redactor provides face redaction functionality. By using face redaction, you can modify your video to blur faces of selected individuals. You might want to use the face redaction service in news media or when public safety is involved.

Azure Media Content Moderator: This processor helps you detect potential adult and racy content in videos.

Azure Media Video Thumbnails: Azure Media Video Thumbnails can help you create summaries of long videos by automatically selecting interesting snippets from the source video. This ability is useful when you want to provide a quick overview of what to expect in a long video.

Media Analytics Use Cases

Call Centers: Call Centers have customer interaction which results in large amount of Audio Data. Using Azure Media Indexer organizations can extract text and build search indexes and dashboards. Then they can extract intelligence around common complaints, sources of complaints, and other relevant data.

Surveillance: With the growth in use of IP cameras comes a growing inventory of surveillance video. Manually reviewing surveillance video is time intensive and prone to human error. Media Analytics provides services such as motion detection, face detection and Hyperlapse to make the process of reviewing, managing, and creating derivatives easier.

User-generated content moderation: Many organizations have public-facing portals that accept user-generated media such as videos and images. The volume of content can spike due to unexpected events. In these scenarios, it is difficult to conduct effective manual reviews of content for appropriateness. Customers can rely on the content-moderation service to focus on content that is appropriate.

Azure Media Service Pricing

Encoder Pricing for Video on Demand

Encoding Tasks will be charged based on the total duration in minutes, of all the media files produced as output.

Standard Encoder	Premium Encoder
$0.015 per output minute	$0.035 per output minute

Output Minute Multipliers

Quality	Multiplier	Example
SD (less than 1280×720)	1x	10 minutes of SD output count as 10 SD minutes
HD (1280 × 720–1920 x 1080)	2x	10 minutes of HD output count as 20 SD minutes
UHD (more than 1920 x 1080, up to 4096 x 2160)	4x	10 minutes of UHD output count as 40 SD minutes
Audio only output	0.25x	4 minutes of output audio count as 1 SD minute

Media reserved units Pricing

Media Reserved Unit type determines the speed with which your media processing tasks are processed by the Cloud Encoder. There are 3 types of Media Reserved Unit: S1, S2 & S3.

S1	S2	S3
$0.02 per hour	$0.04 per hour	$0.08 per hour

Live Channel without Encoding (Uses on-premises Encoder) Pricing

Price (per channel)	$0.0165/minute

Live Channel with Live Encoding (Uses Cloud Encoder) Pricing

First 20 hours/month	$0.056/minute
Next 80 hours (20-100 hours)/month	$0.048/minute
Next 150 hours (100-250 hours)/month	$0.043/minute
Over 250 hours/month	$0.04/minute

Streaming Endpoint Pricing

You are only billed when your Streaming Endpoint is in running state.

Deliver on-demand and live video streams to customers in multiple formats and at scale.

	STANDARD STREAMING ENDPOINT	PREMIUM STREAMING UNITS
Trial	15 Days	NA
Bandwidth	Upto 600 Mbps	Upto 200 Mbps
Price	$2.09/day	$4.49/day

Content Protection

Secure your assets with Microsoft PlayReady digital rights management (DRM), Google Widevine Modular license delivery, Apple FairPlay Streaming, or clear key Advanced Encryption Standard (AES) encryption.

Pricing is based on the number of licenses or keys issued by the service.

MS PlayReady	Google Widevine	Apple FairPlay	AES
$0.20/100 licenses	$0.20/100 licenses	$0.20/100 licenses	$0.10/100 keys

Chapter 17 Locks, Tags & Resource Groups

This Chapter covers following

- Resource Groups
- Tags
- Locks

This Chapter Covers following Lab Exercises to build below topology

- Create Resource Groups
- Create Tags for a Resource

Resource Groups

Resource Groups are logical containers in which resources are grouped. All Resources in Azure are created in Resource Group.

Resource groups allow you to manage related resources as a single unit. Using Resources Groups you can monitor, control access and manage billing for resources that are required to run an application.

Design Considerations for Resource Groups

1. A resource group can contain resources that reside in different regions.
2. All the resources in a resource group must be associated with a single subscription.
3. Each resource can only exist in one resource group.
4. You can move a resource from one resource group to another group.
5. Ideally all the resources in a resource group should share the same lifecycle. You deploy, update, and delete them together. If one resource, such as a database server, needs to exist on a different deployment cycle it should be in another resource group.
6. A resource group can be used to scope access control for administrative actions.

Exercise 53: Create Resource Group

Resource Group can be created independently or can be created along with resource creation.
In Azure Portal click Resource groups in left pane>Click +Add>Add Resource Group blade opens>Enter as per your requirement and click create.

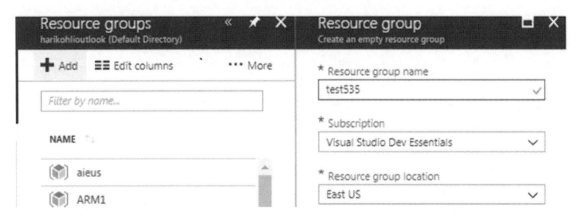

Architecting Microsoft Azure Solutions Study & Lab Guide Part 1: Exam 70-535

Tags

You can tag resources with name/value pairs to categorize and view resources across resource groups and across subscriptions. Using tags you can logically organize Azure resources by categories.

Each tag consists of a name and a value.

Tags enable you to retrieve related resources from different resource groups. This approach is helpful when you need to organize resources for billing or management.

Each resource or resource group can have a maximum of 15 tag name/value pairs. If you want to associate more than 15 values with a resource, use a JSON string for the tag value.

Exercise 54: Create Tags

In Azure Portal go to any Resource (wvm535) and click Tag in left pane groups>Add Tag opens in Right Pane> Enter as per your requirement and click save.

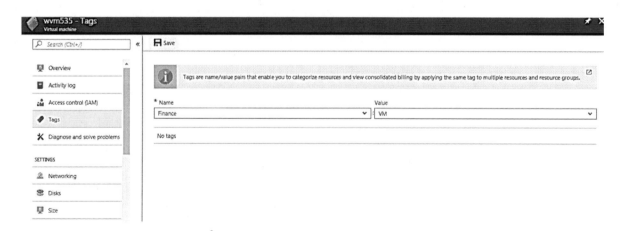

Locks

Locks are applied at subscription, resource group, or resource level to prevent users from accidentally deleting or modifying critical resources.

You can set the lock level to **CanNotDelete** or **ReadOnly**.

CanNotDelete means authorized users can still read and modify a resource, but they can't delete the resource.
ReadOnly means authorized users can read a resource, but they can't delete or update the resource.

When you apply a lock at a parent scope, all resources within that scope inherit the same lock.

Resource Manager Locks apply only to operations that happen in the management plane, which consists of operations sent to https://management.azure.com. The locks do not restrict how resources perform their own functions. Resource changes are restricted, but resource operations are not restricted.
For example a ReadOnly lock on a SQL Database prevents you from deleting or modifying the database but it does not prevent you from creating, updating or deleting data in the database. Data transactions are permitted because those operations are not sent to https://management.azure.com.

Chapter 18 Azure Global Infrastructure

This Chapter covers following

- Regions
- Geography
- Paired Regions

Azure Regions

A region is a set of datacenters (Availability Zones) deployed within a latency-defined perimeter and connected through a dedicated regional low-latency network. As of writing Microsoft has 50 Regions Worldwide.

Geography

A Geography typically contains two or more regions within the same country, that preserves data residency and compliance boundaries. There are exceptions such as some Regions with EU are considered as same geography.

Geographies allow customers with specific data-residency and compliance needs to keep their data and applications close. Geographies are fault-tolerant to withstand complete region failure through their connection to dedicated high-capacity networking infrastructure.

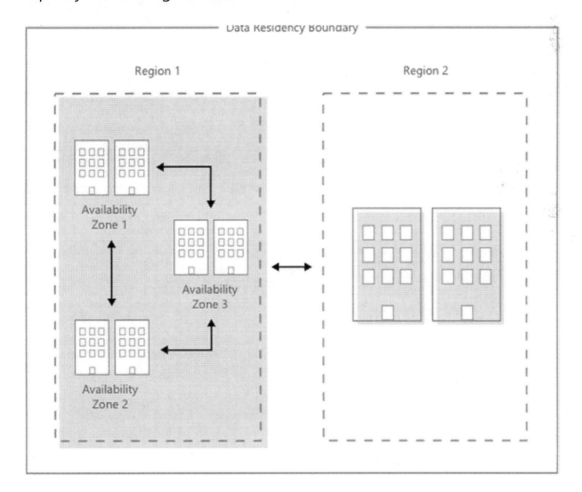

Paired Regions

Each Azure region is paired with another region within the same geography, together making a regional pair. The exception is Brazil South, which is paired with a region outside its geography.

Microsoft recommends that you replicate workloads across regional pairs to benefit from Azure's isolation and availability policies. For example, planned Azure system updates are deployed sequentially (not at the same time) across paired regions. That means that even in the rare event of a faulty update, both regions will not be affected simultaneously. Furthermore, in the unlikely event of a broad outage, recovery of at least one region out of every pair is prioritized.

Table below shows some of the Azure Paired Regions

Geography	Paired Region	Paired Region
North America	East US	West US
North America	East US 2	Central US
Canada	Canada Central	Canada East
Germany	Germany Central	Germany Northeast
India	Central India	South India
China	China North	China East
Japan	Japan East	Japan West
Korea	Korea Central	Korea South

Architecting Microsoft Azure Solutions Study & Lab Guide Part 1: Exam 70-535

Chapter 19 Case Studies Consolidated

This Chapter Covers following Case Studies

1. Designing Virtual Networks and Network Security Groups
2. User Defined Route
3. Workload Isolation with Hub and Spoke VNETs using VNET Peering
4. Availability Set
5. Choosing VM size and Designing IOPs
6. Load Balancing e-commerce server
7. Highly Available Multisite Website
8. Federating On-premises Active Directory and Azure AD
9. Website authentication using on-premises ADFS as SAML Identity Provider
10. Identity Management
11. Licensing Case Study 1
12. Licensing Case Study 2
13. Secure Remote Access to on-premises Application

Case Study 1: Design Virtual Network and Network Security Groups

Design a virtual network (KNET) with 2 subnets (App & DB) using Class A address of 192.168.0.0/16. App subnet will have 2 application servers - Production Application Server (App-Prod) and Test Application Server (App-Test).

Design Network Security groups to satisfy following requirements:
Traffic allowed to Production Application Server (App-Prod) is https and RDP.
Traffic allowed to Test Application Server (App-Test) is http and RDP.

Solution

Subnet VNET network address space 192.168.0.0/16 into 192.168.1.0/24 and 192.168.2.0/24 and assign it to App and DB subnets respectively as shown below.

We will create 3 Network Security Groups – NSGSubnet, NSGProd & NSGTest.
- NSGSubnet will be associated with App Subnet and add 3 inbound allow rules - http, https & RDP.
- NSGProd will be associated with Network Interface of App-Prod Server and add 2 inbound allow rules - https & RDP
- NSGTest will be associated with Network Interface of App-Test Server and add 2 inbound allow rules - http & RDP

NSG Working: NSGSubnet will only allow inbound http, https and RDP traffic and will block any other traffic. NSGProd will allow https & RDP and will block http. NSGTest will allow http & RDP and will block https. From above you can infer that 2 levels of Firewalls (NSG) are Protecting Virtual Machines.

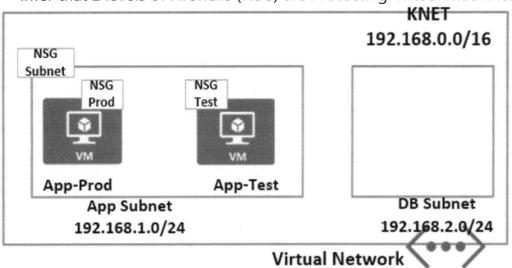

Case Study 2 UDR: Routing Traffic between 2 Subnets to pass through another Subnet.

Route traffic between Web-Subnet and DB-Subnet to pass-through a network virtual appliance located in another Subnet. The idea behind this exercise to clear UDR concepts and this is not a step by step Exercise.

Pre-Req for this Exercise:

10. It is assumed that Virtual Network with 3 Subnets – Web, Db and DMZ is already created as per addresses shown in figure below.
11. Windows Server 2016 NVA VM (myvm-nva) is created in DMZ subnet with Private IP (192.168.3.4) only.

Solution

Figure below shows the architecture of the solution.

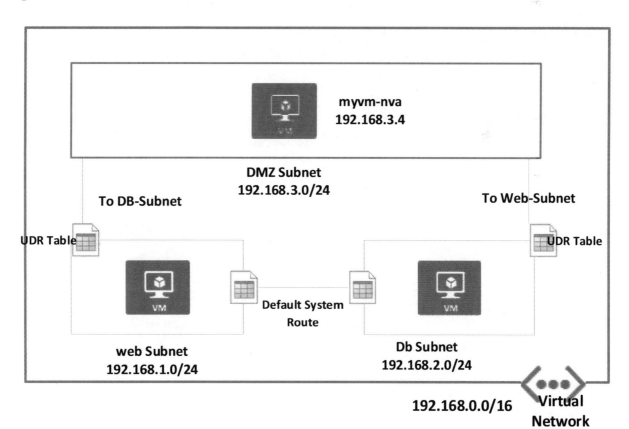

Step 1: To allow NVA Virtual Machine in DMZ subnet to receive traffic addressed to other destinations, enable IP Forwarding for the NVA VM.

Enable IP Forwarding in NVA Virtual Machine in DMZ subnet: Go to NVA VM Dashboard> Click Networking under settings> In Right pane click Private Network Interface attached to NVA VM>Network Interface Dashboard opens>Click IP Configuration in left Pane>In Right Pane Click Enabled.

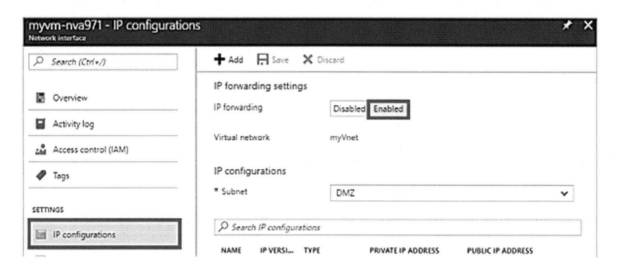

Step 2 Create Route Table: Click + Create a Resource> Networking> Route Table> Create Route Table Blade opens>Enter Information and click create.

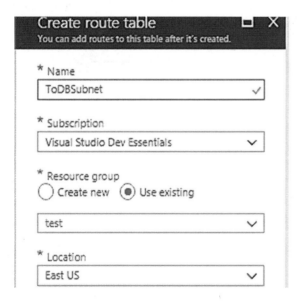

Step 3 Add a route in Route Table (ToDBSubnet): Go to ToDBSubnet Route table Dashboard> Click Routes in left Pane>Click +Add> Add Route Blade opens > Enter information and click ok.
Address Prefix: Network Address of DB-Subnet 192.168.2.0/24
Next Hop Address: IP Address of NVA VM (myvm-nva) 192.168.3.4

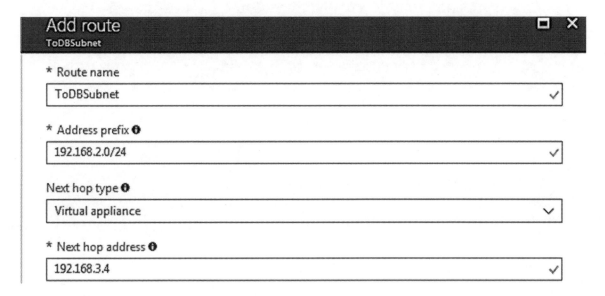

Step 4 Associate Route Table (ToDBSubnet) with Web Subnet: Go to Virtual Network knet Dashboard>click Subnets in left pane>In Right pane click Web-Subnet>Web-Subnet Blade opens>Click Route table>In Right Pane select ToDBSubnet>Click Save in Top left.

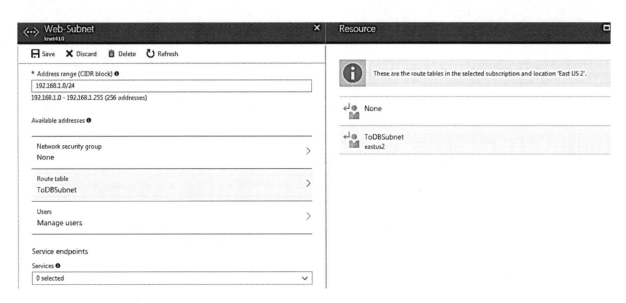

Step 5, 6 & 7: Similarly create Route table ToWebSubnet, add a route to Route Table and associate Route Table with DB Subnet.

Result 1 of above actions: We have both default routes and User defined Routes associated with Web Subnet & DB Subnet.
Result 2 of above actions: Network traffic between any resources in the Web-Subnet and DB- Subnets flows through the network virtual appliance. Though system route specify that Traffic can flow directly between Web and DB subnet but Traffic flows through NVA **as UDR is preferred over System Route.**

Case Study 3: Workload Isolation with Hub and Spoke VNETs using VNET Peering

Spoke VNETs will be used to isolate workloads such as Production & Dev & Test.

Hub VNET will run shared workloads such as DNS, AD DS & Security Appliances.

Spoke VNETs will peer with Hub VNET. Hub VNET will also provide hybrid connectivity to on-premises Data center over internet using Virtual Network Gateway.

Hub VNET acts as a central point of connectivity for on-premises network and spoke VNETs.

Figure below shows Spoke 1 and Spoke 2 VNETs are peered with Hub VNET. Hub VNET is also connected to on-premises network using VPN Gateway.

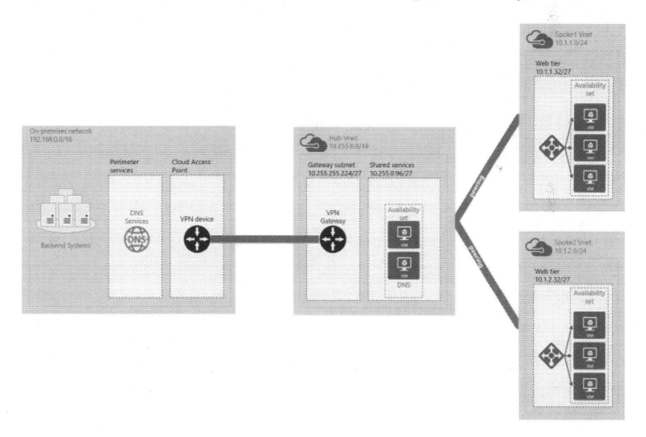

Spoke VNET to Spoke VNET Connectivity (Optional)

If Spoke to Spoke connectivity is required then User Defined Route (UDR) and Network Virtual Appliances (NVA) will be used.

UDR attached to Subnet in the Spoke VNET will forward traffic to NVA VM in Hub VNET. NVA VM will route traffic to other spoke VNET.

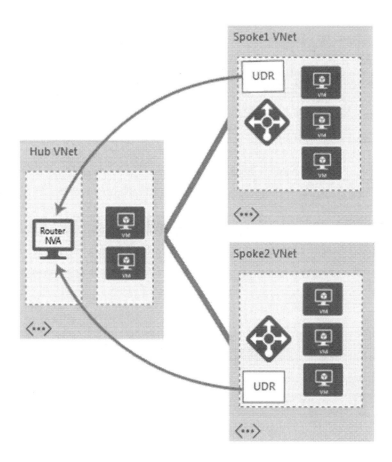

Enterprise use case for this architecture include following:

4. Workloads requiring isolation such as development, testing, and production, but require shared services such as DNS, IDS, NTP, or AD DS. Shared services are placed in the Hub VNET, while each environment is deployed to a spoke VNET to maintain isolation.
5. Enterprises that require central control over security aspects, such as a firewall in the hub as a DMZ, and segregated management for the workloads in each spoke.
6. Require secure Hybrid connectivity to on-premises Data Center.

Benefits of this Architecture include following:

3. **Cost savings** by centralizing services such as network virtual appliances (NVAs) and DNS servers in Hub VNET, that can be shared by multiple workloads in Spoke VNETs.

4. **Separation of operations** between central IT (SecOps, InfraOps) and workloads (DevOps). Central IT Managing Hub VNET and Application owners managing Spoke VNETs.

Case Study 4: Placement of Virtual Machines in Availability Set

Consider a scenario where we have 5 Virtual Machines in Availability Set with 3 Update Domains (UD) and 2 Fault Domains (FD) are configured. Show the possible placement of Virtual Machines.

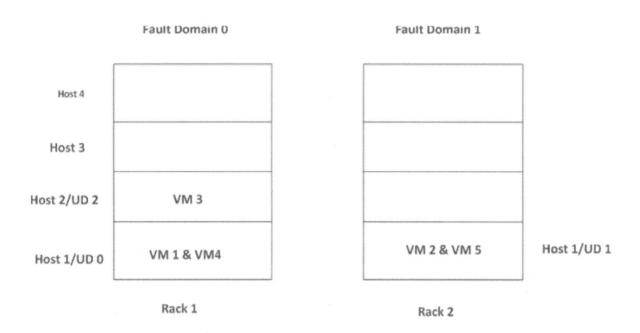

AS is configured with 2 Fault Domains which means VMs will be spread across 2 racks. AS is configured with 3 Update Domains which means VMs will be placed across 5 hosts.

VM1, VM2 & VM3 will be placed in UD 0, UD 1 and UD 2 respectively. VM4 will be placed in UD 0 and VM5 will be placed in UD1.

VM1, VM3 & VM4 will share FD 0 and VM2 & VM5 will share FD 1.

In case of host failure, maximum of 2 VMs out of 5 VMs will be affected. In case of Rack Failure (PS/TOR Switch) maximum of 3 VMs out of 5 VMs will be affected.

Case Study 5: Choosing VM size and Designing IOPs

A company is shifting test & Dev app to cloud. It's a 2 Tier application – Web/App & Database tier. Application & Database owner have specified following requirements for the Virtual Machines.

Feature	Application	Database
vCPU	8	4
Memory	16 GB	64 GB
IOPS		1200
Database Size		100 GB

They want to use latest Generation Dv3 VM. To save on cost they want use Magnetic HDD for storage. They want Database Data to be on separate Data Disks and not on OS Disk.

Suggest size and configuration for Dv3 VM for Application and Database server.

Solution

Following Sizes are available in Dv3 series.

Size	vCPU	Memory	Max NICs	Temp Storage SSD	Max Data Disks	Max IOPS	Price/ hour
D2 v3	2	8	2	50 GB	4	4X500	$0.188
D4 v3	4	16	2	100 GB	8	8X500	$0.376
D8 v3	8	32	4	200 GB	16	16X500	$0.752
D16 v3	16	64	8	400 GB	32	32X500	$1.504
D32 v3	32	128	8	800 GB	32	32X500	$3.008
D64 v3	64	256	8	1600 GB	32	32X500	$6.016

For App Server We will choose D8v3 to satisfy both vCPU and Memory Req.

For DB Server we will choose D16v3 to satisfy both vCPU and Memory Req.

We need to add 3 Data disks to the instance to satisfy IOPS requirement of 1200. 3 Data Disks will give an IOPS of 1500 (3X500). Note 2 Data disks will give an IOPS of 1000 only. Data will be stripped across 3 Hard Disk to achieve the required IOPS.

Case Study 6: Load Balancing e-commerce server

You are connected to e-commerce website through a wired broadband connection. This internet connection goes down during your purchase cycle. You now re-connect to e-commerce website by connecting your computer to internet using mobile phone as hot spot.

Which Load Balancer you will use to load balance e-com application – layer 4 Azure Load Balancer or Layer 7 Azure Application Gateway so that client session reconnect to same e-com application server.

Note: Both layer 4 and layer 7 load balancer support session Persistence.

Solution

We will use Azure Application Gateway to load balance e-com application.

If e-commerce website is load balanced with Application gateway you will be re-directed to the same backend server because of cookies stored in client computers irrespective of which internet connection you use.

If e-commerce website is load balanced with azure layer 4 load balancer configured with client IP affinity, you will not know which e-com server you will be re-directed as in this case client IP has changed. If client IP was not changed then client will be re-directed to same e-com application.

Case Study 7: Highly Available Multisite Website

An IT giant located in Pala Alto, California does business with customers and partners located across the world.

There existing website on a single server is located in Palo Alto and is heavily accessed. End users (Customers and Partners) are complaining about slow performance of the website.

They want to give best experience to customers and partners visiting there website. They have short listed 3 locations for their website. Palo Alto serving North America and South America region, Germany serving EMEA region and Singapore serving APAC region including Australia and New Zealand.

There requirement is that each region should have highly available website and should be accessed by the users of that region only. Load Balancing solution in each region must support cookie based session affinity, SSL termination & URL based content routing.

Suggest a solution which satisfies above requirement.

Solution

We will use combination of Traffic Manager and Application Gateway to satisfy the customer requirement.

Each region will have multiple servers hosting the website to provide highly available website.

Application gateway in each region will provide round robin distribution of incoming traffic to the servers hosting the website. Application Gateway will also provide SSL termination, cookie based session affinity and URL based content routing.

Traffic Manager will provide DNS based Load Balancing and will route the user request to the Application Gateway in the respective region using Geographic routing method.

Architecting Microsoft Azure Solutions Study & Lab Guide Part 1: Exam 70-535

Figure below shows the Architecture of the solution.

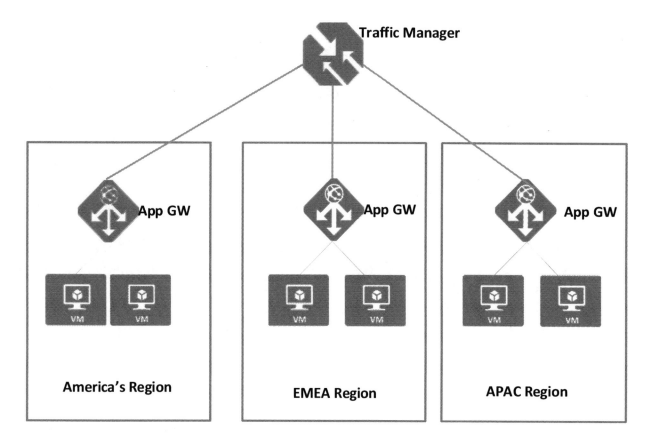

ADFS Case Study 8: Federating On-premises Active Directory and Azure AD Directory for Authentication and Single sign-on

Organization A has application workloads running in Azure. Organization A has a security requirement that user logging to Azure AD for resource access need to be authenticated by on-premises Active Directory Infrastructure. The Solution should also provide single sign-on. Users already logged on to on-premises Active Directory should be able to access Azure cloud resource without logging again. Suggest a Solution which satisfies above requirement.

Solution

AD connect installed on-premises with Federated identity option will synchronize on-premises active directory users to Azure. This will also install a component of ADFS in AD connect. Figure below shows Architecture of the solution.

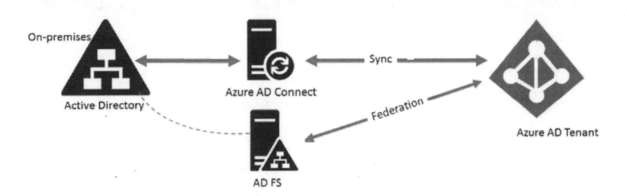

Active Directory Federation Services (ADFS) server installed on-premises and ADFS component in AD Connect will federate the 2 directories which will results in one-way trust with Azure AD **Trusting** on-premises ADFS. User Login happens in cloud but user authentication is redirected to on-premises ADFS.

ADFS also enables single sign-on. Users who are already logged on to their corporate network can sign on to Azure AD without entering there on-premises password again.

Requires AAD Subscription, AD Connect, AD DS and AD FS.

ADFS Case Study 9: Website authentication using on-premises ADFS as Identity Provider (Not in the context of Azure)

There are 2 organisations – Org A and Org B. Org B has a website which will be used by Org A users. Website requires authentication before a user can be allowed to surf. Org B does not want to maintain Authentication infrastructure. Org A already has Active Directory Infrastructure. Suggest a Solution which satisfies above requirement.

Solution

Install ADFS server in Org A as SAML Identity Provider. Website in Org B will be configured to pass user authentication to ADFS server in Org A using either WS Federation, or SAML or OAuth2 protocol.

The Org B website will be service provider or relying party. ADFS will act as identity Provider (IP). ADFS server in Org A will authenticates the users against Active Directory Domain Services and will issues a token containing a series of claims about user.

Using ADFS as an identity provider means that user accounts don't need to be set up and managed in Org B website, greatly reducing the administrative effort of maintaining user accounts.

Case Study 10: Identity Management

A major cricket franchise of Indian Premier League (IPL) wants to engage its fans and monetize its website. The website has details of IPL matches, interview with cricket players, video highlights of the matches, Analysis by cricket experts, off field entertainment gossips, Sale of Merchandise and advertisement by their sponsors.

Fans who register with website, get access to additional contents, can post comments and are eligible for Prices.

They want fans to register with their social accounts – Facebook, Linkedin or Twitter or by registering with their email-id and password. They expect 250000 fans to register.

There requirement is that they do not want to maintain user accounts details. Another requirement is that user registration with the website should be very simple.

Suggest a solution which satisfies the above requirement.

Solution

We will use Azure Active Directory B2C for user identity Management.

With Azure Active Directory B2C, fans can sign up with website by using their existing_social accounts (Facebook, Google or Linkedin etc) or by creating new credentials (email address and password, or username and password).

One of the advantage of B2C is that you need not maintain user account and password details and associated infrastructure (Like hardware, Databases and Directory services).

Advantage for consumers is that they don't have to go through lengthy process of sign up.

Sign-in Protocol: IPL Website will redirect user authentication to Facebook, Google or Linkedin using Sign-in protocols such as oauth2 or SAML or WS-Federation.

Case Study 11: Licensing Case Study 1

A customer wants to invite 50 B2B collaboration users to its Azure AD tenant. B2B users require features of Azure AD Basic edition only. How many licenses customer should have for 50 B2B Collaboration users.

Solution: B2B licensing states that for each paid license of Azure AD (Basic or Premium) you can add 5 B2B Users.
Based on 5:1 Ratio you will require 10 licenses of Azure AD Basic Edition.

Case Study 12: Licensing Case Study 2

A customer wants to invite 100 B2B collaboration users to its Azure AD tenant. 50 of the B2B users require features of Basic edition. 30 users require MFA feature. 20 Users require both MFA & identity protection feature. How many licenses customer should have for above 100 B2B Collaboration users.

Solution: MFA feature require Azure AD Premium P1 license. Identity Protection feature requires Azure AD Premium P2 License.
Using 5:1 ratio you will require 10 licenses of Azure AD Basic, 6 licenses of Azure AD Premium P1 and 4 licenses of Azure AD Premium P2.

Case Study 13: Secure Remote Access to on-premises Application

A regional confectionary company in USA manufactures and sells its products like cookies, cakes & chocolates to consumers in the state of California. Products are sold to consumer's indirectly through retailers.

There sales people visit the retailer for order booking every week. The stock is then delivered directly to retailers by the company. To clear the stock they also offer promotional schemes to retailers.

They have custom developed core business application which shows the stock position, retailer payment due & promotions. The application is hosted in on-premise Data Center. On-premise Data Center has one Cisco firewall.

All IT Resources are accessed from within the internal network except for core business application and Mail which accessed by sales reps and top management both on desktop & mobile (Android & Apple) from internet. To provide access to Business application from internet, SSL VPN has been setup on Cisco ASA Firewall. Total 15 users access the Business application from outside the corporate network.

Recently they had a security breach where in excel worksheet containing details of retailers and inventory was downloaded.

They don't have big IT budget. They have one system admin who manages everything. There VAR is small time IT Company which lacks skills to implement security solutions.

They recently got a quote from a big IT VAR for implementing security solutions. It consists of new firewall, IPS and identity management and cost was around 40000 USD. This was beyond their budget.

They are looking for a solution to protect their applications from security breaches. They want a simple and cost effective solution. They also don't want skilled resources and administrative overheads of managing the security solution.

Suggest a solution which satisfies above requirement with cost breakup.

Solution

We will use Azure Active Directory (AD) Application Proxy for protecting on-premises Business application.

With Azure Active Directory (AD) Application Proxy all access to Business application will happen through Application Proxy service running in Azure cloud. Application Proxy service obviates the need to setup VPN on-premises.

Figure below shows internet users accessing on-premises application through Application Proxy service.

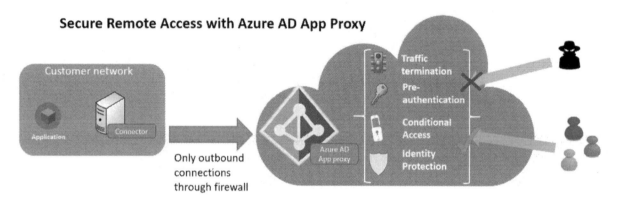

Application Proxy Security Features

Traffic termination: All traffic is terminated in the cloud. Back-end servers are not exposed to direct HTTP traffic.

All access is outbound: You don't need to open inbound connections to the corporate network. Azure AD connectors maintain outbound connections to the Azure AD Application Proxy service, which means that there is no need to open firewall ports for incoming connections.

Authenticated access: Only authenticated connections can access the on premises network. We will configure only 15 users who can access Business application from outside the corporate network.

Conditional access: With conditional access, it is possible to further define restrictions on what traffic is allowed to access your back-end applications. You can define restrictions based on location, strength of authentication, and user risk profile.

Cost of the Solution

We will use Azure AD Basic or Premium P1 Licenses or Premium P2 License. All the 3 license options provide Application Proxy feature. Azure AD Premium P1 license provides additional capability of conditional Access. Azure AD Premium P2 license provides additional capability of identity protection.

License	License cost (USD)/Month	Number of users	Total Cost/Month (USD)	Total Cost/Year (USD)
Basic	1	15	15	180
Premium P1	6	15	90	1350
Premium P2	9	15	135	2025

The above costing was submitted to the company management and they decided to go with Premium P1 License.

Advantages of the solution

The biggest advantage of application proxy is that we don't need to configure any advanced firewall & IPS features and VPN on-premises for remote users to access the applications. Installing & Configuring VPN is a complex job and requires professional services from the system integrator.

Solution is very cost effective as compared to on-premises cost of implementing the solution which was USD 40000.

You also don't require skilled resources to manage the solution.

Made in the USA
San Bernardino, CA
26 June 2018